THE
GREATEST STORIES
NEVER TOLD

Reader's Digest SPECIAL EDITION

THE
GREATEST STORIES
NEVER TOLD

230 *Tales from History to* ASTONISH,
BEWILDER, *and* STUPEFY

Rick Beyer

Reader's
Digest

The Reader's Digest Association, Inc.
Pleasantville, NY/Montreal

Reader's Digest Home & Health Books

President, Home & Garden and Health & Wellness
Alyce Alston
Editor in Chief
Neil Wertheimer
Creative Director
Michele Laseau
Executive Managing Editor
Donna Ruvituso
Associate Director, North America Prepress
Douglas A. Croll
Manufacturing Manager
John L. Cassidy
Marketing Director
Dawn Nelson
Cover Designer
Erick Swindell

The Reader's Digest Association, Inc.

President and Chief Executive Officer
Mary Berner
President, Consumer Marketing
Dawn Zier

Project Management
Joan Krellenstein,
Maius Minus llc

Grateful acknowledgment to Rick Beyer for writing additional stories.

Library of Congress Data has been applied for.

ISBN 978-0-7621-0554-0

Address any comments about *The Greatest Stories Never Told* to:
The Reader's Digest Association, Inc.
Editor in Chief, Books
Reader's Digest Road
Pleasantville, NY 10570-7000

To order copies of *The Greatest Stories Never Told*, call 1-800-846-2100. Visit our website at **rd.com**

Printed in the United States of America

1 3 5 7 9 10 8 6 4 2

US 4916/L

Note to Readers: The information in this book has been carefully researched, and all efforts have been made to ensure its accuracy.

Introduction
History is filled with unpredictable people and unbelievable stories.

Consider: The Pilgrims landed in Plymouth because they ran out of beer. Three cigars changed the course of the Civil War. The stethoscope was invented by a modest French doctor reluctant to put his ear to a female patient's bosom. Teddy Roosevelt is the father of football's forward pass. And believe it or not, actress Hedy Lamarr not only appeared in the movies' first nude scene, but also later patented an idea that formed the basis for cell phone encryption. That's the kind of wonderfully surprising history you'll find in this book.

I am a life-long history enthusiast lucky enough to be earning a living doing what I love: making history documentaries. Some years ago I had the chance to produce a series of history minutes for THE HISTORY CHANNEL®. The Timelab 2000® series, hosted by Sam Waterston, was so well received that it led to *The Greatest Stories Never Told* books. This Reader's Digest edition combines selected stories from the first three books in the series, along with new ones written for this volume.

"History would be a wonderful thing" said Leo Tolstoy, "if only it were true." Ascertaining the veracity of these stories involved lots of history detective work. Many a seemingly good tale has gone by the boards because it didn't hold up under scrutiny. Ones that made it in, crazy as they might seem, are as true as I know how to make them.

There are people in the world who think history is boring. My answer to them is on the pages that follow. To my mind there's nothing more entertaining than history. Where else, after all, can you find so much courage, cowardice, hope, triumph, sex, intrigue, folly, humor, and ambition? And if that doesn't make for good stories, I don't know what does.

Rick Beyer

CONTENTS

Daniel Boone: American hero or treasonous betrayer?

Chapter 1

Heroes and Villains

Untold Stories of the Great and Terrible

No matter the story, the most compelling part is always the people involved. And that's especially true of the extremes: heroes and, even more intriguing, villains. These are the people who are responsible for mankind's pivotal moments. The most familiar names—Attila, Joan of Arc, Daniel Boone—have little-known stories behind them that contribute depth and color to the common facts. Even more compelling, however, are the stories of the people you don't know: Ibn Battuta, Israel Bissell and Hsi Kai, to name a few. These are the amazing men and women who, whether you know them or not, changed the course of history.

Warrior Princess

She takes on the armies of Rome…and almost beats them.

Hell hath no fury like a woman scorned. And Queen Boudicca had been worse than scorned by the Romans. After the death of her husband, who was king of a Celtic tribe known as the Iceni, Roman authorities moved in to annex his kingdom, plunder his property, and humiliate his family. When Boudicca dared to protest, she was flogged and her daughters were raped.

The Romans discovered the error of their ways. Boudicca vowed vengeance, and raised a huge army. She attacked a Roman colony at Colchester, slaughtering its residents. Informed that the Roman Ninth Legion was rushing

Archaeologists have found a three-foot-thick layer of ash that testifies to the destruction Boudicca wreaked upon London.

"She was…most terrifying, in the glance of her eye most fierce."

—ROMAN HISTORIAN DIO CASSIUS, DESCRIBING BOUDICCA

to the colony's aid, she ambushed and annihilated 1,500 elite Roman infantrymen.

When the Roman governor heard she was marching on London, he and his forces abandoned the city. Boudicca's angry army murdered and mutilated everyone they found there, and burned London to the ground.

The Romans were terrified of Boudicca. Though no strangers to the brutality of war themselves, her bloodlust astounded them. "The British could not wait to cut throats, hang, burn, and crucify," wrote Roman historian Tacitus, who estimated that her army killed 70,000 Roman soldiers and civilians.

Eventually the Romans scraped together an army to meet Boudicca in battle, and defeated the Celts. Tens of thousands of Boudicca's soldiers were slaughtered, and she chose to take poison rather than be captured.

Rome would rule Britain for three more centuries—but they never forgot the warrior woman who almost voted them off the island.

Kidnapped

A young boy rises from slavery to sainthood.

In the fading days of the Roman Empire, a 16-year-old boy was abducted and sold into slavery by savages outside the border of the civilized world. These savages often formed raiding parties and kidnapped hundreds of people at a time. They took the boy to a remote land, where he labored under the harshest conditions.

The boy had never been very religious, but in desperation he began to pray every day that he might survive his horrible ordeal. After more than five years in bondage, he was able to escape. He walked 200 miles to a seaport, where he found passage on a ship. Eventually he returned home to joyous parents who begged him never to leave.

But night after night he was tormented by dreams and visions. Voices beckoned. They told him he must return to the land of his kidnappers and bring the word of Christ into this savage land.

And that's exactly what he did.

The boy lived in what is now England. His kidnappers were Celtic tribesmen from across the water in Ireland. And that's how a young Briton named Patricius grew into an old Irishman named Patrick. Saint Patrick, to be exact. The patron saint of Ireland: an Englishman by birth.

JUST A TALE?

The slave business flourished in Ireland for centuries before Patrick's arrival on the scene. Celtic raiding parties would kidnap hundreds of people at a time. Boys were brought back to be sheepherders and girls to be sex slaves. One of Patrick's accomplishments was to largely put an end to this slave trade. But Saint Patrick did not drive the snakes out of Ireland. In truth, the island nation is too cold for snakes. That legend is believed to be a metaphor for Patrick's spectacular success in driving the idol-worshiping Druid religion out of Ireland and converting almost the entire population to Christianity.

"We beg you to come and walk among us once more."

—VOX HIBERNIAE, "THE VOICE OF THE IRISH," SPEAKING TO PATRICIUS IN HIS DREAMS

The Death of Attila

A warrior is poised to conquer the world, until marriage proves his untimely undoing.

Attila the Hun. Even today the name conjures up images of pillage and destruction. King of the Huns for 20 years, he commanded an army of half a million men, made all of Europe tremble, and threatened to capture Rome itself.

But the terrifying Attila died before he completed his conquest of the civilized world—and it wasn't on the battlefield. It was on his wedding night. In the year 453, Attila took a new wife: a young girl named Ildico, who was widely renowned for her beauty. After a night of drunken revelry in celebration of the wedding, he retired with his bride to the bedchamber, where he promptly passed out on his back.

The following day servants became alarmed when Attila didn't rise at the normal time. After their shouts failed to wake him, they knocked down the door. Inside they found the body of their chieftain sprawled out on the bed beside his bride who was weeping and wailing.

Was he the victim of murder at the hands of his new wife? Not at all. It seems that for all his power and might, the great conqueror had a weakness— he suffered from chronic nosebleeds.

Atilla's massive empire was centered in today's Hungary, which is the traditional home of the Hunnish people.

One apparently came upon him in his drunken state, and he choked to death.

At Attila's funeral, his body was laid out in a silk tent, and horsemen rode in circles around it. Many of his followers gashed their faces so that it would appear they wept blood at his death. His men went so far as to murder his burial party so that his grave might never be found.

And so it was that one of history's most fearsome warriors died not from a terrible wound received in a great battle but from a simple bloody nose on his own festive wedding night.

Attila (right) may have killed his brother Bleda to avoid sharing the crown.

During his two-decade reign, Attila the Hun conquered the Eastern Roman Empire, then moved west though Austria, Germany, Gaul and Italy, before stopping outside Rome. So how did he become such a force to be reckoned with? It seems he employed a combination of tactical bribery and modern warfare. Using the spoils of his plunders as a reward he was able to maintain the loyalty of diverse tribes of people throughout Europe and Asia. And his fighters, the Huns, were able horsemen and excellent archers. There is debate over whether or not the Huns used stirrups on their horses to deliver deadlier blows during battle. Historians disagree on the origin of this truly powerful tool. But it is agreed that the Huns developed at least one deadly new weapon—the Hun bow. It's a large, asymmetric bow that can be switched quickly from one side of the horse to the other, giving warriors a greater range. The Huns used this bow with great impact in their quest to conquer the Romans.

Daring Dancer

This circus girl saves an empire.

Theodora was a striptease dancer with one heck of an act. Crowds flocked to the circus in Constantinople to watch her dance half-naked with lions. One of those who found himself mesmerized by Theodora (shown at left portrayed by 19th-century actress Sarah Bernhardt) was Justinian, nephew of the emperor and next in line to rule the Byzantine Empire. He fell in love with the beautiful Theodora and wanted to marry her. However, men of senatorial rank were forbidden to marry actresses and dancers, who were considered little better than prostitutes. Justinian had to convince his uncle, the emperor, to repeal that law so he could marry Theodora. When Justinian eventually became emperor, Theodora became his beloved empress.

Lucky for him—because her fearlessness would one day save his empire. A few years into Justinian's reign, a tax revolt broke out. There was chaos and rioting in the streets. It seemed the end of Justinian's reign might be at hand. Shaken, the emperor prepared to flee. A ship was ordered to stand by, ready to take him and his wife into exile.

Justinian and Theodora reigned together for another 21 years after the uprising, and Justinian for 17 more years after her death.

"May I never be separated from this purple."

—THEODORA, EXPRESSING HER FIERCE DESIRE TO HOLD ON TO HER ROYAL STATUS

But Theodora wouldn't have it. The one-time circus girl made it clear she would rather die than surrender her royal rank. "Royalty is a good burial shroud," Theodora calmly told her husband.

Her words filled Justinian with new resolve. Instead of fleeing, he sent out his imperial guard to fight the rebels, who were eventually crushed.

The Least Curious Man

If Bjarni Herjulfson had gotten out of his boat, he'd be one of the most famous explorers in history!

Herjulfson was lost at sea. On his way to Greenland in 986, fierce autumn storms had buffeted his ship for days. They had blown him so far off course that he had no idea where he was. Once the weather cleared, he was relieved to see land. But this land looked totally unfamiliar. It had no mountains or glaciers as Greenland did, only small hills and forests. Herjulfson didn't know it, but he had crossed the Atlantic and sailed to what is now called Canada.

His crew begged him to land. If only he had the spirit of a Christopher Columbus, this might have been a defining moment in exploration. But Herjulfson was simply intent on going home, not going down in history. So without even leaving his boat, he turned right around and headed out to sea. He and his crew finally made it to Greenland a week later.

Years afterward, he told his tale of adventure to a friend, who decided to retrace Herjulfson's course. In fact, not only did that friend question Herjulfson closely about his journey—he actually purchased Herjulfson's ship and used it for his own

Herjulfson's journey (above), as well as Eriksson's are described in the *Flateyjarbok,* the Norse saga written in the 1300s.

> *"Many thought he lacked curiosity, and for this reason he was somewhat slandered."*
>
> —THE NORSE SAGAS, DESCRIBING VIKING REACTION TO HERJULFSON'S JOURNEY

trip. And so it was that Leif Eriksson staked his claim as the first European to walk on the American continent.

Herjulfson went down in history as the man whose curiosity did not get the better of him.

Ibn Battuta

Take a journey of heroic proportions with the greatest traveler you've never heard of.

We've all heard of the amazing travels of Marco Polo. But Ibn Battuta, who began a lifetime of wandering in 1325, the year after Polo's death, traveled even farther. From his home in Morocco he set out on a one-year pilgrimage to Mecca that turned into a 30-year adventure and made him the foremost frequent traveler of medieval times.

After crossing the Sahara to visit Mecca, he toured Iraq and Persia. Then he embarked on a sea journey down the coast of Africa as far as modern Tanzania. Deciding to travel by land to India and seek employment with a sultan, he took a detour to visit Constantinople in the company of a Turkish princess.

Reaching India, he settled down for eight years, working as a judge for the sultan of Delhi. The sultan then made him an envoy to China, but his mission ended in a disastrous shipwreck off the coast of India. After visiting Sri Lanka and the Maldive Islands, he finally found his way to China before beginning the long journey home.

Upon his return to Morocco, the itch to travel led Battuta on two more voyages: one northward to modern-day Spain, the other southward to Mali and its famous city, Timbuktu.

The pilgrimage to Mecca that began Battuta's wanderings was made by every Muslim who could manage it, a tradition that continues to this day.

Traveling by foot, camel and ship in an age when even 100 miles seemed a vast distance, Battuta logged an astonishing 73,000 miles, visiting what today are 44 different countries.

Ibn Battuta visited Egypt at least twice, and learned of the riches of East Africa during his stays.

OTHER PLAYERS, OTHER PLACES

While today's voyager may romantically aspire to the exploits of early explorers, modern travel concerns center more on how to find cheap airplane seats and a clean hotel room. A word of thanks is needed then, to Thomas Cook—the world's first travel agent. The Englishman, born in 1808, was a strict Baptist, active in the temperance movement. In 1841 Cook organized a train excursion taking 500 people from Leicester to Loughborough in England to attend a temperance meeting. He charged the passengers one shilling for the 24-mile round-trip journey—effectively giving birth to the travel agent industry. After his initial success Cook began organizing longer rail excursions—taking English subjects with wanderlust across Britain and Europe. In 1865 he opened an office in London and, seven years later, led the first round-the-world tour, covering 25,000 miles in 222 days. Along with arranging travel and accommodations, Cook sold guidebooks, luggage and restaurant coupons. His company lives on today as Thomas Cook Group, employing tens of thousands of travel agents around the world.

Admiral Zheng's Voyages

This little-known Chinese explorer makes Columbus look like a real homebody.

The Age of Discovery conjures up images of intrepid Europeans seeking passage to the mysterious East. But starting in 1405, Chinese Admiral Zheng led a series of spectacular voyages to the West.

Zheng commanded a fleet of 300 vessels, some nearly five times the size of Columbus's ships. His ships were served by 28,000 men (as compared with the 90 men on the *Niña, Pinta,* and *Santa Maria*). Admiral Zheng's biggest ship was the treasure ship. Measuring 440 feet long and 180 feet in beam, it was powered by nine masts carrying billowing red silk sales. The ship was loaded with gold, silver, oils, and silks, which the Chinese gave as gifts to the other countries they visited to show off their own wealth and power.

Over the course of seven voyages, Zheng's fleet journeyed as far as the southern tip of Africa—not in search of treasure or trade, but to show off the

might and power of the Ming Dynasty. Recent research holds out the tantalizing possibility that he may have gone even farther, sailing a huge fleet around the Cape of Good Hope and piloting it as far as Europe or even across the Atlantic to the Caribbean—all more than 75 years before the famous voyages of the Italian Christopher Columbus.

Just as remarkable as the boldness of these exploits is the speed with which they came to an end. In 1433, shortly after Zheng's last voyage, Confucian scholars convinced the emperor that such expeditions were too costly, that China should turn its focus inward and isolate itself from the rest of the world. By 1500 the Chinese court had made it a capital offense to build an oceangoing ship, and even went so far as to strike Admiral Zheng's accomplishments from the official record.

So just about the time Europe was broadening its horizons and sending explorers out on the seas across the globe, China was slamming shut its doors to outsiders.

God Is in the Details

Joan of Arc's name may be familiar, but do you know her truly amazing story?

Joan of Arc was just a 17-year-old girl when she led a French army to victory against the English at Orleans in 1428.

Joan had been hearing voices since the age of 13, and they told her that God wanted her to help Charles, the Dauphin (heir to the French throne), defeat the English and be crowned king. What she did next—in a time when women were regarded as property—beggars the imagination.

She talked her uncle into taking her to the local military commander. and convinced him to provide a military escort to take her to the Dauphin.

She convinced a group of priests that God was really speaking to her, and that she should be allowed to meet with the Dauphin.

In less than five minutes she talked Charles into giving her an army. She persuaded grizzled veterans of the war against England that they should take orders from a young girl. Further, she got them to give up cursing and sex while serving under her.

In an age when war meant hand-to-hand combat, even for commanders, Joan survived numerous battles while never wielding a weapon.

Not only did she lead her army to victory at Orleans, she also liberated dozens of French towns and defeated another British army at Patay.

Was Joan actually inspired by God? Her soldiers thought so, and so did the Catholic Church, which made her a saint. If divine inspiration didn't actually play a role, Joan certainly had amazing powers of persuasion and one hell of a run of luck until she was captured by opposition French forces, handed over to the British and tried for heresy. The trial was rigged and the verdict certain, though the prosecution could not produce a single witness to speak against her. Nonetheless, she was burned at the stake on May 30, 1431.

"Here begin the proceedings in matter of faith against a dead woman, Jeanne, commonly known as the maid."

—OPENING WORDS FROM THE RECORD OF JOAN OF ARC'S HERESY TRIAL

End of an Empire

An infamous commander pulls off one of the most extraordinary feats in military history.

In 1533, a highly advanced civilization lie spread across the Andes Mountains. The Incas commanded an empire that stretched 3,000 miles and was about twice the size of Texas. It boasted paved roads, intricate fortifications as good as any in the world and an army of 80,000 men. Over the centuries this empire had also accumulated a vast supply of gold.

That's what attracted Spanish conquistador Francisco Pizarro. After arriving on the scene, however, his band of soldiers became terrified by the numbers and might of the Incas and feared for their lives. Still, their thirst for riches knew no bounds, and they were willing to risk everything to get their hands on all that gold.

So Pizzaro conceived a plan that was breathtaking both in its daring and in its ruthlessness. He and his men tricked Atahualpa, the all-powerful emperor of the Incas, into meeting with them. Then they staged a bloody ambush, killing thousands of Atahualpa's men so they could capture the emperor himself. It proved to be a masterstroke that threw the Incas into disarray and eventually enabled the Spaniards to subjugate the entire empire. The cities and fortifications of this once-proud people were reduced to ruins.

The most amazing thing is that Pizarro had the nerve to undertake this conquest, never mind succeed at it. True, the Spaniards had superior weapons—crossbows and guns—but only enough for a handful of their soldiers. It remains an astonishing fact that he toppled a well-defended empire of 6 million warlike people with just 150 men.

Pizzaro was ultimately killed by his own associates.

MORE OF THE STORY

Desperate to negotiate his release, Atahualpa offered the Spaniards a stupendous ransom: a room full of gold in return for his freedom. They took the gold, and then took his life. They were ready to burn him at the stake until he made a last-minute conversion to Christianity, which prompted them to show a unique brand of mercy: They hanged him instead.

Move Over, Paul Revere

Listen, my children, and you shall hear of a rider even greater than the well-known horseman.

Everyone's heard of Paul Revere. His midnight ride on the eighteenth of April in 1775 to warn of British troops marching toward Lexington and Concord has become a part of American folklore. But another epic ride, which began the following day, has been largely forgotten.

Hours after hearing that British troops had opened fire on colonial farmers in what became known as the Battle of Lexington, the Massachusetts Provincial Congress issued a call to arms, asking neighboring colonies for help. Israel Bissell, a 23-year-old dispatch rider, was sent south to spread the news of the revolution.

Under his spurs his horse seemed to take wing. Local legend has it that he made Worcester—a full day's ride—in just two hours, and that his horse dropped dead when he got there. With a new horse Bissell was off again. Through Connecticut he raced, then to New York, and on to Philadelphia. He rode 350 miles in just six days, a record time.

Paul Revere, by contrast, rode only 20 miles. But Revere's effort to "spread the alarm to every Middlesex village and farm" was immortalized by Henry Wadsworth Longfellow. Nobody wrote a poem about Israel Bissell, so he wound up one of history's secrets.

> *"To arms, to arms, the war has begun."*
>
> —DISPATCH RIDER ISRAEL BISSELL

The largely forgotten Israel Bissell spread the word much farther than Revere.

Trick or Treason

A frontier folk hero is accused of being a traitor.

Daniel Boone: charged with treason and facing the gallows. It doesn't quite fit with his heroic image, but that's what happened to him during the American Revolution.

Captured by Shawnee Indians in 1778, Boone convinced the other members of his hunting party to surrender to the Shawnee without even firing a single shot. He was then overheard conspiring with the Shawnee and British officers to surrender the town of Boonesboro, Kentucky, which he himself had founded. One of the captives even said Boone took an oath of allegiance to the British. While other captives were treated badly and forced to run the gauntlet, Boone was adopted by the Shawnee chief and given the name Big Turtle. This alone

"We were ordered by Colonel Boone to stack our guns and surrender."

—MEMBER OF THE HUNTING PARTY, TESTIFYING AT THE TRIAL

convinced several of the other captives, who were later ransomed, that Boone had betrayed them.

All of this painted a picture of treachery and betrayal. After returning to Boonesboro, Boone was placed under house arrest, charged with treason, and court-martialed.

Surprisingly, Boone denied none of the facts. But he said it was part of a "stratagem" to deceive the British and save Boonesboro. He got captured by the Indians, he said, because he was in his mid-forties and not as fast as he used to be. He also said that he surrendered the hunting party rather than see them all killed. He had spun tales to the British and Indians to buy time so that he could escape and warn the town.

Boone must have been convincing, because he was found innocent on all charges. But hard feelings remained. The famous frontiersman moved away from Boonesboro a year later, leaving the treason charges behind him and traveling a path that would one day see him elevated into an American legend.

Bulldog of the Black Sea

The globe-trotting Admiral Pavel has his final cruise.

In 1788, Catherine the Great appointed a combative new commander to a squadron of Russian warships. "One more bulldog for the Black Sea," said the Russian empress, who charged Rear Admiral Pavel Dzhones with the task of liberating that body of water from the Turks.

Admiral Dzhones took command of 12 warships at the mouth of the Dnieper River and quickly lived up to Catherine's expectations. His mastery of tactics enabled him to prevail over larger Turkish forces in several engagements, and he demonstrated great courage by leading his own

ship alongside a Turkish galley to engage in extremely fierce hand-to-hand combat.

The admiral hoped his efforts would bring him great fame. "Loving glory," he wrote to Catherine, "I am perhaps too attached to honors." But it wasn't to be. Backstabbing colleagues reaped the credit he deserved. He was dismissed from his command and never went to sea again.

But while political intrigue denied Admiral Dzhones the chance to become a revered Russian hero, he is remembered for earlier exploits on different oceans. For the man who fought his last battles under the Russian flag was Scottish by birth and American by choice, a fighting captain whose stirring victories in the American Revolution live on to this day.

His service as Russian admiral Pavel Dzhones is long forgotten by everyone but his immortal words spoken as America's first naval hero, John Paul Jones, "I have not yet begun to fight" can never be forgotten.

JUST A TALE?

Did Jones really utter the phrase, "I have not yet begun to fight"? An officer aboard the *Bonhomme Richard* recalled those were the words Jones used—but his account came 46 years later. Several accounts written shortly after the battle have Jones saying, "I may sink, but I'll be damned if I strike." And another eyewitness wrote that Jones shouted, "Yankees do not haul down their colors until they are fairly beaten." Whatever his actual words, his spirited refusal to give up was more than clear.

Matchmaker

A good boy gets the fun girl, thanks to one of history's bad boys.

History has tagged Aaron Burr (right) as a scoundrel, and history has it right. He tried to steal the presidency from Jefferson while serving as his running mate. As vice president, he shot and killed Alexander Hamilton during a duel. Later he was involved in a conspiracy against the U.S. government.

But he did make one positive contribution to the country and the presidency. Surprisingly it was as a matchmaker.

Burr served as a senator from New York in 1794 when the nation's capital was still Philadelphia. When in town he often stayed at Mary Payne's boardinghouse, which is where he met her widowed daughter, Dorothea.

Like many, Burr was charmed by Dorothea's vivacious personality. Had the two become romantically involved, history might have turned out very different. Instead, Burr introduced her to a friend: a shy Virginia congressman who was still a bachelor at age 42: James Madison.

That's how Dorothea "Dolley" Payne became Dolley Madison, the legendary First Lady who won over Washington and the world with her charm and pluck. It never would have happened but for a scoundrel.

JUST A TALE?

A bigger-than-life First Lady, Dolley Madison was famous for her wonderful parties and her amazing gowns. She played cards for money, used rouge and wore fancy jewelry—all shocking in her day. Legend has it the feisty lady saved Gilbert Stuart's famous portrait of Washington (the one that now appears on the one-dollar bill) from burning with the White House during the War of 1812 when British soldiers torched the building. That's absolutely true. When it proved too difficult to unscrew the eight-foot-frame from the wall, she coolly ordered the glass broken and the canvas taken out. She rolled it up and escaped with only minutes to spare.

Warrior Queen

This Chinese lady pirate's navy becomes a world power.

The most successful pirate of all time was a woman. She commanded more men and ships than any other pirate in history. Best of all, from her point of view she retired undefeated, kept all of her plunder and was allowed to live peacefully into old age.

The name of this remarkable woman was Hsi Kai. Plucked from a Canton brothel by the notorious pirate Ching Yih, she rapidly became much more than just another concubine. Stunningly beautiful, she was also a wily negotiator and an organizational genius. In return for her hand in marriage she demanded and got a 50-percent share of her husband's wealth. Upon his death in 1807 she took complete control of the fleet.

For three years, Hsi Kai commanded more than 50,000 men and women and more than a 1,000 ships. Hers was a pirate navy larger than that of most world powers. She ruled much of the South China Sea with an iron hand, terrorizing shipping, attacking seaside villages and defeating every naval force sent to intercept her.

By 1810 Britain, Portugal, and China were so fed up that they assembled a combined force to attack Hsi Kai. To avoid the massive loss of life such an assault would entail, the emperor of China offered amnesty: "If there is anything of a woman's heart in you, you will someday want peace and offspring. Could it be now?" She wasn't interested in children, but she knew a good deal when she saw one. Under terms she personally negotiated with the governor general of Canton, she and 17,000 of her men gave up their ships and weapons but were allowed to keep their stolen treasures. She lived another 30 years and died wealthy—nobody ever got the better of Hsi Kai.

Davy's Death

The last moments of an American hero may not be what you think.

For many the enduring image of the Battle of the Alamo is Davy Crockett fighting like a wildcat to the bitter end. According to one dramatic account shortly after his death his body was found encircled

by "17 dead Mexicans, 11 of whom had come to their deaths by his dagger and the others by his rifle and four pistols."

So goes the legend. What about the truth?

While the 189 Texans who fought at the Alamo in 1836 were all killed, numerous Mexican soldiers wrote accounts of the battle. They paint a far different picture of Crockett's last moments.

Mexican general Antonio López de Santa Anna ordered his troops to "give no quarter" when they stormed the Alamo, and the hand-to-hand fighting that followed was bloody, desperate, and lasted until dawn. That's when Crockett and six other men were found, quite alive, in a back room, to which they had retreated. Crockett, by one account, then tried to talk his way out, telling his captors he had planned to become a loyal Mexican citizen and had done no fighting at the Alamo.

When the men were brought to Santa Anna, the general was so enraged that his "take no prisoners" directive had been disobeyed, he ordered his soldiers to execute the captives on the spot. "With swords in hand," wrote one Mexican officer, they "fell upon these unfortunate, defenseless men just as a tiger leaps upon his prey."

The truth was known within weeks of the battle and published in many newspapers. But the myth proved far more appealing, and so it has endured from that day to this.

Forgotten Fillmore

This overlooked president forces an issue—and affects the world.

Every time we buy a product that's made in Japan—a car, a camera, a digital chip—we would do well to reflect on the overlooked president who made it possible.

Millard Fillmore is perhaps the most obscure chief executive of the United States. He was a little-known ex-congressman when selected as Zachary Taylor's running mate. Taking over after Taylor died in office, the 13th president served two and a half years and never ran for reelection. He is generally remembered for being just another in a long series of inept presidents unable to stop the drift toward Civil War.

But Fillmore did one thing that changed the world. For centuries the Japanese had closed off their country, discouraging trade or any kind of relations with the rest of the world. Fillmore wanted to open up trade with Japan and secure permission for U.S. ships to obtain supplies there. He sent Commodore Matthew Perry and a fleet of warships to force a change in policy.

Perry's mission led to a treaty that established diplomatic relations with Japan. It also made the Japanese realize just how far behind the West they were and led the country to embark on a crash course of modernization. Japan's subsequent rise to power, first through military might and later through its role as an economic powerhouse, is due in part to the president no one recalls.

MORE OF THE STORY

Several other U.S. missions to Japan had failed, and Fillmore decided an American show of force was necessary. Commodore Perry sailed into Nagasaki harbor in four steam-powered warships that became known to the Japanese as the "Black Ships." Refused permission to land, he threatened a bombardment. The Japanese realized that they lacked the military power to resist. Perry delivered a letter from President Fillmore as well as gifts that emphasized the West's technological prowess, including a scale model of a steam locomotive that could travel 20 miles per hour. A treaty followed two years later.

Admiral Perry was already in his 60s when he undertook this mission, which was to be his last.

Red Cross

A businessman's empathy gives birth to a mission of mercy.

Little remembered today, the Battle of Solferino was one of the most terrible in history to that date. On June 24, 1859, French and Italian forces under Napoleon III attacked an Austrian army. Three hundred thousand men engaged in furious fighting for more than 15 hours.

A Swiss businessman named Henry Dunant (below), who was trying to arrange a meeting with Napoleon III, found himself a witness to the battle.

"Is it not a matter of urgency, since...we cannot avoid war...to alleviate the horrors of war?"

—HENRY DUNANT

He was shocked by the horrifying carnage. "Every mound, every rocky crag, is the scene of a fight to the death," he wrote later. "It is sheer butchery."

What came next was even worse. A staggering 40,000 were left wounded on the field of battle and medical care for them was totally inadequate. Dunant threw himself into the effort to help the wounded, despairing when many died for lack of care. He recalled one wounded soldier who spoke bitterly of his fate: "If I had been looked after sooner I might have lived, and now by evening I shall be dead." And he was.

Moved by what he had seen, Dunant wrote a book about his experiences and called for the formation of an international organization to provide aid. His work led to the first Geneva Convention and the formation of an international relief agency.

To protect doctors and nurses on the battlefield, the nations who formed the agency also agreed on a symbol that would proclaim its neutrality. In a fitting tribute to this compassionate Swiss businessman, they reversed the colors of the Swiss flag to create: the Red Cross.

Fighting Joe

Good guy or not—whose side is he on, anyway?

Wheeler had no problem taking the commission; it was seen as a sign the nation was whole again.

After the sinking of the battleship *Maine* in Havana Harbor, the United States mobilized for war with Spain. Many prominent people clamored for a chance to join the army as high-ranking officers. Assistant Secretary of the Navy Theodore Roosevelt was one. Another was a powerful congressman named Joe Wheeler. President William McKinley appointed Wheeler a major general of volunteers.

OTHER PLAYERS, OTHER PLACES

Wheeler was a Confederate general at age 26 and a U.S. Army general at age 61. He stayed in the service after the Spanish-American War. In 1902 former Confederate general James Longstreet was visiting West Point when he ran into Wheeler in full regalia. Recalling a deceased Confederate comrade, the feisty Jubal Early, Longstreet said: "I hope Almighty God takes me before he does you for I want to be within the gates of hell to hear Jubal Early cuss you in the blue uniform." Wheeler died in 1906 and was buried in Arlington National Cemetery, one of only two former Confederate generals buried there.

It made perfect sense: Wheeler, after all, had military experience, having served as a general during the Civil War. Of course, at that time he had been fighting against the United States.

"Fighting Joe" Wheeler was a cavalryman who had earned his stars in the Confederate Army. Now he was trading in the old gray uniform for a brand-new blue one, to serve as a general in the Army he had once considered an enemy.

Wheeler was a bantam rooster of a man, five-foot-two and all fight. "A regular gamecock," Theodore Roosevelt called him. At times he seemed to think he was fighting the Civil War all over again. "Let's go, boys!" he reportedly cried at the Battle of San Juan Hill. "We've got the damn Yankees on the run again!"

Wheeler's appointment was greeted by many in the North and the South as a sign that the War Between the States was thing of the past.

A Tale of Two Generals

Meet the heroic general you never heard of.

General Douglas MacArthur (left) was one of the most talented, flamboyant and controversial men ever to put on a military uniform. His remarkable achievements in World War II and the Korean War have led many to regard him as the greatest military man of all time. And he certainly was a one-of-a-kind figure.

Well, not exactly.

There's another general from an earlier era whose career was remarkably similar. Like Douglas MacArthur, he earned his reputation fighting in the Pacific. Like Douglas MacArthur, he thrilled the nation with his exploits in the Philippines. Like Douglas MacArthur, he rose to become the highest-ranking general in the Army. And, like Douglas MacArthur, he was eventually removed by the president for insubordination and brought home, triggering a national controversy.

Both men came within a hairsbreadth of being killed on the battlefield. Both were nominated as young officers for the Medal of Honor, but didn't actually receive the award until decades later.

Is it just an odd coincidence that Douglas MacArthur's career so closely mirrored the life of this earlier military hero? Just a random happenstance? Unlikely.

Because that man was General Arthur MacArthur (right), Douglas MacArthur's father—whose greatest legacy may have been the son who spent a lifetime trying to live up to his dad.

MORE OF THE STORY

Arthur MacArthur fought in the Civil War, the Indian Wars, and the Spanish-American War. His son, Douglas, saw action in World War I, World War II and Korea. They were great military men, with their joint careers spanning nearly a century, but neither man's ego was able to handle being subordinate to civilian authority. When President McKinley appointed a civilian governor of the Philippines, Arthur MacArthur, then military governor, accused him of "unconstitutional interference." Douglas MacArthur labeled his own sacking by the president as one of the most "disgraceful plots" in U.S. history.

Double-O Powell

Meet the man of mystery who founded the Boy Scouts.

The Boy Scout movement was launched by Robert (later Lord) Baden-Powell back in 1908. But the revered scout leader had another side. He was a spy for the British military—the James Bond of his day. He was so proud of his undercover exploits and his mastery of spy techniques that he detailed them in a book entitled *My Adventures As a Spy*.

He was a master of disguise and developed many novel espionage tactics, including the coded sketch—an innocent-looking drawing that contained hidden military secrets.

He spied for Britain on several continents, barely escaping capture several times. Espionage was a game to him, and he pursued it with great zest. "Spying would be an intensely interesting sport, even if no great results were obtainable from it," he said. "For anyone who is tired of life, the life of a spy would be the very finest recuperation."

After his spying days were over, Baden-Powell went on to become a bonafide military hero. His defense of Mafeking in South Africa during the Boer War made him a national hero in Britain. It was after all this that he created the scouting movement. Later in his life, when asked what he had loved most about spying, he replied, "romance and excitement."

The Black Swallow of Death

He's the first African-American military pilot, a heroic fighter and one heck of a drummer, too.

Gene Bullard's last job was working as an elevator operator in New York's RCA Building. He probably had the most amazing résumé of any elevator operator in history.

Born the grandson of a slave in 1894, Bullard (left) stowed away on a transatlantic freighter when he was just 10 years old. He was found on board and put ashore in Scotland. From there, he worked his way south to England, where he eventually started prizefighting at age 16. Upon journeying to France for a bout, he fell in love with the country he'd heard stories about—a fascinating and beautiful place where blacks were not second class. When World War I broke out in 1914 he took up arms for his adopted country and joined the French Foreign Legion. His infantry unit was known as the "Swallows of Death."

Bullard spent two years at the front. In his very first action in the Battle of Artois, more than half of his unit was wiped out. He was badly wounded at

the Battle of Verdun. While recuperating, he volunteered for the new French Air Service and became the world's first black combat pilot, in 1917. Involved in countless air skirmishes he had one confirmed kill and another unconfirmed one. Afer one battle, he landed to find his plane riddled with 78 bullet holes.

After the war he became a well-known character in Paris. He took drumming lessons to get in on the jazz craze and got a job as a bandleader at Zelli's Zig Zag bar in Montmartre, France. He would later own his own club, but his days of military service weren't over.

In 1939 Bullard was recruited to gather information for French intelligence. When the Germans invaded in 1940, he picked up a rifle to fight for his adopted homeland and was severely wounded once again. He was smuggled out of Europe through Spain and returned to the United States he had left so many years ago.

Bullard, a native of Columbus, Georgia, was awarded more than 15 medals for his service to France. In 1954, when the French were relighting the eternal flame at the Tomb of the Unknown Soldier at the Arc de Triomphe, to whom did they give that honor? A New York elevator operator.

He emblazoned his plane with the motto *"Tout le sang qui coule est rouge!"* — *"All blood runs red."*

OTHER PLAYERS, OTHER PLACES

Unlike Bullard, who fled the racism he encountered in the United States, Benjamin O. Davis, Jr. (right) worked within the existing system of the day to become the first commander of an all-black flying unit and one of the most influential officers of any color. The son of an Army officer in an all-black cavalry unit, the younger Davis was sponsored for West Point by the only black member of Congress at the time, Representative Oscar De Priest of Chicago. When he received his commission as a second lieutenant in 1936, he and Benjamin O. Davis, Sr. were the only two black line officers in the armed forces. He was assigned to teach military tactics at Tuskegee Institute to avoid having him command white soldiers. It was there that he received his flight training and became commander of the 99th pursuit squadron—the first Tuskegee Airmen. When the Air Force integrated in 1948, it was following the plan written in part by then-Colonel Davis, the military man who fought the fascists abroad and the racists at home.

Gunfighter Golden Years

The final days of two real-life Western heroes are very modern.

Wyatt Earp and Bat Masterson: legendary lawmen of the Old West. Masterson, the mild-mannered Dodge City sheriff, was said to have killed 26 men before he turned 30. Earp, his onetime deputy, achieved undying fame after the gunfight at the OK Corral. They walked tall, shot fast, and each earned a reputation that soon became enshrined in myth and legend.

And then they rode off into the sunset, right? The truth is, both men outlived the Wild West by many years.

After years in Alaska, Wyatt Earp headed to Hollywood and spent his last days in showbiz. One of the people Wyatt Earp befriended in Hollywood was a young propman named Marion Morrison, who as an actor took the name John Wayne. Wayne later said he based his portrayal of Western lawmen on his conversations with Earp. Earp became great friends with early Western star William Hart and spent hours teaching him how to quick-draw before dying in 1929.

Bat Masterson went back east and settled down in New York City. He lived until 1921, ending his multifaceted career as a sports columnist for the *New York Telegraph*, where he died at his desk—literally with his boots on.

In this 1883 photo of the Dodge City Peace Commission, Wyatt Earp is seated second from the left in the front row and Bat Masterson is standing at the far right in the back.

The Good Man of Nanking

A Nazi businessman becomes a savior for thousands.

Japanese forces sweeping through China reached the capital city of Nanking on December 13, 1937. After taking control, they began to execute Chinese prisoners of war and the killing quickly spiraled out of control. Men were rounded up for bayonet practice. Women were raped by the tens of thousands. People were beheaded for sport. Snapshots taken by Japanese soldiers captured the frenzy of violence known as the Rape of Nanking.

A surprising hero emerged during this reign of terror: an unassuming German businessman named John Rabe.

The small group of Westerners still in Nanking created a "safety zone," hoping to make it a safe haven for refugees of war. They elected Rabe their leader in the belief that his Nazi Party membership would afford him influence with the Japanese.

"You hear of nothing but rape. If husbands or brothers intervene, they're shot."

—JOHN RABE

Desperate Chinese began to flood the safety zone to escape the massacre. When Japanese soldiers pursued them even there, Rabe assumed the role of protector. He fearlessly confronted Japanese commanders, demanding that they control their soldiers. He threw his own property open to refugees. He began patrolling the safety zone himself, pulling Japanese soldiers off rape victims and chasing them away without using any weapons. His only defense: an armband sporting a Nazi swastika. "They don't want to tangle with a German," he wrote in his diary. "Usually all I have to do is shout 'Deutsch' and 'Hitler' and they turn polite."

Japanese troops went on an eight-week orgy of murder and violence in Nanking, killing an estimated 300,000 men, women and children in what some have called the forgotten holocaust. But more than 250,000 who crowded into the safety zone were spared, thanks in no small part to a good man named John Rabe.

Rabe (third from left) is pictured with other Westerners still present in Nanking during the conflict.

Japan's Schindler

An obscure Japanese diplomat saves thousands from death in the Holocaust.

When Hitler's blitzkrieg exploded into Poland in 1939, thousands of Polish Jews fled to neighboring Lithuania. But it was only a temporary refuge. By the summer of 1940, with the Soviet Union occupying Lithuania and the Nazis on the march, danger was closing in.

The dilemma the refugees faced was that they needed travel documents to get out—and no government was prepared to issue them. A sympathetic Dutch diplomat hatched an unlikely plan to get them out via the Soviet Union and Japan. But his scheme hinged on refugees being able to get hard-to-obtain Japanese transit visas—quickly. Without those visas the refugees would be trapped.

At this dark hour a surprising savior appeared: Chiune Sugihara (left), the Japanese consul general in Kaunas, Lithuania. Against the express orders of his government, he began to issue precious travel visas to any desperate refugees who applied, regardless of whether or not the applicants had the proper documents. He issued thousands of transit visas even as his superiors ordered him not to. Finally, Tokyo told him to leave the coutnry, but he continued to hand lifesaving visas out the window of the train.

Ultimately, Sugihara's efforts saved at least 5,000 Jews from the Holocaust—and cost him his job with the Japanese Foreign Ministry. Why did Sugihara defy his government and destroy his career? "They were human beings, and they needed help," he said. "I'm glad I found the strength to give it to them."

Susan Bluman had an invalid passport (top) but Sugihara still issued the transit visa (bottom) that saved her life.

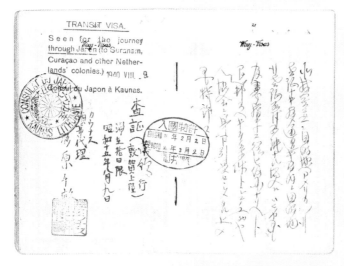

Germany and Japan today seem unlikely allies in the goal of world domination. But by the time Hitler invaded Poland in 1939 Japan had been skirmishing with China since 1931 in the second Sino-Japanese War. Japan saw China's Manchurian region as a limitless source of natural resources and as a buffer zone against the hated Soviet Union. Hitler saw Europe as a source of raw materials and its domination by Germany as a natural by-product of Germany's growth. Both nations were chafing under what they believed was unfair treatment at the end of World War I. Realizing their mutual goals led to the signing of the Tripartite Pact in 1940 with Italy as a third partner. In the pact, the three nations agreed to "establish and maintain a new order of things," with the plan being that Germany and Italy were to gain joint control of all of Europe and Japan was to rule all of Eastern Asia. During the time Sugihara was writing exit visas, his country was an ally of Germany and already technically at war with the Soviet Union, which then controlled Lithuania. He was working feverishly against his ally, and rightly so: it is believed that 91 percent of Jews in Lithuania were slaughtered.

The Man Who Saved the Palace

An RAF pilot rescues the royals.

The air-raid sirens sounded at 9:30 that Sunday morning. As Big Ben struck noon the skies over London began filling with warplanes.

It was September 15, the fiercest day of the Battle of Britain. More than 400 German bombers attacked London. Buckingham Palace was a prime target. The official residence of the royal family had been hit twice in recent days, suffering minor damage. It seemed only a matter of time before it suffered a direct hit.

Royal Air Force fighter pilots battled desperately all day to protect the city. Toward the end of the battle, Sergeant Ray Holmes shot down one bomber and then saw another German plane making an unobstructed run straight toward the palace. Holmes was out of ammunition, but he didn't hesitate for a minute.

He flew his Hurricane fighter directly into the German plane, slicing off its tail and sending it hurtling to the ground below. Then he managed to parachute out of his own plane before it crashed on Buckingham Palace Road.

Street crews later paved over the remnants of Holmes's plane, which remained buried for more than 60 years until archaeologists recovered the engine and some other parts in 2004. The 89-year-old Ray Holmes looked on with interest.

"What goes through a young pilot's mind as he confronts the Germans?" he was asked. "Nothing particularly," answered the man who saved the palace. "Except he just has to go and have a bash at him. That's all."

Queen Elizabeth and King George V survey the wreckage outside Buckingham Palace.

The Lady Is a Spy

Josephine Baker goes from banana dancer to decorated hero.

American-born Josephine Baker was a dancer, singer and daring sex symbol, as well as a highly successful intelligence operative. After arriving in Paris in the 1920s, her provocative dancing took the town by storm. In 1940, when war broke out, she offered her services to the French Resistance. She told a Free French leader, "Parisians have given me everything, especially their hearts. Now I will give them mine."

One of her superiors was skeptical: "I was afraid she was one of those shallow show-business personalities who would shatter like glass."

But she proved cool as a cucumber. When the Germans invaded Paris, Baker let members of the Resistance hide in her remote château. Dispatched to neutral Lisbon to establish contact with the Free French, she set up concerts as a cover story and carried vital information written with invisible ink on her sheet music. "The destiny of the Free French," said her boss, Colonel Paolle, "was written in part on the pages of *Two Loves Have I*."

Invited to diplomat's parties, she acted the part of a ditzy dancer, then wrote down everything she heard. "My notes would have been compromising if

Baker is pictured here during her heyday in the 1920s.

discovered," she said later, "but who would dare search Josephine Baker to the skin?"

After the war Charles de Gaulle officially recognized her contributions, awarding her the *Légion d'Honneur* and the *Medaille de la Résistance* for her efforts. When she died, the sensation who had once shocked Paris with her banana dance became the only woman ever to receive a 21-gun salute in France.

> *"France has made me what I am."*
>
> —JOSEPHINE BAKER

Beautiful Brains

This pioneer of on-screen nudity revolutionizes electronic communications.

Hedy Lamarr was just a teenager when she shocked the world in 1933 by appearing nude in the Czech film *Extase* (which means "ecstasy" in English). It was the movie industry's first nude scene that actually made it into a film.

When Lamarr hit Hollywood she was billed as "the most beautiful woman in the world." But after World War II broke out she was determined to put her brains to work for her adopted country.

In August 1942 Lamarr got together with composer George Antheil and patented a secret communications system to prevent the jamming of radio-controlled torpedoes. At its heart was an innovation Lamarr dreamed up on the back of a cocktail napkin: frequency hopping. In other words, radio signals that constantly switched frequencies to make interception impossible.

> *"Any girl can be glamorous. All you have to do is stand still and look stupid."*
>
> —HEDY LAMARR

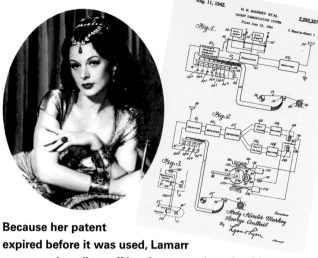

Because her patent expired before it was used, Lamarr never made a dime off her frequency-hopping idea.

It was way ahead of its time and wasn't put to use until the Cuban missile crisis, 20 years later. Today it has a fancier name—spread spectrum technology—and is a critical part of cell phone systems, satellite encryption and other modern marvels. A testament to the actress who was "heady" in every sense of the word.

MORE OF THE STORY

In *Extase's* famous nude scene, Lamarr is skinny-dipping when she discovers her horse has run off. She goes trotting after him, naked, until she comes face-to-face with a strange man in the woods. Tame by today's standards—its most risqué shot is a glimpse of Lamarr's breasts—the sequence led to the film being condemned by the pope and banned in the United States.

Heroes O'Hare

Chicago's O'Hare Airport is named after a hero—which one?

Butch O'Hare was America's first ace of World War II. On February 20, 1942, he spotted a Japanese bombers preparing to attack the carrier USS *Lexington* in the waters off New Guinea.

Diving into their midst he shot down six of them single-handedly, saving the ship and the lives of thousands aboard. This action earned him the Medal of Honor.

Butch died in combat the following year. In 1949 the citizens of Chicago honored O'Hare by naming their airport after him.

That's not all there is to the story, however.

O'Hare's father was a lawyer and racetrack owner named Eddie O'Hare. "Artful Eddie," as he was known, got involved with Chicago mob boss Al Capone in the 1920s. That connection made him a ton of money, but he was worried about the impact on his then-teenage son. Eddie was dead-set on Butch getting into the U.S. Naval Academy and he figured he would have to break away from Capone before that could happen.

So "Artful Eddie" cut a deal. For the sake of his son's future he volunteered to risk his life and inform on Capone. He detailed the mobster's

Butch O'Hare waves to the cheering crowds.

"One of the most daring, if not the most daring, single action in the history of combat aviation."

—FRANKLIN D. ROOSEVELT, AWARDING BUTCH O'HARE THE MEDAL OF HONOR

operations for IRS agents and led them to a bookkeeper who could testify about Capone's illegal income. As a result prosecutors were able to convict Capone on charges of tax evasion and finally send him to prison in 1931. Butch received an appointment to the Naval Academy a year later. So while O'Hare Airport bears the name of a famous hero of World War II, it also commemorates the name of the father who was willing to do anything for his son—and the man who helped prosecutors win their war against Capone.

An Offer He Couldn't Refuse

A notorious mobster plays a part in America's war effort.

War can make for some strange bedfellows. None stranger han when U.S. naval intelligence hooked up with the Mafia during World War II.

It began when the SS *Normandie,* a French ocean liner being converted into a troop ship, burned at its New York City moorings in February 1942. The Navy thought it might be sabotage. Concerned about dockside security and always looking for ways to gather information, naval intelligence decided to seek help from New York's most powerful mobster: Charles "Lucky" Luciano.

Luciano was serving a 30-year jail term, but he agreed to cooperate. He "encouraged" his gangland associates to work with the Navy. Mob *capos* passed the word to dockworkers and fishermen that they should report any suspicious activity—or else. When the U.S. was getting ready to invade Sicily, Luciano put them in touch with people who had connections to the Sicilian underworld.

After the war the Navy tried to cover up its wartime marriage to the mob. All records were destroyed, and the Navy denied that they had gotten much in the way of help from Luciano. To this day it is unclear how useful he was.

But consider this: despite a huge public outcry, Luciano was released from prison and deported to Sicily less than six months after the war was over, though he was years away from completing his sentence. A reward, perhaps, to a man whose contribution the government could never afford to officially recognize.

Mug shot of mobster Charles Luciano

"The greater part of the intelligence…was from the Charlie 'Lucky' contact."

—LIEUTENANT COMMANDER CHARLES HAFFENDEN,
NAVAL INTELLIGENCE

The Youngest Hero

A boy is determined to do a man's job for his country.

Graham holds a photo of himself as a boy-sailor.

In August 1942, Calvin Graham walked into a recruiting station in Fort Worth, Texas. He was shipped out to the Pacific, where he joined the crew of the USS *South Dakota* as a gunner.

It wasn't long before Graham found himself in harm's way. First came the Battle of Santa Cruz in October. Two weeks later it was the Battle of Guadalcanal, in which the battleship took 47 hits in a desperate night action. Graham was knocked down a stairway by an explosion that peppered his jaw with shrapnel. Though seriously wounded he worked through the night, fighting fires and pulling fellow crewmen to safety.

And how did the Navy reward Graham's heroism in battle? They shipped him stateside, put him in the brig for three months, stripped him of his veteran's benefits and gave him a dishonorable discharge. It seems that after the battle, Graham carelessly let slip that he had lied on his enlistment papers. Specifically he had lied about his tender age.

Calvin Graham was 12 years old. He is believed to be the youngest of the thousands of underage servicemen who fought for the United States in World War II.

The Navy didn't quite know what to do with Graham. Eventually his sister got him sprung by threatening to go to the papers. Two days after his 13th birthday, he rejoined his Fort Worth classmates in the seventh grade—undoubtedly the only veteran in the group.

JUST A TALE?

The man to whom Graham admitted his true age was his gunnery officer on the *South Dakota*, Sargent Shriver, who later married JFK's sister Eunice Kennedy before heading to the Peace Corps and running for president in 1976. But was that the end of the story—was his heroism never made public? Graham never stopped fighting to have his navy service recognized. In 1978, President Jimmy Carter ordered the Navy to grant him an honorable discharge. And in 1994, the Navy finally agreed to give him a Purple Heart for his injuries suffered off Guadalcanal. Graham didn't live to see it, having died two years before.

A Country of Heroes

The citizens of tiny Denmark stand up to Adolf Hitler.

In September 1943, Adolf Hitler signed an order for Denmark's Jewish population, as yet largely untouched by the Holocaust, to be deported to the death camps.

Nazi officials planned to begin the roundup on the night of October 1. More than 1,000 German police and Gestapo officers came to Denmark to handle the action. Ships and trains were readied to whisk the Jews away.

The response of the citizens of little Denmark deserves to be remembered for all time.

The Danish government, tipped off about the roundup by German diplomat Georg Duckwith (left), warned Jewish families to go into hiding. Many non-Jewish Danes risked their lives to hide and protect their Jewish neighbors. That led to a spontaneous nationwide effort to smuggle Denmark's Jews to safety in Sweden—"a conspiracy of decency," one author has called it. Haphazard at first, the rescue mission soon became an organized effort of the Danish underground. Churches and hospitals were used as gathering points. Universities closed down for a week—and students worked with resistance fighters to get the country's Jews secretly to the coast.

From there more than 300 fishing boats ferried Denmark's Jews to Sweden, which welcomed them with open arms. More than 90 percent of Denmark's 7,000 Jews managed to escape the German sweep through their country.

There was no single hero in this country of heroes, which is why Israel's Holocaust memorial Yad Vashem honors the entire Danish people as "righteous among nations" for risking the wrath of Germany to help their Jewish countrymen in their hour of need.

When Sweden offered asylum to Danish Jews, an official German communiqué referred to the Swedes as "Swine in dinner jackets."

Oddly enough Denmark was not officially at war with Nazi Germany for most of WWII. Instead, the Danish government had agreed to a peaceful occupation by German forces in 1940, in effect remaining an independent country with a few not-very-welcome "guests." Although the Danish government accepted the Germans, many Danish citizens did not—and the resistance movement was born. Its tactics consisted primarily of sabotaging German equipment and became increasingly daring until August 1943. At that point Germany demanded that the Danish government sentence to death any captured saboteurs. When Denmark refused, the Germans seized power, officially overthrowing the government. Germany then attempted to subject Denmark's Jews to the same treatment as those in the other countries it had occupied.

Like Father, Like Son

The tours of duty of these brave men have an unusual twist.

During World War II, Mike Novosel flew a B-29 and participated in the fire-bombing of Tokyo. At age 42, with three children, he found himself so inspired by President Kennedy that he volunteered to fly heli-copters for the Army in the Vietnam War.

He thought he would be used as an instructor, but found himself shipped off to combat, flying in the company of pilots half his age. Eventually he served two tours as a "Dustoff" MEDEVAC pilot in Viet-nam, airlifting wounded soldiers from the battlefield. He flew more than 2,000 missions and evacuated more than 5,000 wounded. One very dangerous mission earned him a Medal of Honor.

His son, Mike Novosel, Jr., graduated from Army Flight School 27 years to the day after his father. The year was 1969 and he asked to be assigned to his dad's unit—the 82nd Medical Detachment. "At the time I just wanted my dad to

During the mission for which Mike Novosel, Sr. (left), was awarded the Medal of Honor, he braved heavy fire to save 29 lives.

be proud of me," said Mike, Jr. But it was the first and only time in U.S. history that a father and son ever flew together in the same combat unit. And each would have the chance to save the other's life.

When Mike, Jr.'s helicopter was forced down by enemy fire, his father flew to the scene and rescued him. Less than a week later, Mike, Jr, rescued his father under similar circumstances.

In 1971, Mike, Sr., was awarded the Medal of Honor by President Nixon, who told father and son that they wouldn't be going back to Vietnam. "The Novosels have done enough," he said.

The Code of the Service

Could an old movie save a president's life?

In 1939, Ronald Reagan made a film called *Code of the Secret Service*. It was one of a series of movies in which he played a tough-guy Secret Service agent named Brass Bancroft. It wasn't one of Reagan's more memorable pictures. He said more than once that it was the worst film he was ever in. But he ended up being very glad he did make it.

Reagan (right) on screen as the movie hero Bass Bancroft in *Code of the Secret Service*.

The film captured the imagination of a 10-year-old boy in Miami. "I made my dad take me to that movie quite a few times," recalled Jerry Parr. He vowed that when he grew up, he would become a Secret Service agent And he did.

Forty-two years later, on March 30, 1981, Secret Service agent Jerry Parr was part of the detail guarding President Reagan when would-be assassin John Hinckley opened fire. It was Parr who braved the hail of bullets to tackle Reagan and push him into the waiting car, which sped off toward the White House. And it was Parr who saw Reagan coughing up blood and made the split-second decision to head straight for the hospital.

Unbeknownst to either of them, a ricocheting bullet had sliced into Reagan's chest, causing massive internal bleeding. Parr's decision to seek immediate medical care saved the president's life. Brass Bancroft could have done no better.

Reagan waves moments before the shooting. Parr is at his immediate left.

Second Chance

An Olympic champion fights the battle of a lifetime.

When Rulon Gardner won a gold medal in wrestling at the 2000 Olympics the announcers called it the "Miracle on the Mat." After all, Gardner was facing one of the most fearsome Olympic champions of all time. Russian wrestler Alexander Karelin had won 13 consecutive world championships and three consecutive Olympic gold medals in the event. No one had even managed to score a point against "The Russian Bear" in more than six years. Gardner shocked the world by defeating the man who was considered unbeatable.

Yet that only ranks as the second-biggest miracle in Gardner's life.

Two years later Gardner became separated from friends while snowmobiling in a Wyoming forest. His snowmobile flipped him into the freezing waters of the Salt River. The water was shallow, but Gardner was left soaked and stranded. Night was falling and the temperature was dropping.

The situation looked bleak. Gardner's soaking-wet boots soon froze into solid blocks of ice. But he drew on the

"I had won the most important match of all…for my life."

—RULON GARDNER, ON SURVIVING HIS SNOWMOBILE ACCIDENT

mental discipline that made him a champion and refused to give up. He ran feebly in place to keep warm. He positioned himself so that if he fell

Gardner (in blue) defeats Karelin at the 2000 Olympics.

Gardner rebounded from his injury to win a bronze medal at the 2004 Olympic games, after which he retired from wrestling.

asleep he would fall down and wake up again. He narrowed his focus to a single, critical goal: surviving until dawn.

The mercury dipped to 25 below zero. When Gardner was rescued the following morning his core temperature was down near 80 degrees and his body was sheathed in ice. For a while it was touch and go. Doctors believed that they would have to amputate part of his feet and that he might never walk again.

Rulon Gardner had other plans.

His recovery was painful and difficult. Only one toe had to be amputated, but it damaged his balance. He ruined several pairs of shoes because his swollen feet bled through the leather. But just as he did on that frozen night, he persevered.

Not only did he walk again, not only did he wrestle again, not only did he make it to the Athens Olympics in 2004—he managed to win another medal, taking a bronze.

After the match Gardner left his shoes in the middle of the ring, signaling the end of his extraordinary wrestling career.

Truly a miracle—on and off the mat.

MORE OF THE STORY

Perhaps vying for the title of "Luckiest Man in the World," Gardner also cheated death in 2007 by surviving a harrowing plane crash. After their single-engine Cessna nosedived into a lake on the Utah-Arizona border, Gardner and two friends spent more than an hour swimming in 44-degree water to reach shore, then had to spend the night huddling for warmth without shelter. Gardner has also survived a motorcycle crash and the accidental puncturing of his abdomen with an arrow.

The Hindu goddess Kali inspired a cult whose name lives on today.

Chapter 2

Word Work
Words and Names That Stood the Test of Time

Our language is rich with history—with expressions born of exciting times, places named for famous people, and objects given the monikers of their creators. There are ominous examples, too: actions that echo across generations, carrying the spectre of long-forgotten players and nefarious characters whose very names inspire fear and loathing. But also present here are the words written by the famous (and not so famous) whose ability to withstand the test of time and remain meaningful today speak volumes about the author. These are the stories of words that have stood the test of time.

History's Hitmen

Could this frightening group be the world's first terrorists?

During the 11th century, a rebellious Islamic sect took command of a castle outside Teheran. They set about trying to win converts and soon held a chain of castles across the Middle East.

This group of radical Shiites waged war against the rulers of the Islamic world, chiefly through acts of terrorism and "hits" carried out on leaders. Their weapon of choice was the dagger; they murdered princes, crusaders, and caliphs—whoever were their enemies of the moment.

In many ways, they were the Al-Qaeda of their day. Their specialty was dramatic, high-profile

A legend tells of how the assassin leader ordered two followers to jump from a tower to their deaths to demonstrate his total authority.

MORE OF THE STORY

The word "assassin" is actually a corruption of the group's original name, the Hashishi. Crusaders thought that meant the terrorists were hashish eaters, which added to their fearsome reputation. The founder of the Assassins was Hassan-I-Sabbah. His sect could be flexible in its allegiances. They executed crusader leaders but also carried out execution attempts on behalf of the crusaders when it suited them.

killings—sometimes for the purpose of advancing their agenda, other times to raise money. Members of the group believed that the murders they carried out would earn them eternal bliss.

For more than 150 years they held sway. In the 1200s, Mongol warriors, led by Genghis Khan's grandson, Hulagu, captured their mountain strongholds and their long reign of terror was finally over for good.

Crusaders brought tales of this faction back to Europe. Their very name evoked shivers of terror and it is still remembered today. Whenever a political leader is murdered, it evokes the memory of this ancient cult whose methods seem all too modern. Their name? The Assassins.

Divine Wind

What do you call the storm that saved Japan?

This was war on an unprecedented scale. Kublai Khan had already completed the conquest of China begun by his grandfather, Genghis Khan. In 1281 he had assembled 140,000 warriors to invade the Japanese islands. A fleet of 9,000 ships carried them to Japan. It seemed that nothing could stop them from defeating Japan and absorbing it into the Mongol Empire.

But everything changed when the winds suddenly rose with a fury and a powerful typhoon slammed into the Japanese coast, wreaking havoc on the invasion force. Ships were dashed upon the rocks. Thousands drowned. Chinese warriors who managed to stagger ashore were easy prey for the Japanese, who slaughtered them at will. It is thought that as many as 100,000 of the invaders perished in the storm.

Japan was saved. The Japanese people gave credit to the gods, calling the incredible typhoon that wrecked the invasion force "The Divine Wind."

It was a name that would become familiar in another war centuries later when it was adopted by Japanese warriors willing to sacrifice their own lives in a last-ditch bid to turn defeat into victory. They too referred to themselves as "The Divine Wind." Or, in Japanese: *kamikaze.*

A *kamikaze,* or divine wind, plane attacking the USS *Missouri* in April 1945.

Kublai Khan tried twice to invade Japan but was stymied on both occasions by a typhoon.

Count Vlad

The name of this murderous prince will live in legend forever.

In the 1450s, there lived a prince known as Vlad the Impaler. He was ruler of Walachia, a small principality in what is now Romania. Much of what we know about Vlad comes from his enemies, and it paints a rather dark picture. He ruled with an iron hand and had no mercy for those who disobeyed him. He impaled people by the thousands and even washed down his meals with their blood.

Stories of his unbridled cruelty abound. He is said to have skinned unfaithful lovers alive. When two visiting ambassadors refused to remove their hats, saying it was not the custom in their country, Vlad replied with grim humor that he would like to support their customs— and he ordered the hats nailed to their heads. A charming fellow, this Prince Vlad.

After his death, in 1476, people tried hard to forget him—but the scary stories of his short time in power never really went away.

In the 1890s Vlad achieved a special sort of immortality when a writer doing research at the British Museum came across an old manuscript about him. Its tale of unvarnished evil inspired Bram Stoker to create one of the darkest characters of all time.

Vlad's father was known as Dracul, which in Romanian means "Dragon" or "Devil." Vlad was the son of the Devil. Or, as we know him: Dracula.

Vlad never lived in Bran Castle, commonly considered "Dracula's Castle," but he did spend some time imprisoned in the dungeon.

"The shocking story of a MONSTER and Berserker called Dracula."

—TITLE PAGE FROM A 15TH-CENTURY ACCOUNT OF COUNT VLAD

Dracula, as portrayed by Bela Lugosi in the 1931 film of the same name.

MORE OF THE STORY

In 1459, an invading Turkish army came across a gruesome warning left by Vlad: the decaying bodies of perhaps 20,000 Turkish captives, impaled on stakes. But Vlad also impaled his own subjects as punishment for almost any crime. One estimate says he may have personally authorized the killing of as many as 10,000 of the 500,000 people in his principality. Although he was prince of Walachia, Vlad was actually born, appropriately enough, in nearby Transylvania. He spent more time as a prisoner of other rulers than he did on his own throne. His longest stretch of rule lasted only six years. He was eventually killed in battle, trying, unsuccessfully, to retake his land from the Turks.

War of Jenkins' Ear

An oddly named conflict inspires an American landmark.

No war in history has a more striking title than the 1739 War of Jenkins' Ear. Robert Jenkins was a British sea captain whose ship was boarded by the Spanish coast guard in the Caribbean. According to Jenkins, the Spanish captain tied him up and cut off his ear with a sword. He was so angry that he brought the severed ear to Parliament, prompting the prime minister to declare war on Spain.

Actually things were a little more complicated than that. Jenkins didn't exhibit his ear to Parliament until seven years after he said it was cut off. Some people wondered aloud if that shriveled thing in the box really was his severed ear. Critics claimed he had lost his ear in a bar fight, and that the whole thing was a political stunt designed to force a war the prime minister didn't really want.

Whatever the truth, the alleged brutality inflamed public opinion. England was enraged, and war was waged.

The British hero of this little-known war was Admiral Edward Vernon. Today we remember him less for his exploits, perhaps, than for what he inspired.

One of his officers was a young colonial who owned a farm in Virginia called the Little Hunting Plantation. Lawrence Washington was so impressed with his superior officer that he

Jenkins displays his ear to Lord Walpole.

OTHER PLAYERS, OTHER PLACES

Admiral Vernon was known as "Old Grog" because he wore a grogram cloak in stormy weather. After he diluted his sailors' rum ration with water, the disgruntled seamen named the watered-down drink after their commander: grog. Vernon achieved fame for his attack on the Spanish colonial town of Porto Bello, now a part of Panama. The Spanish considered it the finest port in the Americas. Gold and silver mined in Peru and elsewhere in South America were collected and stored there pending shipment to Spain, so the fortifications surrounding the port were impressive. It was quite a prize. Vernon attacked with just six men-of-war and emerged victorious. All of England celebrated the Spanish defeat and

Londoners are reminded of the battle (or should be) when they go shopping on London's very tony Portobello Road.

Admiral Vernon takes Porto Bello.

renamed the farm in Vernon's honor. But he died a few years later and his half-brother George inherited the place.

The farm is Mount Vernon, America's only tribute to the War of Jenkins' Ear and home to the first president.

Mount Vernon, built by George Washington's older half brother

From Sin to Grace

A reformed slave trader's writing is an amazing legacy.

John Newton started in the slave trade at age 20 and eventually became captain of his own slave ship. "I was once an active instrument in a business at which my heart now shudders," he later wrote.

On May 10, 1748, his ship was foundering in a storm. Until then, Newton had never been a religious man, but as the storm threatened to capsize the ship, he fell to his knees and began to pray. "God have mercy," he begged as wave after wave crashed violently over the deck. When the storm suddenly died down, he fervently vowed to devote himself to God.

That moment changed his life forever, and one day it would touch the lives of millions.

Newton continued in the slave trade for five years after his conversion, finding it disagreeable but not yet considering it morally wrong. "What I did, I did ignorantly," he said later. He was at first rejected for ordination to the ministry because of his checkered past but was eventually allowed to become a minister in 1764 and continued in the ministry for the next 43 years. Newton eventually started to speak out against slavery and turned into a crusading supporter of abolition. He lived long enough to see the slave trade entirely abolished by the British Empire in 1807—in part because of his tireless efforts.

He also became well known for writing beautiful hymns. One song we remember particularly well today celebrated his own amazing transformation:

> *Amazing Grace, how sweet the sound,*
> *That saved a wretch like me.*
> *I once was lost, but now am found,*
> *Was blind, but now I see.*

> *"I awaited with fear and impatience to receive my inevitable doom."*
> —JOHN NEWTON, DESCRIBING THE STORM

Doctor Death

A medical man's name becomes a symbol of terror.

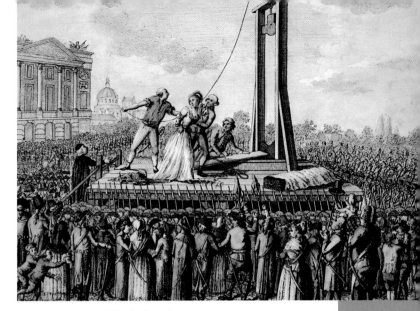

The execution of Marie Antoinette

After the outbreak of the French Revolution, a doctor and member of the National Assembly beseeched his fellow revolutionaries to outlaw inhumane forms of execution. He described in detail gory executions of the past and advocated a less-painful method. He painted a vivid picture of what he had in mind: "The mechanism falls like lighting; the head flies off; the blood spurts; the man no longer exists."

Dr. Joseph Guillotin became an instant celebrity after championing this new means of execution, in 1789, and although he neither invented nor designed the device that was subsequently built, his name was quickly attached to it. The guillotine soon took center stage in the Revolution, as 14,000 "enemies of the state" were brought before huge crowds to lie beneath its blade—including the young King Louis XVI and his hapless queen, Marie Antoinette.

After the doctor's death, in 1814, his children changed their names, appalled that their once-proud family moniker was now synonymous with bloody decapitation and revolutionary terror.

> *"With my machine, I'll take off your head in a flash, and you won't even feel the slightest pain."*
>
> —DR. JOSEPH GUILLOTIN, DESCRIBING HIS PROPOSED METHOD OF EXECUTION

OTHER PLAYERS, OTHER PLACES

Before the guillotine was adopted, Paris executioner Charles-Henri Sanson wrote a memo complaining that death by decapitation was becoming, well, a bit of a headache. Each beheading blunted his blade, he owned only two swords, and there were just too many people to be executed. The result, he said, was that many executions were unavoidably cruel.

The Gospel According to Thomas

A president rewrites the Bible to suit his personal vision.

When Thomas Jefferson found himself at odds with the writings of Matthew, Mark, Luke and John, he took a unique approach: He decided to write his own gospels.

Jefferson valued the ethical teachings of Jesus but he didn't buy into what he called the "corruption of Christianity." He thought the New Testament gospels were filled with material that shouldn't be there. So he cut and pasted the original gospels of the New Testament to create his own version, known today as the Jefferson Bible.

Jefferson's pasted-together gospel consists largely of the teachings of Jesus as told in parables and sermons. The Jesus of this book performs no miracles. He does not proclaim himself the Son of God. And he does not rise to heaven after dying on the cross. Jefferson thought all these things had been added through the "stupidity" or "roguery" of Jesus' disciples. Jefferson's Jesus was a man, spiritual and prayerful, but simply a man.

Jefferson did the work at night in 1802 during his first presidential term. He hid his radical

Jefferson was well known to work late into the night.

rewriting of the Bible because he thought it might arouse controversy. "I not only write nothing on religion," he told a friend, "I rarely permit myself to speak on it." Jefferson kept his views under wraps during his lifetime. The Jefferson Bible wasn't published until 75 years after his death.

Although Jefferson wasn't willing to share his views on his personal religioisity, he was vehement in his defense of religious freedom. "It does me no injury for my neighbor to say there are 20 gods or no gods," he wrote. "It neither picks my pocket nor breaks my leg."

Jefferson considered Jesus a philosopher and was bold enough to point out where his own philosophy differed. "I am a Materialist; he takes the side of Spiritualism," he wrote. But whether Jefferson adhered to a particular religion, he was a great

believer in Jesus' moral teachings. As he wrote in 1803 to Benjamin Rush, "To the corruptions of Christianity, I am indeed opposed; but not to the genuine precepts of Jesus himself. I am a Christian, in the only sense in which he wished any one to be; sincerely attached to his doctrines, in preference to all others...." And so he took the trouble to make sure his Good Book reflected this philosophy.

MORE OF THE STORY

Thomas Jefferson was a prolific writer and a careful curator of his own records. Jefferson maintained categorized filing cabinets full of papers. Even tiny scraps and scribbled notes were preserved by the former president, creating a comprehensive historical profile of his life and times. But the Jefferson papers also give Americans a glimpse into the creative mind of this founding father. Jefferson's archives include some 80 of his architectural drawings. They relate to the building of his Monticello home, the Virginia

Governor's mansion and the dormitories for the University of Virginia. He looked after every detail, even drawing a design for a desk and sharing his own personal recipe for cement. In his slightly sloppy but precise handwriting, Jefferson wrote that builders should use "equal parts of pulverized brick, lime and wood ashes, carefully sifted through a fine sieve and brought to a proper consistency with oil." Jefferson was a statesman, philosopher, scientist, architect and—so it would seem—a bit of a micro-manager.

Shell Shock

A revolutionary weapon—and the name to go with it— changes warfare forever.

At the start of the 1800s, a new weapon appeared on the battlefields of Europe. It was the brainchild of an English officer who had spent 30 years perfecting it. A hollow artillery shell was filled with smaller musket balls along with a charge of gunpowder ignited by a fuse. The shell could be launched from long distances at the enemy's lines. When it exploded in midair it spread a deadly carpet of metal shards over a wide area.

The inventor of the shell devoted all his free time to perfecting it, pouring his life savings into the project. The British army finally adopted the shell in 1803 and first used it in the Napoleonic

Shrapnel's shells (below, left) were the "bombs bursting in air" that Francis Scott Key saw during the bombardment of Fort McHenry (above) in the War of 1812.

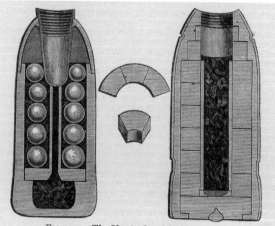

FIG. 102.—*The Shrapnel and Segment Shells.*

Wars. It proved frighteningly lethal on troops and so terrified French soldiers that they believed the British had poisoned their cannonballs.

Sir George Wood, commander of the British artillery, credited the new shell with playing a critical role in the defeat of Napoleon at the Battle of Waterloo. "On this simple circumstance hinged entirely the turn of the battle," he later wrote in a letter to the shell's inventor.

Artillery became infinitely more terrifying and the name of the man who invented the shell became known around the world: Henry Shrapnel.

Political Monster

This vice president's name really has staying power.

Many vice presidents are quickly forgotten. One has been remembered for about 200 years because his name became a permanent part of the American language.

In 1812, Elbridge Gerry was governor of Massachusetts. He signed into law a redistricting bill that rearranged state senate districts in a way that gave the Jeffersonian Republicans a huge advantage over the Federalists.

One district in particular was stretched into a tortuous shape in order to make sure that a majority of its voters were Jeffersonian Republicans. Federalists howled that it was an abuse of power. Political observers joked that the odd-shaped district looked like a salamander. Engraver Elkanah Tisdale seized on that idea, added claws, wings and fangs, and published a cartoon in the *Boston Gazette* showing the monster that Gerry created.

What did he call it? A Gerrymander.

While the redistricting kept Republicans in power, many in Massachusetts were outraged, and the political backlash swept Gerry out of office later in the year. But Republicans appreciated his efforts and he was picked to run as vice president with James Madison.

Now when anyone tinkers with redistricting to give an unfair advantage to one party, it's called gerrymandering. And Elbridge Gerry is remembered one more time.

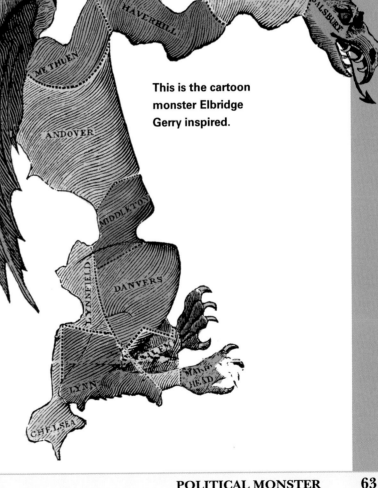

This is the cartoon monster Elbridge Gerry inspired.

A Capital Idea

An American president lends his name to a foreign city.

Immigrants depart for Liberia in March, 1896.

In the early 1800s, James Monroe (left) was one of many people who thought the best solution to the problem of slavery was to remove blacks from the United States entirely. In December 1816, Monroe and others founded the American Colonization Society. Its goal was to form a new colony in Africa and encourage free blacks who lived in America to emigrate there.

Some of the people who founded the society were idealists who thought blacks would be happier in Africa. Others were slave owners who considered free blacks troublemakers and wanted to get rid of them. "Of all classes of our population," said Speaker of the House Henry Clay, another founder of the organization, "the most vicious is that of the free colored."

Shortly after the society was formed, Monroe became president of the United States and used his new position to support the effort. He secured $100,000 from Congress and the colony of Liberia was founded in 1822. In honor of Monroe's efforts, the capital city was named after him.

It was called Monrovia.

In all, 13,000 free blacks were transported to Liberia, but the idea of colonization never really caught on. Today Monrovia is a city of 500,000 that recalls a president's failed effort to solve a problem that would one day plunge the United States into civil war.

FOOTNOTE TO HISTORY

Colonization was highly controversial among both blacks and whites. Shortly after formation of the society, 3,000 free blacks protested against it in Philadelphia. Abolitionists loudly condemned the idea in the 1830s, but many saw it as the only answer to the problem of race relations in America. Abraham Lincoln was a big supporter of colonization and tried in vain to promote it during the Civil War.

Budding Statesman

The U.S. Secretary of War plants the seed for a Christmas tradition.

Joel Poinsett (right) was an ambassador, a congressman and eventually Secretary of War from 1837 to 1841. He holds the distinction of being the only U.S. statesman whose name was made into a word in two different languages—meaning two entirely different things.

During Poinsett's years as ambassador to Mexico, he got a little too embroiled in the political intrigue swirling about Mexico City—some even said he was plotting with revolutionaries who wanted to bring down the government. Mexican authorities grew angry at his heavy-handed interference in Mexican affairs, and they coined a new and not very flattering word to describe his officious and intrusive manner: *poinsettismo.*

He was eventually asked to leave Mexico, but not without bringing back something we use to commemorate Christmas to this very day.

Poinsett wasn't all bad. He was an avid botanist and he became enchanted with a flower he found that grew only in southern Mexico. The Aztecs called it *cuetlaxochitl.* He began growing the flowers in his greenhouse and shipped samples back to the United States. Eventually the winter-blooming plant became a holiday hit and the season of peace became a little brighter thanks to the flower that bears the name of a Secretary of War. We call it, in his honor, the poinsettia.

In the Name of Kali

This group of hooligans influences the way you talk.

In Hindu tradition there is a goddess named Kali who is considered the mother of all goddesses. This goddess was so engrossed in fighting evil, however, that she got a little carried away, destroying everything in sight. Fortunately the god Shiva was able to stop her by laying down under her foot.

The city of Calcutta (originally Kalighata) got its name from Kali. It is the site of a large temple dedicated to the goddess who has long been worshiped by a wide variety of ordinary people.

But in 13th-century India, there arose a secret Hindu sect that worshiped Kali as the goddess of destruction. This sect remained a powerful and greatly feared force for more than 500 years.

This particular sect was far from ordinary. Members lived typical lives most of the year, but in the autumn they roamed the countryside in bands, looking for wealthy travelers to kill and sacrifice to their goddess. Their *modus operandi* was to have one member of the band become friendly with the intended victim while the others awaited an opportunity to strike. They liked to decoy a victim to a secluded spot, sneak up from behind, and kill him with a scarf especially reserved for that purpose. Because the goddess did not like to see blood spilled, victims were usually strangled. The group picked wealthy victims for sacrifice so they could provide a source of revenue as well. Women and musicians, interestingly enough, were considered exempt from attack.

They became known as the Phansigars ("the stranglers") but that wasn't their real name.

DESCRIPTION

OF THE

HABITS AND SUPERSTITIONS

OF THE

THUGS;

A SECT WHO PROFESS TO BE DIVINELY AUTHORIZED TO

PLUNDER AND MURDER.

PUBLISHED BY CALEB WRIGHT.

This illustration of a band of Thugs (apparently between attacks) appeared in *Harper's Weekly* in 1857. The accompanying article introduced readers to the tactics of the sect, which often used beautiful women as decoys and schooled its young in murder.

After the British colonized India, they made a decision to destroy the group. From 1833 to 1837, more than 3,000 of its members were arrested. Nearly 500 were hanged, and thousands more imprisoned for life. The last known member was executed in 1882. What was the real name of this feared band? The Thugs.

Although victims were killed by strangulation, each thug carried a pickax and used it to dig a grave to hid the victim's body.

The museum is affectionately known as "the nation's attic."

The Bastard and the Brahmin

Unravel the story of how an American institution, championed by an ex-president, came to be named after a dead Brit.

In 1835, the United States received some startling news. An eccentric British chemist named James Smithson had died and left all his money to the United States—a country he had never even visited. Smithson was the bastard son of the duke of Northumberland and a wealthy man in his own right. His will directed the U.S. government to use the money to "increase knowledge among men."

President Andrew Jackson and numerous other prominent American politicians were dubious about accepting a gift from the son of a British nobleman. After all, the British had put Washington to the torch less than 20 years earlier. Senator John Calhoun spoke for many when he said it was "beneath the dignity of the United States to receive presents of this kind."

But one prominent American statesman stood up to advocate acceptance of the gift. Former president John Quincy Adams (left), scion of the famous Adams family, was now serving as a representative from Massachusetts. Through much of his career Adams had advocated government support of the arts and sciences. He said the country had "an imperious and indispensable obligation" to put Smithson's money to good use. Adams eventually convinced a reluctant Congress to accept the grant and spent years making sure it was put to good purpose.

Smithson's legacy was about half a million dollars, the equivalent of more than $10 million today. After the money was accepted a 10-year fight took place over how to spend it. Ideas floated included a national university, a botanical garden and a celestial observatory.

In the end, the gift the United States thought about possibly turning down led to the museum that may be John Quincy Adams's greatest legacy: The Smithsonian.

OTHER PLAYERS, OTHER PLACES

Smithson had an older half brother, Hugh Percy, the legitimate son of the duke of Northumberland. In one of history's ironies, Percy was a British general who had led troops against America in the early days of the American Revolution. So one brother fought to keep the United States from becoming a country, while the other gave the States one of its most enduring institutions.

Old Kinderhook

A president helps launch the world's most popular expression.

People all over the world know what "O.K." means. But few of them realize it was born from a wordplay craze and a presidential election.

It all started in Boston in 1838. People there started using humorous initials, sometimes combined with purposeful misspellings, just for fun. Newspapers picked up the fad, and writers had a high old time throwing around all sorts of silly or fantastic abbreviations.

This cartoon depicts Van Buren, "Old Kinderhook," being expelled from the White House by William Henry Harrison.

For example:

g.t.d.h.d.	give the devil his due
n.g.	no go
s.p.	small potatoes
O.W.	Oll Wright (all right)
G.T.	Gone to Texas

And there was another expression that started gaining some currency: Oll Korrect, or O.K.

The fad spread quickly to New York, but the phrase "O.K." didn't come into national use until the presidential campaign of 1840. Democrats trying to reelect Martin Van Buren were casting around for political slogans. Van Buren, sometimes known as "The Little Magician" and "The Fox of Kinderhook" because of his political skills, was from Kinderhook, New York. He was also called "Old Kinderhook." O.K. Political operatives seized on that coincidence. Democrats started forming O.K. clubs and staging O.K. balls. The campaign catapulted the expression into national circulation.

Van Buren lost his bid for reelection. But "O.K." won in a landslide and is still used billions of times a day around the globe.

Dressed to Kill...or Be Killed

A military fiasco goes down in history as a fashion boon.

The Charge of the Light Brigade in 1854 took place during the Battle of Balaklava in the Crimean War. Both battle and war have been largely forgotten, but the charge lives on, thanks to Alfred Lord Tennyson's famous poem.

> *Into the valley of Death*
> *Rode the six hundred.*

There was some confusion about the orders and 673 British cavalrymen were sent on a doomed charge up a long valley with Russian artillery firing on them from all sides.

> *Theirs not to reason why;*
> *Theirs but to do and die.*

In less than 20 minutes the Light Brigade was decimated. More than 200 men were killed. Militarily, it was a terrible blunder. But it quickly captured the imagination of the British public, who regarded it not as a disaster, but instead as something glorious and noble. The commander of the Light Brigade, James Thomas Brudenell was lionized as a national hero.

He also inspired a piece of clothing we still use today. Brudenell bought his men button-down collarless sweaters they could wear under their uniform to keep warm. After the battle, the style became all the rage, and it was named after him.

Never heard of the Brudenell sweater, you say? That's because it was named after his title. Thomas Brudenell was an earl. In fact, he was the seventh Earl of Cardigan.

OTHER PLAYERS, OTHER PLACES

The cardigan wasn't the only garment to emerge from the battle. The balaclava, a knitted hood that covers the head and comes down over the face and neck with holes for the eyes and mouth, was first worn there by soldiers. Cardigan's superior officer, who gave the order for the charge, was also a fashion inspiration. After he lost an arm at the Battle of Waterloo, Lord Raglan began wearing a cape-like coat with sleeves extending to the neck. The raglan sleeve is still a popular style today.

Not Whistling "Dixie"

The most famous song of the South is born and bred in the North.

"Dixie," the anthem of the South, was actually written in a New York hotel room by a man from Ohio. The year was 1859 and composer Daniel Decatur Emmett (right) wrote the song on a rainy Sunday afternoon for Bryant's Minstrels, one of the blackface minstrel shows popular at the time. A contemporary of Stephen Foster, Dan Emmett also wrote "Jimmy Crack Corn."

But it was Dixie that was played in 1861 at the inauguration of Jefferson Davis as president of the Confederate States of America. Soon it became the marching song for the Confederate Army. "It is marvelous," wrote one Southern soldier, "with what wildfire rapidity this tune 'Dixie' has spread across the whole South."

This was an outrage to Emmett, a staunch Union supporter. "If I'd known to what use they were going to put my song," he reportedly said, "I'll be damned if I'd have written it."

Prior to the Civil War, the actors in minstrel shows were whites in blackface. After the war, blacks often appeared in the shows wearing the standard makeup.

> *"It made a tremendous hit and before the end of the week everybody in New York was whistling it."*

—DAN EMMETT, ON THE FIRST PERFORMANCE OF "DIXIE," IN 1859

So Emmett, the creator of "Dixie," was actually a damned Yankee!

The day after Robert E. Lee surrendered, President Lincoln asked a band outside the White House to play "Dixie." "I have always thought 'Dixie' one of the best tunes I ever heard," Lincoln said. "Our adversaries over the way attempted to appropriate it, but we have fairly captured it."

After the war Emmet came to cherish the South's love of "Dixie." In 1895, at the age of 80, he made a farewell tour and sang the song to standing ovations. He even occasionally restored the original first verse, which the wife of the original show's promoter was worried might be offensive:

> *Dis worl' was made in jiss six days,*
> *An' finished up in various ways;*
> *Look away! Look away! Look away! Dixie Land!*
> *Dey den made Dixie trim and nice,*
> *But Adam called it "paradise,"*
> *Look away! Look away! Look away! Dixie Land!*

"Dixie" remains a popular Southern anthem to this day and a true American folksong.

OTHER PLAYERS, OTHER PLACES

A little later, a woman wrote a poem that was set to music and became a popular Civil War song—this time for the North. Julia Ward Howe, a prominent Abolitionist and social activist first heard the music in Washington, D.C., as a marching song for a battalion of the Massachusetts Infantry. The tune stayed with her that night and, upon waking early the next morning, she wrote new words for the music. Her song became the now-famous "Battle Hymn of the Republic," first published in *Atlantic Monthly* in February 1862 and sung at the funerals of such figures as Robert Kennedy, Richard Nixon and Ronald Reagan.

Unleaded Zeppelin

Name the man whose Civil War experience changes the course of aviation history.

Count Ferdinand von Zeppelin was a young Prussian military officer when he was sent to the United States in 1863 as a military observer attached to the Union Army. The enthusiastic young lieutenant rode along on several missions with the Union cavalry and was almost captured by the Confederates a week before the Battle of Gettysburg.

Having come so far von Zeppelin set out to explore the breadth of the United States. And so it was that he ended up in Minneapolis, where he ran into something that changed his life: A ride in a hot-air balloon.

The balloon was being operated by John Steiner, who had spent a year as an aeronaut for the Union Army. On August 19 he let von Zeppelin go up on a tethered ascent. The young nobleman rose 600 feet into the air. He was hooked.

Steiner regaled von Zeppelin with tales of military reconnaissance over Confederate lines, noting that the biggest problem was the inability to steer the balloon. The answer, Steiner thought, would be to create a cigar-shaped balloon with a rudder that could be guided through the air.

Von Zeppelin was soon on his way back to Germany, but he never forgot that balloon ride or Steiner's idea. Twenty-five years later, after he retired from the army, he set out to build a rigid, steerable balloon. The first zeppelin made its maiden flight on July 2, 1900, launching a new age of lighter-than-air travel that owed its birth to the War Between the States.

The most famous of Von Zeppelin's ships was the ill-fated *Hindenburg*.

Land War

Meet an English landlord who unwittingly gives his name to a revolutionary form of protest.

Irish tenant farmers were outraged over high rents set by their English landlords. So in 1880 they organized. They called themselves the Land League and their movement swept the nation overnight. Along the way it gave birth to a new tactic that became a staple of nonviolent organizations down through the decades.

One of the first and most notorious targets was a British estate manager in County Mayo. The Land League demanded that he reduce his rents to his tenants because of a bad harvest. His response was less than conciliatory—he brought in constables to evict them instead.

The Land League responded in a manner that would soon be the talk of the world. Local residents refused to sell him supplies, pick his crops or even talk to him. Instead they hooted and jeered at him whenever he appeared in public. He was compelled to use his wife and daughters to harvest the estate's crops under the watchful eye of the local constabulary. His nerve soon broke and he fled the country for the safety of England.

The estate manager is now long dead, but his name has lived on, attached to the revolutionary tactic first used against him: Charles Cunningham Boycott.

Within a month, the press had picked up the term "boycott."

"No laborer dared to work for him, no tradesman to serve him with goods."

— *HARPER'S WEEKLY*, DECEMBER 1880

A Reasonable Doctor

A superstar fictional character is born of a doctor's well-honed power of observation.

Dr. Joseph Bell (below) was a professor of medicine at the University of Edinburgh. His students were amazed by his astonishing powers of observation. He seemed able to determine what patients did for a living or what illness they might have, simply by glancing in their direction. One time he concluded that a patient had walked across a golf course on the way to the doctor, simply by looking at his shoes. Another time he was able to determine not only that a patient had been in the army but also which regiment he served in.

One of Bell's students was particularly impressed with his teacher's abilities. He became Bell's lab assistant—his Dr. Watson, if you will. He filled up notebooks with examples of what he called Bell's "eerie trick of spotting details." For example, Bell studied the way a man walked. A sailor moved very differently than a soldier. And if a man was indeed a sailor he probably had tattoos that might illustrate his travels. Thus, Bell could learn a lot just by observing details. But to Bell, it wasn't just a parlor trick, it was an important part of a doctor's trade, one he was very serious about teaching his students. This particular student eventually went into practice himself outside London. When business was slow he filled his spare moments by writing stories.

In 1886 he took Dr. Bell's powers of perception and gave them to a character of his own making—a character who made the young doctor Arthur Conan Doyle famous the world over. And so the professor who made even the most complex diagnosis seem "elementary" became the inspiration for fiction's greatest detective: Sherlock Holmes.

> *"It is most certainly to you that I owe Sherlock Holmes."*
>
> —ARTHUR CONAN DOYLE TO JOSEPH BELL

Holmes and Watson confer in a first-class train carriage in this illustration by Sidney Paget of the 1892 story, *The Adventure of Silver Blaze.*

MORE OF THE STORY

Arthur Conan Doyle (right) was quick to credit Bell with the uncanny power of deduction that was Sherlock Holmes's trademark: "I do not think that his analytical work is in the least an exaggeration of some of the effects I have seen you produce." Bell himself took a more modest view of his role: "Dr. Conan Doyle, by his imaginative genius, made a great deal out of very little." Once it was revealed that Bell was the model for the great detective, the Edinburgh doctor found himself deluged with fan mail and interview requests. He relished the attention but sometimes found it tjust a bit iresome. "I am haunted by my double," he wrote a friend. And that's not surprising—Doyle wrote at least 60 stories about Holmes. He even brought him back from the grave in response to the public outcry over the character's untimely death.

Presidential Phrasemaker

One president truly has a way with words.

Theodore Roosevelt was more than an activist president. He was perhaps the greatest phrasemaker ever to inhabit the White House. His contributions to the English language still affect the way we talk.

It was Roosevelt who first called the White House "a bully pulpit," a great stage for someone to use to make his views heard round the world. He is also famous for the proverb "Speak softly and carry a big stick."

It didn't stop there. TR also came up with "lunatic fringe" to refer to the extremists who populate all political parties. Asked in 1912 whether he would run for president again, he introduced yet another enduring phrase. This one referred to frontier boxing, when a man ready

to take on all challengers would toss his hat into the boxing ring.

"My hat's in the ring."

Roosevelt has also been credited with accidentally authoring one of the enduring marketing slogans of the 20th century. In 1907 he visited the Hermitage, the Tennessee home of President Andrew Jackson. Given a cup of coffee, he drank it down it and then supposedly exclaimed:

"Delighted! Good to the last drop!"

The coffee was a local brew served at the Maxwell House, one of Nashville's hotels. Within a decade, Maxwell House coffee began using the slogan to turn the coffee into a powerhouse national brand. TR had struck again.

JUST A TALE?

There's some disagreement over whether Roosevelt actually uttered, "Good to the last drop," although at least one eyewitness said he did. There is no doubt, however, that he raved over the coffee he was served. A local paper captured this quote: "This is the kind of stuff I like to drink, by George, when I hunt bears." And yes, the teddy bear really is named after him.

Thank You for Smoking

A hotel room and a phrase enter the history books together.

George Harvey arrived at Chicago's Blackstone Hotel in June 1920. He was there to attend the Republican National Convention. The prominent GOP leader from New York City checked into a spacious two-room suite. Harvey's name has faded from public memory but the reception room of suite 404 was destined to become the most famous hotel room in American political history.

It was the original "smoke-filled room."

After four ballots, the convention found itself with a deadlocked vote between two presidential candidates, General Leonard Wood and Illinois governor Frank Lowden. A distant fourth in the balloting—out of the picture, really—was another candidate, Ohio senator Warren G. Harding.

Through the hot and sultry night that followed, a group of party leaders met in Harvey's room, looking for a way out of the deadlock. Bypassing the front-runners, they seized on the little-known Harding as the candidate least offensive to all. They summoned Harding and told the surprised candidate that they were giving all their support to him.

As the dawn broke, Associated Press reporter Kirke Simpson filed a story saying, "Harding of Ohio was chosen by a group of men in a 'smoke-filled room' early today." Harding went on to win

OTHER PLAYERS, OTHER PLACES

A political boss from Ohio who backed Harding was most likely the person who originated the phrase. Harry Daugherty predicted the outcome of the convention with amazing accuracy weeks before: "After the other candidates have gone their limit, some 12-15 men worn out and bleary-eyed for lack of sleep, will sit down around two o'clock in the morning, around a table in a smoke-filled room in some hotel, and decide the nominations. When that time comes, Harding will be selected."

Perhaps as a reward, Daugherty (right) was a frequent guest at the Harding White House.

the nomination and become president. And the "smoke-filled room"—describing a back room where political operators pull the strings out of public view—became an indispensable part of our political lexicon.

The Name Game

One president's name comes to stand for two very different things.

In 1918, everyone in America knew the meaning of the word "Hooverize." It meant to cut back on your consumption so that you might be able to share the bounty with others. The word paid tribute to the most respected humanitarian in the world: Herbert Hoover (right).

Little more than a decade later, his surname would take on a much darker meaning.

Hoover made millions as an engineer and businessman. After the outbreak of World War I, he turned his attention to humanitarian efforts. He organized a massive relief program to save millions in Europe from starvation. He convinced Americans to voluntarily conserve food with "Meatless Mondays" and "Wheatless Wednesdays" so that there would be plenty of food to share overseas. His relief efforts also gave him a great name in Europe. In Finland beef that came in the humanitarian assistance packages was known as a *Hooverin pintaa* which translates into "Hoover treat."

In 1919, Hoover's success at humanitarian efforts led a well-to-do New Yorker to say: "He is certainly a wonder and I wish we could make him president. ... There could not be a better one." And indeed, Hoover's fame and kindness led him to the White House and the tragic irony of his life.

Hoover's popularity garnered him 58 percent of the vote in the 1928 election, but only a dismal 39.7 percent in 1932, when he lost to Franklin Roosevelt.

A stock market crash in 1929 sent the nation's economy into a tailspin. Millions were thrown out of work. Many expected the great humanitarian to mount relief efforts. But Hoover was strongly opposed to government handouts. He seemed paralyzed in the face of disaster. Soon shantytowns full of homeless people became known as "Hoovervilles." The newspapers they wrapped around themselves to keep warm were known as "Hoover blankets." The thin gruel handed out by soup kitchens was known as "Hoover soup."

A name that once stood for generosity and sharing had now become synonymous with poverty and despair. And that New Yorker who thought Hoover would be a great president? It was none other than Franklin Delano Roosevelt, who drove Hoover from the White House.

"I can Hooverize on dinners, and on lights and fuel too, but I'll never learn to Hooverize when it comes to loving you."

—WORDS FROM A POPULAR CONTEMPORARY SONG

Live and Let Spy

Reality and fiction come together in the world of espionage.

William Donovan became famous as the founder of the Office of Strategic Services Society (OSS), the World War II spy agency that was the forerunner of the CIA. When Donovan was setting up the agency in 1941 he consulted with a trusted friend, a British naval officer who was the assistant to the head of British Naval Intelligence.

The officer was eager to help Donovan. Furthermore he was a man of great imagination with a keen eye for detail. He stayed in a spare bedroom at Donovan's house in Washington, D.C., and

Fleming on his Jamaican estate, Golden Eye, in 1964

drafted several detailed memos advising Donovan how to organize an American intelligence agency. Donovan went to work and the rest is history.

The British officer was Commander Ian Lancaster Fleming. Donovan clearly valued Fleming's contributions. He presented Fleming with a .38-caliber police revolver engraved with the words "For Special Services." After the war Fleming moved to Jamaica, where he drew upon his wartime experiences and fantasies to write a series of novels about an espionage agent who knew no equal and who, like Fleming himself, was a bit of a ladies' man. He also gave the character many of his own distinctive tastes: vodka martinis, for instance—shaken, not stirred. And his secret designation in Navy Intelligence was Agent 17-F. His creation, of course, was 007. So it is that the man who had a hand in creating the CIA also created the world's most famous fictional spy. And his name? Bond. James Bond, of course.

Sean Connery as James Bond in the film version of *Casino Royale*.

MORE OF THE STORY

When Fleming saw a bird-watching book, *Birds of the West Indies*, written by an ornithologist named James Bond, he knew it was the perfect name for his spy: "brief, unromantic, yet very masculine." Later, when the ornithologist's wife, Mary, jokingly threatened to sue Fleming, he wrote back: "I can only offer your James Bond unlimited use of the name Ian Fleming for any purpose he may think fit." So while the bird expert may be the real James Bond, who was the first fictional one? Sean Connery is often credited as the first actor to play James Bond, but he was actually preceded by two other men. It was an American thespian, Barry Nelson, who was the first-ever Bond. He portrayed the enigmatic and handsome spy on an American TV version of *Casino Royale*, which was broadcast October 21, 1954, on the CBS network. The first British James Bond (and officially the second actor to request his martini shaken) was Bob Holness, who played the secret agent in a 1957 radio dramatization of *Moonraker*, broadcast in South Africa.

Gadzooks!

Jazz, the Marines, radio and a weapon all help win World War II.

Sergeant Bob Burns was a champion rifleman in the Marine Corps during World War I. But as good a marksman as he was, he was a better musician. Burns organized a Marine Corps Jazz Band that was a favorite of General John Pershing and played to troops across Europe.

Burns was especially known for playing an instrument he invented himself that was made of two pieces of gas pipe and a whiskey funnel. It was sort of a combination of a trombone and a slide whistle and it became Burns's trademark. He even coined a funny name for it.

After World War I, Burns became a radio entertainer and a movie star. He was known around the country as "The Arkansas Traveler," casting himself as a homespun rube telling tales of the Ozarks. But the cornerstone of his success was that wacky instrument of his. In the late 1930s and early 1940s, at the height of his popularity, thousands of toy versions were manufactured and sold across America.

Burns's instrument is forgotten today but the name he dreamed up for it lives on—with a very different meaning. In the early days of World War II the army was testing a new shoulder-mounted antitank gun called the M1A1 at the Aberdeen Proving Ground. The soldiers trying it out thought it bore a remarkable resemblance to the odd contraption Burns had made so famous. And so the gun got the nickname by which it is still remembered: the bazooka.

Bob "bazooka" Burns plays his creation.

MORE OF THE STORY

Where did Burns get the name? He said once he took it from the now-obsolete slang word "bazoo," meaning mouth, as in "He blows his bazoo" (he talks too much). He told other people that the name mimicked the sound the strange instrument made. It sounded like a low-tone saxophone with a range of about six notes. Burns was equally adept at playing the instrument for laughs or turning in virtuoso jazz performances with it.

Where Does It Stop?

Words start in a prison paint shop and end up in the Oval Office.

In the fall of 1945, a burly federal marshal named Fred Canfil paid a visit to a federal prison in El Reno, Oklahoma. As he was talking to Warden L. Clark Schilder, a sign on the warden's desk caught his attention. Canfil made an admiring comment about the sign and mentioned that he thought a friend of his would just love it.

No problem, said the warden. The head of the prison's paint shop had designed the sign and it would be easy enough to have him run up another. Warden Schilder promised to send the duplicate sign to Canfil as soon as possible, and he was as good as his word.

Fred Canfil was a lifelong political hack once described by an associate as "loudmouthed, profane, vulgar, and uncouth." But on this day he

MORE OF THE STORY

The expression comes from the phrase "passing the buck," which in turn comes from frontier poker playing. The buck was a marker showing who had the next deal. If somebody didn't want the responsibility of the deal, he could "pass the buck" to the person on his left. Sometimes a silver dollar was used as the marker—which is where we get the slang word "buck" for a dollar.

made a contribution to popular culture and presidential lore that will live forever.

Canfil's longtime friend was fellow Missourian Harry Truman, who had become president just a few months before. The sign he gave to the president contained four words that would become a part of Truman's legacy: "The Buck Stops Here."

The sign made quite an impact given that it was on the president's desk only a short time. It was put on display at the Truman Presidential Museum in 1957.

Ich Bin Ein Berliner

There's a little-known story behind the words, "I am a Berliner."

You may have never heard of Robert Lochner. But he played a part in creating one of the most memorable lines ever uttered by an American president.

Lochner was an American who grew up in Germany before World War II and went back afterward to work for the American government. Fluent in German, he was chosen as a translator when President John F. Kennedy visited in 1963.

Lochner came to the States to help JFK prepare for the trip and tried to teach him several German phrases. But Kennedy's pronunciation was

"All free men, wherever they may live, are citizens of Berlin, and, therefore, as a free man, I take pride in the words 'Ich bein ein Berliner'!"

—JOHN F. KENNEDY, JUNE 26, 1963

terrible, so he decided not to attempt any German speaking on the trip. "Let's leave foreign languages to the distaff side," he said, referring to his wife's fluency in French.

The president changed his mind when he got to Berlin, where he was to give a speech within sight of the Berlin Wall. As his entourage walked up the steps of the city hall he called Lochner over and asked him to write out a single phrase in German. It was from the speech he was about to give, designed to express his solidarity with beleaguered West Berliners. Lochner wrote it out phonetically and coached the president on how to say it. Then Kennedy went out and gave a speech that would live in memory forever—largely because of that one line.

"If you ever heard the tape, it wasn't exactly perfect," Lochner recalled, "but with those few words you couldn't go wrong."

Robert Lochner (center) translates for President Kennedy.

Anatomy of a Great Line

Another president speaks groundbreaking words in Germany.

It started with Ingeborg Elz, a Berlin woman who was hosting a party for speechwriter Peter Robinson, who was researching a speech Ronald Reagan was going to give at the Berlin Wall. Talking about Soviet premier Mikhail Gorbachev she said that if he were serious about *perestroika*, "He can prove it. He can get rid of this wall."

Robinson seized on the idea as the cornerstone for the speech. Then came writer's block. He couldn't get the line the way he wanted it. "Herr Gorbachev, bring down this wall." The "Herr" was to please his German audience. But it didn't quite work. "Herr Gorbachev, take down this wall." Still not right. He even tried taking the whole line out, replacing it with a challenge, in German, to open the Brandenburg Gate: *"Herr Gorbachev, machen Sie dieses Tor auf."* Not exactly a line to resonate through the ages.

Eventually he got it right. Then it turned out that everybody seemed to hate it. Secretary of State George Schulz, National Security Adviser Colin

> ## *"Mr. Gorbachev, tear down this wall."*
> —RONALD REAGAN, JUNE 12, 1987, AT THE BERLIN WALL

Powell and others declared that it was too provocative, that it should be taken out. News drafts of the speech were written with the line omitted. The point was argued for weeks, right up to the day of the speech.

One man never wavered in his support of the phrase: the president. The line stayed in. And less than three years later, the wall came down.

JUST A TALE?

Could one sentence really cause such a stir? Yes. Opposition to the line was so fierce that Deputy White House Chief of Staff Ken Duberstein decided it was up to the president to make the call, which led to this memorable exchange:

Reagan: *I'm the president, aren't I?*

Duberstein: *Yes, sir, Mr. President. We're clear about that.*

Reagan: *So I get to decide whether the line about tearing down the wall stays in?*

Duberstein: *That's right, sir. It's your decision.*

Reagan: *Then it stays in.*

British civilians successfully rescued thousands at Dunkirk.

Chapter 3

Success and Failure
History's Incredible Highs and Lows

Imagine conquering most of the known world, inventing a simple tool that's in everyone's home, losing at the greatest games, tying in a debate with Kennedy, saving the city you love, botching an assassination, hitting home runs that don't make the record books, or plotting to overthrow FDR. All of these stories have at least one thing in common: They relate the summit or valley of someone's life. From tremendous personal achievement to heart-wrenching disappointment, the steady march of time demonstrates again and again that even history's losers can achieve greatness and today's winners may not always be on top.

Water World

A legendary city, founded by refugees, rises from a swamp.

Rape and pillage. Houses torched, crops stolen and hasty graves for bloody corpses. This was the legacy of Attila's Huns, sweeping across northern Italy and wreaking havoc and destruction on the remnants of the Roman Empire. But they unintentionally left a more positive legacy as well.

People fled from burning cities, desperate to find refuge. Some literally took to the swamps, finding sanctuary in a desolate group of islands in a marshy lagoon off the northern Adriatic. When the Huns were followed by other invading tribes, more Roman citizens streamed to the swamps to avoid the carnage and destruction on the mainland.

Over the next few centuries they transformed the inhospitable surroundings into an architectural wonder: Venice. With more than 400 bridges and almost 200 canals, it became a center of trade and a seafaring power. Built out of misfortune, Venice eventually turned into one of the richest and most beautiful cities in the entire world.

Harsh necessity can be the mother of glorious invention. The city of Venice was built on 118 islands two and a half miles from the mainland. Its streets are a

IMRE KIRALFY'S GREAT REALISTIC REPRESENTATION OF VENICE OF T... AT OLY...

·THE·RIALTO·BRIDGE·

COPYRIGHTED BY IMRE...

"You live like sea birds."

—ROMAN STATESMAN CASSIODORUS, IN A LETTER TO VENETIANS, CIRCA 537

precarious few inches above sea level and are currently sinking at a frightening level: about an inch every 10 years. Efforts are currently under way to protect the city from being overcome by the sea.

The gondolas that dot the waterways of Venice have been around for at least a 1,000 years, with the first known mention of them appearing in 1094.

OTHER PLAYERS, OTHER PLACES

Venice isn't the only city to be built on wetlands. St. Petersburg, Russia (below), is one of the most ambitious of the marsh-towns. In 1703 during the war with Sweden, Tsar Peter the Great ordered the building of a fortress to protect the newly conquered lands around the River Neva. Thousands of peasants toiled in very primitive and dangerous conditions to bring Peter's vision to fruition. The death rate for workers was high and St. Petersburg's morbid nickname, "The City of Bones," endures today. Despite its perilous beginnings St. Petersburg was transformed from a swamp to the capital of Russia within nine years. America has its own boggy center—Washington D.C.—which was built at the suggestion of George Washington on a floodplain near the Potomac River. Washington believed the location would be good for the tobacco trade. And China's Shanghai was founded centuries ago on a swamp at the mouth of the Yangtze River. Of all the spongy cities Shanghai is the most unstable. Thousands of high-rise buildings are exacerbating the city's subsidence problem. It's sinking 1.5 centimeters yearly.

Drebbel's Dream

This long-forgotten vessel is the first of its kind.

Not long after the Pilgrims set sail from England aboard their ship *Mayflower,* a far different vessel ventured forth on a journey up London's Thames River. It traveled only a few miles, but it did something the *Mayflower* did not—and could not—do: it traveled underwater.

The vessel, designed by Dutch inventor Cornelius Drebbel, was the first successful submarine ever built. Drebbel had been hired as a court inventor for England's King James I and was trying to convince the Royal Navy that this was the vessel of the future.

Drebbel took a fishing boat and built a wooden roof over it. Then he covered the whole thing with greased leather. It was powered by 12 oarsmen, who breathed air through a snorkel tube. A sloping foredeck acted as a diving plane, and the vessel moved up the river about 12 feet underwater. Observers said it traveled a distance of about four miles in three hours.

The DREBBEL

"A conceit of that deservedly Famous Mechanician and Chymist Cornelius Drebbel."

—DESCRIPTION OF DREBBEL'S BOAT BY
SIR ROBERT BOYLE IN 1662

The successful test of the boat piqued the king's interest, and Drebbel built two larger versions of his submarine. It is said that the king even took a ride in one of them. But the Royal Navy never did cotton to it. They just couldn't imagine that a vessel that traveled underwater could have any military use.

And poor, disappointed Drebbel himself wasn't much more successful than his unusual boat. A jack of all trades including glassmaker, engraver, alchemist, doctor, and of course, inventor, he died in poverty in 1634, despite his many and varied skills. It would be nearly three centuries before the Royal Navy launched a submarine.

OTHER PLAYERS, OTHER PLACES

The first submarine employed for military purposes was the *Turtle,* designed by David Bushnell of Connecticut. The one-man sub tried to attach a mine to a British man-of-war in New York Harbor in 1776. The effort failed and the mine exploded harmlessly. Wrote George Washington later: "I thought, and still think, that it was an effort of genius." The first submarine successfully used in battle was the *Hunley,* a Confederate submarine that rammed the USS *Housatonic* with an explosive torpedo in 1864. The explosion sank the *Housatonic* but also sent the *Hunley* to the bottom off the coast of Charleston, South Carolina, costing the lives of everyone aboard.

A contemporary illustration of the *Hunley*

Bees in Battle

Battlefields have been buzzing with this successful practice for centuries.

In the closing stages of the Thirty Years' War, a Swedish army assaulted Kissengen, a walled city in Bavaria. The desperate defenders responded by throwing beehives into the ranks of the Swedes, who were forced to retreat in the face of attacks from the angry swarm that enveloped them.

This was hardly unprecedented. When faced with the question "To bee or not to bee?" armies throughout the ages have consistently answered in the affirmative. The Romans frequently loaded their catapults with beehives and launched them upon their enemies. King Richard the Lionhearted did the exact same thing against the Saracens during the Crusades.

Bees have been used at sea as well. There is at least one recorded instance of sailors on a small ship in the Mediterranean climbing the rigging and throwing beehives down onto the deck of an attacking galley, instantly turning the tables on the larger ship.

Louis XII wears the beehive symbol into battle.

Bee warfare hasn't gone out of style, either. Both sides in Vietnam created fearsome booby traps using hives of Asian honeybees, which are larger and more ferocious than their Western cousins. And now Pentagon scientists are trying to recruit bees into the war on terror, training them to sniff out explosives. They hope the bees will be able to uncover land mines and bomb factories. That would be a honey of a trick.

JUST A TALE?

Bees may look fierce, but the truth is that they tend to respond only when provoked. Hives handled with care could be transported or loaded on a catapult with little problem. Once dashed against a wall or on the ground, however, their peace-loving populations turn into winged warriors seeking vengeance. In the so-called "Battle of the Bees" during World War I, both British and German forces fighting for the East African city of Tanga were tormented by swarms of angry bees provoked by machine-gun fire disturbing their nests. Some soldiers were stung hundreds of times.

Old Man's Fight

You're never too old to fight... and prevail!

War is usually considered a young man's endeavor. But on April 19, 1775, the first day of the American Revolution, the older generation got their licks in, too.

At the battles of Lexington and Concord (below), colonial militia clashed with the Redcoats and sent them fleeing back to Boston. One militiaman who answered the call was a gentleman named Samuel Whittemore.

Whittemore was 78 years old and crippled but that wasn't going to stop him. He headed out to join the fight carrying a rifle, two pistols and an old cavalry saber.

As the British approached, he took up a position behind a stone wall and got off such accurate fire that the British sent a detachment to rout him out. As they drew close, the old man killed one with a rifle and shot two more with his pistol. He was reaching for his saber when they finally fell upon him. One British soldier shot him in the face while others bayoneted him repeatedly.

Whittemore suffered 14 separate wounds. When he was brought to a doctor, the man just shook his head. It was clear that Whittemore had little chance of surviving.

But Whittemore defied the odds and lived on. He lived long enough to see the British defeated, the Constitution ratified and George Washington become president. He was 96 when he finally died, a remarkable 18 years after the battle in which that senior soldier fought to make America free.

OTHER PLAYERS, OTHER PLACES

In another episode of geriatric heroism, a group of old men ambushed a British wagon, gunning down two soldiers and driving off the rest. Several of the soldiers fleeing the ambush came upon an old woman named Mother Bathrick and begged her to accept their surrender and escort them to safety. This led critics of the war back in England to pose this question: "If one old woman can take six grenadiers, how many soldiers will it take to conquer America?"

Forgotten Fight

For the Revotionaries, it's a big loss in the Big Apple.

The biggest battle of the American Revolution is, oddly enough, also one of the least remembered. It was fought on the streets of New York. The British invasion fleet contained more than 400 ships and transports carrying 35,000 soldiers and sailors, the biggest British Expeditionary Force until World War I. Facing them were 25,000 inexperienced men under George Washington, who had never led a large army into battle.

It was the only full-scale conflict of the war. From August until November 1776, the two armies clashed in engagements that ranged across Brooklyn, down the streets of lower Manhattan, up into Harlem and Westchester, and across to New Jersey.

It's largely forgotten today for a simple reason: the colonials suffered a crushing defeat. Washington lost more than three-quarters of his army.

The battle, however, deserves to be remembered. This is where America could have lost the fight for independence in an afternoon—but

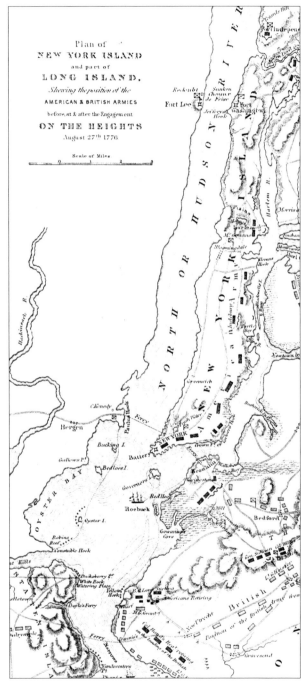

The British came ashore in Brooklyn, then crossed the river into Manhattan.

OTHER PLAYERS, OTHER PLACES

The most famous casualty of the battle was a captain from a Connecticut regiment named Nathan Hale, remembered romantically as the spy who "had but one life to give his country." The British viewed him far less romantically: They believed that in addition to being a spy, Hale was one of the colonial arsonists who had torched New York days before, destroying one-quarter of the city. Without benefit of a trial, Hale was hanged at a site believed to be near what is now the intersection of Third Avenue and 66th Street. As was the custom, his body was left hanging for several days. But his memory lives on—he is the official hero of the state of Connecticut.

didn't. Instead, it became the place where an army of green soldiers—little more than a band of farmers, really—began to learn the trade of war.

The Battle of Trenton, fought by Washington's decimated and hungry army just a few short weeks later in New Jersey, is rightly celebrated as a great American victory. But the Continental Army might not have won that fight without using the hard lessons they had learned in the terrible battle for New York.

The General's Gambit

A bold deception gives George Washington his first victory in the American Revolution.

After spending the winter holed up in neighboring Cambridge, General George Washington was determined to drive the British Army from Boston. One morning when the Redcoats there awoke, they were shocked to find that the hills looking down on Boston were bristling with cannons. Washington was throwing down the gauntlet, his guns poised to blow the enemy to kingdom come.

Even more galling was the fact that the cannons were actually British equipment that had been captured at New York's Fort Ticonderoga in May, 1775. The 50 cannons had been painstakingly dragged more than 300 miles on sleds through snow-covered mountains by Colonel Henry Knox and his men and delivered to Washington at Dorchester Heights.

The British chose not to fight. General Howe ordered the evacuation of 10,000 men and 200 warships to the safe port of Halifax, Nova Scotia. Boston was free without a shot being fired.

But what the British didn't know was that Washington's gambit was simply an enormous bluff. Despite the awesome display of force he lacked just one very important ingredient to back it up: gunpowder.

With Washington's cannons frowning down on them, Lord Howe and his British army completed their evacuation of Boston by sea in less than two weeks.

> *"To maintain a post within musket shot of the enemy for six months together without powder...is more than probably ever was attempted."*
>
> —GEORGE WASHINGTON, IN A LETTER TO CONGRESS, JANUARY 1776

Washington was so short on gunpowder that his army would have been able to throw only a few shots at the British before retreating. So severe, in fact, was the colonial powder shortage that the British could have easily taken Washington's army and crushed the nascent rebellion any time during the previous six months.

If only they had known, American history might have taken a very different turn. Washington may have lacked gunpowder, but he proved to have something more important: the nerve and audacity that would be needed to see the ragtag colonials through to a successful conclusion to their Revolution.

Shortly after taking command of the army in June 1775, Washington discovered that he had only enough gunpowder for each soldier to fire a handful of bullets. Brigadier General John Sullivan described the moment: "The General was so struck that he did not utter a word for half an hour." Gunpowder was in short supply because the British had long discouraged its manufacture in the colonies. The problem was eventually eased by importing large quantities from French traders. But even five years later, just before the Battle of Yorktown, Washington's supply of powder was reported to be in a "wretched and palsied state."

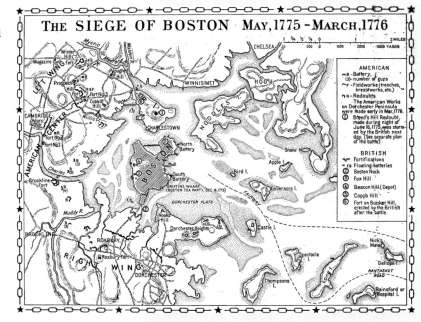

THE SIEGE OF BOSTON MAY, 1775 – MARCH, 1776

The Fever Factor

Grand plans are foiled by an island rebellion and a lowly insect.

Napoleon Bonaparte had big plans for the vast territory that France held in North America. In 1802 he sent an army under the command of General Charles Leclerc, his brother-in-law, to take control of New Orleans and open the door for a new wave of French colonists to populate what he hoped would be a thriving new France.

Napoleon ordered Leclerc to stop off along the way and reestablish French rule in Haiti, which had been wracked by a bloody slave rebellion led by Toussaint L'Ouverture, a former slave who had established himself there as "Governor-for-Life." The Haitians were no match for the crack French troops, who won control of the island in a matter of weeks. L'Ouverture quickly agreed to an armistice with the French. But then a much deadlier enemy emerged: the mosquito.

Spring rains brought clouds of mosquitoes and an outbreak of yellow fever. The local population was largely immune—unlike the French soldiers. Tens of thousands perished. Leclerc himself died in October 1802. Reinforcements arrived, but many of them also succumbed to the disease.

Meantime the freed slaves of Haiti renewed the fight against their weakened enemy, taking a severe toll with persistent attacks.

For France it was nothing short of a debacle. Between the disease and the fighting an estimated 50,000 French soldiers died and the rest finally surrendered in 1803. With his army gone and his brother-in-law dead Napoleon gave up on his

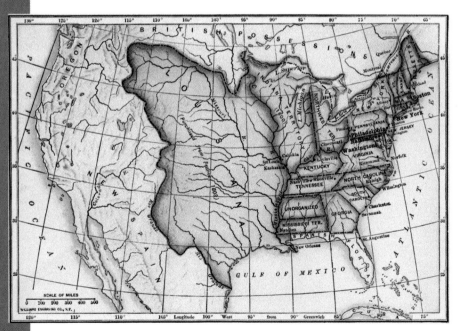

The Louisiana Purchase added 828,000 square miles of land to the United States. The purchase price was $15 million—three cents an acre.

dreams for the New World, deciding instead to sell France's holdings in North America to the United States.

The Louisiana Purchase doubled the size of the young country. But it might never have taken place without the resilient rebels and the unmerciful mosquitoes of Haiti.

L'Ouverture was kidnapped and sent off to a French prison. He died there before he could see Haiti achieve full independence, in 1803.

OTHER PLAYERS, OTHER PLACES

Yellow fever is a viral disease that can cause bleeding from the nose, mouth, and stomach, before eventual liver failure (resulting in jaundiced, yellow skin). It was a ferocious killer not only in the tropics but also in the young United States. As colonies, Boston and New York City were afflicted at times. An epidemic killed some 5,000 people in Philadelphia in 1793, and thousands more died of the disease in the South during the 1800s. But no one knew how it was spread. In 1881 a Cuban scientist, Carlos Finlay, hypothesized that mosquitoes were the culprits, but his work was ignored. It wasn't until 1900 that a U.S. Army physician named Walter Reed met with Finlay to learn more about his mosquito theory, then began his own tests, using human volunteers. In 1901 Reed published his findings. Almost immediately the U.S. government went to work curbing mosquito breeding grounds and successfully limiting instances of infection in U.S. A yellow fever vaccine was developed in 1936, eventually eradicating the virus from the U.S., though outbreaks still occur today throughout Africa and South America.

First Computer

Some (but not all) great ideas are ahead of the times.

Railroads were still brand-new in 1822 when a British mathematician named Charles Babbage dreamed up the idea of a mechanical calculator. He called it a "difference engine." Like the railroad, it was designed to operate by steam.

It took Babbage a decade to build just one section of his difference engine. When it was completed, people marveled at its sophistication. But even as he was working on it he conceived of something even more ambitious: a machine that could be programmed with punch cards to perform even the most complex calculations.

In other words, a mechanical computer.

Babbage made hundreds of drawings outlining his new idea. He envisioned that this "analytical engine" would be about as big and heavy as a small locomotive, containing thousands of finely machined gears. It would be able to add or subtract 40-digit numbers in a few seconds and multiply similarly large numbers in about two minutes or so.

Babbage was a bit ahead of his time, since this was more than 100 years before the first electronic computer was created. In fact he was such a perfectionist that every time he started to build the analytical engine, he came up with an idea that would render obsolete that version.

It increased in complexity until it became nearly impossible to build. Babbage did, however, develop other, practical things, including something for those newfangled railroad locomotives.

You can see it on the front of old steam engines: the cowcatcher.

125,000 to One

It's the first ever attempt on a president's life—and the odds are against him.

Housepainter Richard Lawrence believed that he was an heir to the British throne and that President Andrew Jackson was trying to keep him from claiming his rightful place among British royalty. So he decided to shoot the president.

Richard Lawrence was extremely crazy. And Andrew Jackson turned out to be an unbelievably lucky man.

On a gray Friday in January 1835, Jackson attended a funeral service at the U.S. Capitol. Lawrence was waiting behind a pillar as Jackson walked out. The president was just eight feet away when Lawrence pulled a pistol from his pocket and fired at point-blank range.

He was so close, he couldn't possibly miss—but the pistol misfired. Much to the horror of everyone present, Lawrence pulled out a second pistol. Jackson was raising his cane at Lawrence and lunging at him, still presenting an easy target. But the

Lawrence was prosecuted by Francis Scott Key. The trial took one day; the jury debated five minutes before finding him not guilty by reason of insanity.

second pistol misfired, too. A Navy officer knocked Lawrence down and the first assassination attempt on a U.S. president was over.

There was nothing wrong with the pistols. They were loaded correctly. They just didn't go off. It was later estimated that the odds against both pistols misfiring was 125,000 to one.

"Were I inclined to superstition," wrote one friend of Jackson, "the conviction that the president's life was protected by the hand of a special providence would be irresistible."

An early distributor of P&G's popular products

Family Business

You may not know Alexander Norris, but what he put together touches every one of us.

In 1837, the United States was in the grip of a financial panic. Markets plunged downward. Hundreds of banks closed their doors. People wondered if the economy would ever right itself again. But in the midst of these hard times, in fact because of them, a smart and family-minded Midwestern businessman planted a seed that would flower into a multibillion-dollar business.

Alexander Norris had two daughters. One was married to a maker of candles, the other to a maker of soap. Each man's business depended on a steady stream of animal fats. Rather than see his sons-in-law compete for the same raw materials in a depressed economy, Norris urged them to go into business together. Reluctantly, they agreed.

Today they are recognized around the world for turning animal fat into a fortune. Their small Cincinnati business has become a worldwide powerhouse, with more than 250 brand-name products, from Pepto-Bismol to Pampers. Early sponsors of radio programs to promote their products, the company became well known for the popular "soap operas." The sons-in-law were named William and James. Their last names? Procter and Gamble.

In 1879 a P&G workman left his machine running while he went to lunch, inadvertently creating a new product: Ivory soap. It was well publicized, as in this 1898 ad, and became a top-selling item for the company.

OTHER PLAYERS, OTHER PLACES

In 1886, another iconic American company, SC Johnson, was founded. It made its fortune on a product it created to protect wooden floors: SC Johnson Wax. One of the largest-privately owned companies in the country, it's actually run by the fifth generation of the man who founded it, Samuel Curtis Johnson (below). Even more unusual than the fact the family wants to work at its offices in Racine, Wisconsin is that everyone else does, too. Consistently rated as a "best to work for" company by magazines ranging from *Money* to *Working Mother,* the company has more than 12,000 employees. The company has become very well known for caring for both their employees and their customers. But good luck trying to get a job there; it has an annual turnover of only 2%. That's pretty good for a company that came into being to sell parquet flooring and wound up a success at making products to care for them instead.

Pin Money

This inventive wizard just can't get it right.

In the long history of invention there is no tale of woe quite like that of Walter Hunt. He was an absolute genius at making things but an abysmal failure at making money.

In 1834, he invented the first sewing machine in the United States. But the country was in the midst of a depression and no one was interested in a machine that would put more people out of work, so he didn't bother to file a patent. Bad move. Elias Howe patented a similar machine a few years later and got rich beyond his wildest dreams.

Hunt also patented the first fountain pen and the first repeating rifle but failed to turn them into viable products. Others did so later and reaped amazing profits.

But the most staggering part of the story was yet to come. One afternoon in 1849 he began playing with a piece of wire. In less than four hours he twisted it into a pin with a spring on one end and a clasp on the other: he'd invented the safety pin. A million-dollar idea if ever there was one, and Hunt was quick to patent it. So he finally became rich beyond his wildest dreams—right?

Not exactly. Desperate for some quick cash, he sold off the patent rights—for just $100.

W. Hunt.
Pin.
N⁰ 6281.   Patented Apr. 10. 1849.

Fig. 1. Fig. 2. Fig. 4. Fig. 3. Fig. 5. Fig. 6. Fig. 8. Fig. 7.

Hunt's safety pin design was easy to reproduce—the perfect item for mass production.

JUST A TALE?

So did Walter Hunt actually invent the sewing machine? Not really. There were quite a few patents issued for machines that could sew. The first one was issued in England in 1790 to Thomas Saint, but there's no evidence it actually worked. That was followed by a German device, a French one and at least two American versions. Finally, a French tailor named Barthelemy Thimonnier invented a fully functioning machine in 1830, but he was almost killed in the ensuing tailor's riot. Hunt did create a machine, but the first American patent went to Elias Howe in 1846,

for a machine that sewed with thread from two sources: a top thread from a spool and a bottom thread from a bobbin, the way most contemporary machines still work. So where did Singer come in? He invented the first machine that used an up-and-down needle motion, powered by a foot treadle. It was the first commercially successful machine but there was one little problem: he was infringing Howe's patent. Howe sued Singer and won, forcing Singer to pay him royalties. Howe expired in 1867, the same year as his patent, a wealthy man from Singer's successful sewing machine.

Buchanan's Blunder

Learn the story of the failed pre–Civil War civil war.

In 1857, President James Buchanan (right) declared the Mormons in the Utah Territory to be in rebellion. There had been a growing conflict over federal jurisdiction in the territory and Buchanan decided it was time for a show of force. He appointed a new governor and dispatched a force of 2,500 troops to restore order.

When Mormon leader Brigham Young got the word he began preparing for war. He declared martial law, called up the militia and began gathering arms. Three years before the War Between the States, it looked as if the United States was headed for a civil war.

The American troops Buchanan sent ran into all sorts of trouble. They got a slow start and ran into fierce winter weather. Mormon raids on their supply wagons forced them to hole up for the winter on starvation rations. Back east, criticism began to mount over how Buchanan was managing things. Newspapers began to refer to the venture as "Buchanan's Blunder." It was proving to be a huge embarrassment to the administration.

Eventually negotiators were able to work out a settlement and conflict was averted. The Army entered Salt Lake City peacefully and the new governor was installed.

But the expedition cost Buchanan a large amount of political capital. It crippled his ability to deal with the looming crisis between North and South. When Southern states began to secede he refused to send troops—perhaps mindful of the criticisms he had borne for the Utah effort.

As a result the Southern rebellion remained unchecked until Abraham Lincoln took office. It would eventually cost the lives of more than a million Americans.

OTHER PLAYERS, OTHER PLACES

In the spring of 1857, a wagon train of about 40 families left Arkansas for Southern California. On their way, they were joined by other settlers led by Alexander Fancher, who had made the journey twice before. They reached Salt Lake City and then took a route through the southwestern part of Utah. Running low on supplies they attempted to obtain food from local Mormons, but since Brigham Young had declared martial law only a few days earlier—forbidding outsiders to travel through the area without a pass—most declined to trade with settlers passing through. The party stopped in Mountain Meadow, where all the adults and most of the children were massacred by a group of Indians and Mormons on September 11, 1857. The youngest children, the oldest of whom was just six years old, were sent to live with Mormon families throughout the region. Eventually, the surviving children were reunited with family members in Arkansas. Some 20 years after the incident a Mormon leader named John D. Lee was hanged for massacre, claiming all the while that he had done his best to save the lives of the settlers.

Pony Express

A business flop creates an enduring American legend.

As kids, many of us thrilled to stories of the adventures and romance of the Pony Express. Daring riders galloping thousands of miles across the Western plains, braving Indians, bandits, and natural hazards to bring the mail from Saint Joseph, Missouri, all the way to California in just 10 days.

But guess what? The real Pony Express was a disaster: an impractical, money-losing business that went bankrupt in little more than a year and cost investors nearly a quarter of a million dollars. Founded in 1860 with 80 riders and 500 horses, it was doomed almost before it began by the construction of the transcontinental telegraph. Once the telegraph was

MORE OF THE STORY

Sending a message by Pony Express wasn't cheap. A half-ounce letter cost $5, the equivalent of more than $90 today. Once the telegraph was built, it was both quicker and cheaper, at least for short messages. But while the business went belly-up, the legend rode off into the sunset. One young fellow who reaped its benefits was a Kansas boy named William Cody who became a Pony Express rider at 14. Buffalo Bill (left), as he later became known, turned his Western experiences into a famous Wild West Show that toured the United States and Europe for decades.

completed, in August 1861, the Pony Express was obsolete. It went out of business just two months later.

Amazing Fax

If you think of the fax machine as a modern convenience, consider this: the first one was put into service more than 140 years ago.

Giovanni Caselli was a priest but his neighbors in Florence thought of him as a bit of a mad scientist. He was eternally tinkering with things and his home was always filled with junk.

The telegraph was the hot new technology of the moment and Caselli wondered if it was possible to send pictures over telegraph wires. He went to work in 1857 and over the course of six years perfected what he called the "pantelegraph." It was the world's first practical fax machine. On the transmitting end, a stylus attached to a pendulum would swing back and forth over the original. When it touched the ink it would send an electrical signal to a synchronized stylus passing over chemically treated paper on the other end. This caused the paper to change color wherever electricity touched it. The result was an exact copy.

Emperor Napoleon III of France was so impressed with Caselli's work that he authorized use of the machine on French telegraph lines. By 1868 the pantelegraph was transmitting as many as 110 faxes per hour. But it was viewed as a novelty, not a necessity. When Prussian troops invaded

Standing six feet tall and made up of swinging pendulums, batteries and wires, the pantelegraph worked by passing an electrical current through an image.

France in 1870, the service was interrupted, never to be resumed. It was another 100 years before the modern fax machine became indispensable.

Secret Subway

Believe it—New York's first subway is a quiet affair.

In 1912, construction workers digging a new subway line stumbled upon something almost shocking: a fully preserved station they never knew existed. It was the brainchild of Alfred Beach, editor of *Scientific American*. In the 1860s he became appalled by New York's traffic. His innovative solution: build an air-powered train underground.

The most powerful person in New York, William Marcy "Boss" Tweed, was dead set against the idea. To outsmart Tweed and gain public support, Beach decided to build a 312-foot-long subway beneath Broadway in total secrecy. Furthermore he had the gall to run it right under City Hall. He concocted a clever cover story, claiming that he was building a pneumatic tube to carry messages between buildings. To keep his secret, all the work was done at night. Dirt was carried out through a nearby basement and construction materials came in the same way.

"A tube, a car,
a revolving fan!
Little more is required!"

—ALFRED BEACH

The *New York Times* called Beach's project "certainly the most novel, if not the most successful, enterprise that New York has seen for many a day."

In February 1870, he threw open the doors to an amazed public, which was delighted by the clean-running train and luxuriously appointed station. Frescoes lined the walls, goldfish swam in a sparkling fountain and a grand piano provided background music as passengers lounged in easy chairs. More than 400,000 people paid admission just to see it. But Tweed was outraged and fought tooth and nail against Beach's plan to expand the subway. Eventually Beach got the permission he needed from the governor but a financial panic killed investor interest. Beach reluctantly sealed up the tunnel after the train operated for just a year and it was soon forgotten. New Yorkers would have to wait until the 20th century to commute to work on an underground train.

Who Killed Garfield?

Is it a successful assassination or failed medical procedures?

In July 1881, President James A. Garfield set out for his college reunion. But as he walked through Washington's railroad station he was gunned down by Charles Guiteau, a mentally unbalanced lawyer who was angry with Garfield for denying him a diplomatic post.

Doctors spent the next 80 days trying to remove the bullet. Dr. Willard Bliss stuck a probe into the wound, creating a path that misled other doctors. Then he compounded his error by inserting an unwashed finger in the hole, introducing infection. Another doctor stuck his hand in wrist-deep and accidentally punctured the liver. Together the 16 doctors who poked and prodded Garfield turned a three-inch hole into a 20-inch infected canal.

The president lingered on in great pain throughout the summer, finally dying on September 14. An autopsy revealed that the bullet was lodged in a spot that was not life-threatening.

Garfield would have survived—if they'd left him alone. Guiteau made the doctors' incompetence the centerpiece of his defense, saying he didn't kill

Garfield: "The doctors did that. I simply shot at him." Correct as he might have been, he was nonetheless convicted and hanged.

> *"Assassination can no more be guarded against than death by lightning; and it is best not to worry about either."*
>
> —PRESIDENT JAMES GARFIELD

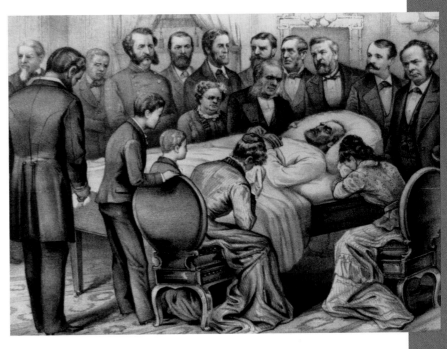

Of Flashlights and Model Trains

A win-win situation: This man gives up a fortune to play with his trains.

Illuminated flowerpots. That was the thing, thought Joshua L. Cowen (facing page), that was going to make him a fortune. Though only in his 20s, Cowen was already an inventor. His latest design consisted of a metal tube with batteries in the middle and a light bulb on the end. He figured you could stick one in a flowerpot so that it would illuminate the plant in a restaurant or store display.

It did wind up making a fortune, but not for Cowen. The problem was that other people were coming up with the idea of a battery-operated light at the same time and everybody was hiring lawyers and threatening to sue. It all became a bit much for Cowen, so he signed over his rights to a business associate named Conrad Hubert. Hubert wasn't interested in flowerpots—he wanted to put the small battery-operated light into people's hands. He started the American Eveready Company and raked in millions selling flashlights and batteries.

But don't feel too badly for Joshua L. Cowen. He always had a passion for railroads and after designing a tiny electric motor for a miniature fan,

MINIATURE

ELECTRIC

CARS

With full accessories for

**WINDOW
DISPLAY**

and

**HOLIDAY
GIFTS.**

Manufactured by

Lionel Manufacturing Co.
Incorporated,

24 and 26 MURRAY STREET.

NEW YORK.

he realized it was just the right size to power a miniature train. He started selling model trains by catalog as eye-catching displays for shop windows, figuring they were at least as good as illuminated flowerpots. He thought the little trains would draw attention to the other goods in the shop window. Imagine his surprise when customers fell in love with the motorized models and began snapping them up as toys for their children.

Cowen wasn't about to let this opportunity pass him by. He began marketing the trains as mature toys for boys and their fathers to enjoy together, particularly around the Christmas tree. And what kind of trains were they? Here's a hint:

The "L" in Joshua L. Cowen's name stood for Lionel. The rest is model-train history.

MORE OF THE STORY

Just to muddy the waters a bit, Cowen's first invention was called a "flash-lamp." It looked like a flashlight, but instead of lighting a bulb at the end, it ignited flash powder for creating consistent light for taking photographs. Most fuses of the day had a tendency to absorb moisture from the air, which made them unreliable. Cowen's invention wasn't a hit with photographers, but because his fuses were almost entirely waterproof, the Navy thought they would make great fuses for underwater mines—which wasn't what Cowen had in mind—but he liked it fine when the government bought 10,000 of them.

Cowen's lifelong interest in model trains such as the one below began at age seven when he carved a locomotive out of wood, then tried installing a tiny steam engine of his own design. It exploded.

Patton rounds to the finish in the running portion of the modern pentathalon. Patton's teammate, Jim Thorpe, won the gold in the event at the 1912 Stockholm games.

Glory Deferred

He misses gold by a hair—but he'll have medals aplenty in the future.

The young military officer had thirsted for glory ever since he was a young boy. After graduating from West Point he was desperate for some way to prove himself.

One problem: there were no wars going on. So he turned to a different arena. He traveled to Stockholm to represent the United States at the 1912 Olympics. His event was the modern pentathlon, which tested competitors in five military skills: horsemanship, fencing, running, swimming and shooting.

The young lieutenant performed excellently in every event except the one he considered his best: pistol-shooting. Most of his shots punched holes right inside the bull's-eye. But for two of his shots the judges ruled that he missed the target entirely. The officer himself believed the shots were so good they went through one of the earlier bullet holes.

The gold medal was hanging in the balance. If the scoring had been done in the American manner—10 points for a bull's-eye, nine for the next ring, and so on—his shooting would have

OLYMPIC GAMES
⊱ STOCKHOLM 1912 ⊰
JUNE 29th — JULY 22nd.

placed him third for that event and the overall gold medal would have been his. But the Swedish method counted any hit on a target equally, so his numerous bull's-eyes did him no good, while his alleged misses ruined his score. Instead of finishing first, he finished fifth, his thirst for glory still unquenched.

But don't feel too badly for the failed Olympian. He would find glory more than 30 years later, leading the tanks of the Third Army across what Shakespeare once called "The vasty fields of France," punching holes in the German lines and making headlines back home. He would become known as "Old Blood and Guts"—General George S. Patton, finally achieving the fame and plaudits he had sought his entire life.

A gold medal from the 1912 games

If Patton were competing in the Olympics today his argument over those bull's-eye shots would be taken more seriously. In 1984 the Court of Arbitration for Sport (CAS) was established, with its headquarters in Switzerland. Its mission is to resolve the growing number of international sports-related disputes, covering everything from doping allegations to conflicts over commercial contracts. But many of the cases it hears involves athletes who feel their victory at an event was hindered—by another player's unfair tactics, a spectator intervening or incorrect judgments by a referee. More than 700 decisions have been rendered by arbitrators of the court since its inception. Though the arbitration process can often take many months a special CAS panel is set up during Olympic Games to quickly handle disputes, especially those involving the awarding of medals. The CAS promises a decision within 24 hours of a case brought to its attention at the Olympics. Had the court been around in 1912 the young George Patton's quarrel with the pentathlon judges would have fit into the CAS's remit, and the Olympic results may have been very different.

The Cab Drivers Who Saved Paris

Here's the story of how a taxi fleet turns sure defeat to victory.

In August 1914, the Germans were driving relentlessly for Paris. They were less than 40 miles away by the beginning of September. That's when French troops made a last-ditch stand at the river Marne. It seemed almost certain the French would be crushed and their capital city captured.

There were 6,000 soldiers in Paris who could help make the difference but there was no way to get them to the front. Then one of the generals realized that if they could mobilize the taxicabs of Paris to carry the soldiers, they could do the job.

The word went out. Patriotic cabbies emptied out their passengers, explaining proudly that they had to "go to battle." Six hundred of them lined up at the appointed hour. General Galliéni, military

Almost all the taxis driven from Paris to the front lines were Renaults.

The Battle of the Marne prevented Germany from winning a decisive victory at the outset of the war. It led, however, to four years of trench warfare that cost millions of lives. Although there had been some very limited trench warfare in previous conflicts, autumn 1914 to spring 1918 was typified by a stalement in which trench war became the standard form of fighting. In the first World War, the trenches on the Western Front ran 475 miles, from the North Sea to Switzerland.

The trenches were horrifying for anyone living in them. Infested with black and brown rats that fed on corpses, lice and even frogs and slugs, there was no escape from the vermin. Add to that the freezing winters and the fact that the trenches were often filled with water just begins to hint at the environment. And, of course, there were the weapons: lung-smothering clouds of poisonous mustard and chlorine gases, artillery that could bury men under tons of mud if they weren't killed by a direct hit, and rows of expert snipers ready to shoot any head that popped above ground. It's no wonder that it was considered hell on earth.

commander of Paris, came out to inspect them. *"Eh bien, voilà au moins qui n'est pas banal!"* he said. Roughly translated: "Here's something you don't see every day."

Each cab could hold five men. Every taxi had to make the 75-mile round trip to the front twice in order to bring up the soldiers. The soldiers were rushed to the front and their presence helped stiffen resistance to the Germans. In what history has come to call "the miracle of the Marne," the French army held firm. Paris was saved—thanks in part to the valor of her heroic cab drivers.

> *"Gentlemen, we will fight on the Marne."*
>
> —GENERAL JOSEPH JOFFRE,
> COMMANDER OF THE FRENCH ARMY

Going...Going...Gone

The best home-run hitter of all time never makes the big leagues.

He was called the black Babe Ruth. But there are those who say Ruth should be known as the white Josh Gibson. In the 1930s and 1940s this powerful catcher was one of the greatest stars of the Negro Leagues. And he may well have been the greatest home-run hitter of all time.

Records are sketchy but Gibson is credited with a total of more than 800 home runs in his 17-year career, hitting 89 in one season and 75 in another. He could also hit for average—he led the Negro Leagues in batting four times.

Gibson hit the ball so hard he is said to have broken the backs of numerous wooden seats in the outfield grandstands. The *New York Daily News* wrote that any team in baseball would benefit from signing him. "He hit the ball a mile," mused Hall of Fame pitcher Walter Johnson. "Too bad Gibson is a colored fellow."

The tragedy of his life was that Gibson never played a day in the majors because during his career blacks were kept out. Several major-league teams came close to taking the plunge and signing Gibson, but none ever did. His friends believed that it broke his heart. He died of a massive stroke in 1947 when he was only 35—just a few months before Jackie Robinson broke baseball's color line forever.

> *"The only way to pitch to him was to pitch behind him."*
>
> —CHET BREWER, NEGRO LEAGUE PITCHER, ABOUT JOSH GIBBONS

The Business Plot

Wall Street may have tried to overthrow the president.

In 1934, during the desperate days of the Depression and little more than a year after Franklin Roosevelt had become president, a decorated military man stepped forward to warn of a plot to take over the White House. Smedley Darlington Butler (right) was a retired Marine Corps general who was twice awarded the Medal of Honor. Known as "Old Gimlet Eye," the colorful officer had a reputation for reckless bravery and blunt outspokenness. He told reporters that he had been approached by a group of Wall Street financiers to lead an army of 500,000 veterans on Washington to overthrow the government.

Leaders of the plot allegedly wanted to overthrow FDR because they thought the New Deal was an assault on capitalism. Butler said he was told that bigwigs J.P. Morgan and Grayson Murphy were ready to finance the plot with $3 million in cash while corporate giants DuPont and Remington would supply the arms and ammunition. Once they had control of the capital, a "Secretary of General Welfare" would be appointed to run the country, reducing President Roosevelt to a mere figurehead.

The supposed plotters ridiculed Butler. The tale seemed far-fetched to many and the media downplayed the story. But other officers said they had also been approached to take part. The House Un-American Activities Committee took Butler's charges seriously enough to hold hearings. It issued a final report that supported the general.

So perhaps we ought to remember Butler as the man who saved the presidency.

MORE OF THE STORY

Only five years earlier, 20,000 veterans seeking money from Congress had marched on Washington and set up camp there. Butler had encouraged the "Bonus Army," which might have led to him being approached for the plot. According to Bulter, middleman Gerald MacGuire told him: "You are the only fellow in America who can get the soldiers together." After leaving the marines, Butler referred to his career as that of "a high-class muscleman for Wall Street and the big bankers. In short, I was a racketeer for capitalism."

The Rescuer

Fate offers him a second chance— and he takes it.

It's called the Miracle of Dunkirk. In May 1940, German forces advancing through France were on the verge of capturing an entire Allied army. Nearly surrounded, British and French soldiers fought their way to the coastal town of Dunkirk in a desperate bid to escape.

The British Admiralty put out the call for every small craft it could find: yachts, fishing boats, motor launches, tugboats—any vessel that could pull men off the beaches—to help stage an emergency evacuation. Despite constant attack by German bombers this motley fleet managed to rescue more than 300,000 men over the course of 10 days and bring them back to England so they could fight again. Winston Churchill called it a "miracle of deliverance."

One of the legion of heroic rescuers was a 66-year-old retiree named Charles Lightoller. Determined to bring home every man possible he crammed more than 120 soldiers on his small motor yacht. Then he piloted the dangerously over-loaded vessel back across the English Channel, dodging bombs and bullets all the way.

The evacuation effort was called Operation Dynamo.

Perhaps his zeal to rescue as many men as possible was driven in part by memories of a harrowing night at sea nearly 30 years before. It was a nightmare he could never forget, a night that lives on in legend: lifeboats launched only half full, cries of distress in the water, despair at not being able to do more. An April night in 1912 when more than 900 people perished in the icy North Atlantic, despite the best efforts of Charles Lightoller (facing page), second officer on the RMS *Titanic*.

MORE OF THE STORY

The story of the little ships rescuing soldiers from the shores of France is firmly planted in British consciousness as a symbol of national pride. The phrase, "Dunkirk spirit," is still used to describe people pitching in to help each other. But at the time of Operation Dynamo, many in Britain thought it would be seen as a great catastrophe of the war. The overpowering of Allied forces by the Germans in 1940 was one of the biggest military disasters in British history. In a speech just after the Dunkirk rescue, Prime Minister Winston Churchill diluted his praise with the warning that "Wars are not won by evacuations." And some of the soldiers who were saved from the French beaches feared they would be jeered upon returning home. But in one of the most successful propaganda campaigns in history, the British newspapers re-framed the military failure at Dunkirk into a victory for British morale. That spirit would become very useful to the British, as the Dunkirk evacuation marked the start of some of the darkest days of World War II.

The Dead Man Who Duped Hitler

The contribution of this corpse helps win the battle before it even starts.

In early 1943, the Allies were getting ready to invade Nazi-occupied Europe from North Africa. Their destination was the island of Sicily. For the invasion to succeed, it was critical that the enemy be caught off guard, so British officers concocted a fantastic scheme. Code name: Operation Mincemeat.

Major Martin was really a homeless man named Glyndwr Michael.

Love letters, over-due bills, an old bus ticket and various personal items all helped convince the Germans that Major Martin was genuine.

They grabbed a corpse from a London morgue and gave him a completely new identity. He was outfitted with a uniform and papers placed in his pockets identified him as Major William Martin, a military courier. A briefcase was chained to his wrist.

Inside, British spymasters planted forged documents suggesting that the target of the invasion would be Greece, not Sicily. Then a British submarine dropped the body of "Major Martin" off the coast of Spain, making it look as if he was a courier who died in a plane crash.

As hoped, Spanish authorities showed the papers to the Germans. They were completely fooled. The news was rushed to Hitler, who made the defense of Greece his top priority. The German High Command sent Panzer units there and Hitler ordered the famed General Erwin Rommel to Athens to mastermind the battle.

But there would be no battle fought in Greece. Instead forces under generals Bernard Montgomery and George Patton came ashore in Sicily, where German forces were ill-prepared for them. Victory was made possible with the help of the man who never was.

Pigeons in a Pelican

This weapons system is controlled by a real birdbrain.

During World War II, the U.S. Navy began work on a rocket-propelled guided missile, but prototypes of the so-called "Pelican" missile were not performing up to expectations. Then stepped forward a scientist who had an unusual idea for how to steer the missile to its target.

A pigeon would control the guidance system.

Behaviorist B.F. Skinner believed he could use positive reinforcement to train the pigeons to guide missiles to the target—although the outcome might not be positive for the bird. He convinced the Pentagon to provide funding for the idea.

Thus began "Project Pigeon" in 1943.

A lens-and-mirror system projected an image of the distant target on a screen directly in front of the pigeon. The bird was trained to peck at the target, activating a mechanism that would turn the missile in that direction.

As outlandish as that might sound, Skinner and his team succeeded in training the pigeons and building a prototype homing device. They were

Skinner never lost enthusiasm for Project Pigeon. Years after the war he was still defending it, suggesting that pigeons could guide a rocket to the moon.

> *"Hell, that's better than radar."*
>
> —MIT EXPERT, REVIEWING PIGEON-GUIDANCE TEST RESULTS

able to demonstrate that it was both highly effective and easy to manufacture. But in the end, the pigeons never got off the ground. Neither scientists nor generals were able to take the project seriously enough to actually put the homing device in a missile and test it.

And so it was that a missile with a birdbrain was shot down for good.

Patton's Prayer

Everybody talks about the weather, but only one general takes much-needed action.

With the armored division sidelined by wet weather, Patton was fuming.

In December 1944, General George Patton's Third Army found itself bogged down in Belgium. The Germans were only part of the problem. Patton's army was also hampered by bad weather: rain, fog, and floods were making advance nearly impossible.

Not content to sit idly by, Patton (left) summoned one of his officers and told him what he wanted: A prayer for good weather.

The officer he called on was chaplain James O'Neill. "I'm tired of having to fight mud and floods as well as Germans," Patton told him. "See if we can't get God to work on our side." O'Neill got right to work. The prayer he wrote beseeched the Almighty to change the weather, to look favorably upon them in battle and to crush the wickedness of their enemies.

When he brought it back to Patton, the general told him he wanted 250,000 copies printed up. "We've got to get every man in the Third Army to pray," Patton said. The soldiers received the prayer card on December 22, the very day they were supposed to launch a desperate counterattack in the Battle of the Bulge. As if by magic, the rain and fog disappeared. Six days of perfect weather followed, during which the Third Army handed the Germans a crushing defeat.

Patton called O'Neill into his office. "Chaplain, you're the most popular man in this headquarters. You sure stand in good with the Lord and the soldiers." Then he pinned a bronze star on O'Neill—a medal for a prayer that worked wonders.

> *"...most merciful Father, we humbly beseech Thee, of Thy great goodness, to restrain these immoderate rains..."*
>
> —FROM THE PRAYER WRITTEN FOR PATTON BY CHAPLAIN JAMES O'NEILL

Fu-Go Attack

These strange intercontinental weapons attack America.

In April, 1942, four months after the Japanese attack on Pearl Harbor, 16 bombers took off from the deck of the aircraft carrier Hornet to conduct a daring bombing raid on Tokyo.

While the attack did little damage it was a psychological blow. Eager to strike back, Japanese war planners searched for a way to hit the American mainland. After two years of intensive top-secret preparation Japan unleashed the world's first intercontinental weapon on the United States in 1944: Bomb-carrying balloons.

While it may sound funny, it was anything but. Over a period of months, the Japanese launched more than 6,000 of the so-called "Fu-Go" weapons against the United States. The balloons were designed to catch the jet stream for a quick crossing of the Pacific before dropping down on America's cities, forests and farmlands. Each one carried four incendiary bombs for starting fires and a shrapnel bomb for sowing terror.

An estimated 1,000 of the balloons came down in the U.S. Some reached as far as Michigan but most came down in the Pacific Northwest. One killed six picnickers in Oregon while another temporarily shut down a plant in Hanford, Washington, that was part of the atomic-bomb project.

The spherical balloons were 33 feet across. Because of the high winds in the jet stream the journey across the Pacific took only about four days.

The damage was minimal but the threat was real. The government's response was to censor all news of the attacks. This "defense of silence" convinced the Japanese high command that the program was a failure and they discontinued it before their new weapon of terror could reach its full potential.

One of Shepperton Studios' rubber tanks, which was used to fool the Germans into thinking an army was massing.

The Greatest Hoax in History

The Normandy invasion requires deception on a grand scale.

In the spring of 1944, Allied commander Dwight Eisenhower gave General George Patton a mighty army to spearhead the invasion of France. The First U.S. Army Group consisted of 11 divisions assembled near the White Cliffs of Dover, readying to cross the English Channel at its narrowest point and invade France at Pas-de-Calais.

But it wasn't a real army—it was a giant con job. The Allies wanted to convince Hitler that the actual invasion they were planning was just a diversion and that the real invasion was going to come more than 100 miles away, near Cherbourg. So began Operation Quicksilver.

Set designers from London's famous Shepperton Studios were brought in to create the illusion of a massive army where there was none. They created battalions of rubber tanks and regiments of wooden soldiers. Canvas airplanes were parked on fake runways, harbors filled with dummy landing craft. Radio operators sent huge amounts of bogus traffic orders to and from units that didn't exist.

A professor of architecture from Britain's Royal Academy used broken sewage pipes and rusty old oil tanks to create a fake refinery. Movie-studio wind machines blew clouds of dust over the scene, making it look as if construction was proceeding at a furious rate.

Numerous other ruses were also employed to thoroughly mislead the Germans. Actor M.E. Clifton-James impersonated British general Bernard Montgomery and traveled to Gibraltar and Algiers shortly before D-Day to convince Germans that something was cooking

The deceptions fooled Hitler completely. Even after the Allies stormed ashore in Normandy on June 6 the Germans held their Panzer divisions in reserve, waiting for a phantom invasion from a ghost army that was purely the product of Allied imagination. That gave the Allies the time they needed to secure the beachhead and make possible the triumph of D-Day.

M.E. Clifton-James as General Bernard Montgomery

OTHER PLAYERS, OTHER PLACES

Deception played a big part in with winning of WWII. The Americans had another ghost army, the 23rd Headquarters Special Troops, which practiced similar deceptions throughout the war. Artists and designers were in great demand to create the illusions needed to fool the enemy. Among the many talented soldiers who paticipated in fooling the enemy was a young man by the name of Bill Blass, who would later go on to great fame and fortune as a fashion designer.

Shades of Gray

A wartime replacement inspires millions.

On Sunday, May 20, 1945, the St. Louis Browns trounced the New York Yankees in both games of a doubleheader. Browns outfielder Pete Gray was the shining star of the day. In the first game he had three hits, driving in two runs and scoring a third. In the second game he scored the go-ahead run and made a spectacular catch in the outfield.

Pretty amazing for a guy with one arm.

During World War II large numbers of baseball players joined the military, so teams had to look for replacements. One of those called up was Gray.

When Gray was six he fell off a farm wagon and his right arm got caught in the spokes. The arm had to be amputated at the elbow. A natural right-hander, Gray learned to throw and bat using only his left hand. His passion for baseball led him to spend untold hours perfecting a way to catch the ball, tuck his glove under his stump, then roll the ball across his chest to his throwing hand in one quick motion.

Eventually he quit school to pursue a baseball career. He joined the pennant-contending Browns in 1945 after a stellar year in the minors, where he batted .333 and hit 6 home runs. His major-league numbers were nowhere near as strong—he played in only 77 games and batted .211. When the year was out and the regulars returned home from the service, he was gone from the majors for good.

But to many baseball fans he was a hero. Pete Gray: a man unwilling to let adversity get in the way of a dream.

Newspapers referred to Gray as "Wonder Boy." Some of Gray's teammates resented him because they thought he was signed as a gimmick bring in fans.

First Debate

Win, lose or draw: it's just practice for a presidential showdown.

When John F. Kennedy and Richard Nixon squared off for their historic presidential debates in 1960, they knew something most of the country didn't.

They had debated before.

Thirteen years earlier, in 1947, both Nixon and Kennedy were freshmen congressmen, still wet behind the ears. They were invited to the industrial town of McKeesport, Pennsylvania, to debate the Taft-Hartley Bill, a Republican-sponsored measure that was designed to limit the power of labor unions.

No one in the hotel ballroom that night knew that the debate was a glimpse into the future.

Ever the fighter, Nixon was aggressive in arguing for the bill. A member of his college debate team, he challenged his opponent on every point. Union members in the audience booed and jeered him, but he kept on nonetheless. Kennedy, ever the charmer, often ignored his opponent as he sought middle ground and tried to win over the crowd. The debate was ruled a draw.

Later that night, the two men took a night train for Washington. They drew straws for the lower berth, and Nixon won. It was the last time he was to beat Kennedy in anything.

Young congressmen Kennedy, 29, and Nixon, 34, are at the back, right in this photo.

A Dog's Life

Meet the space pioneer who is definitely nothing to bark at.

In October 1957, Americans were amazed to discover that the Soviet Union had put up the world's first satellite: Sputnik. The 184-pound satellite orbited the earth every 90 minutes, its signature beeping easily heard on radio sets around the globe.

Less than a month later, the Soviets did it again. They put up a much bigger satellite, with the world's first orbital space traveler: Laika, a mutt picked up from the streets. Moscow radio announced that Laika was riding in air-conditioned comfort as she rocketed through space at 18,000 miles an hour.

Unfortunately the Russians did not yet have the technology to bring Laika back. Her oxygen ran out after a few days and eventually her satellite burned up after its orbit decayed and it reentered the earth's atmosphere.

Laika went up, but never came down.

Although she never got home, Laika proved beyond all doubt that space travel was possible. And the two satellites rocketed into space by the Russians shocked the worried United States into launching its own space program.

The space race was on—thanks, in part, to the dog nicknamed "Muttnick."

Belka and Strelka were the first animals to go to space and come home to Earth again.

OTHER PLAYERS, OTHER PLACES

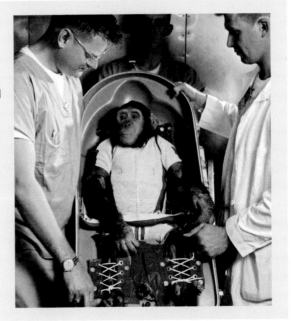

One of America's first astro-animals was a chimpanzee named Ham. He rode a Mercury capsule on a suborbital trip in 1961 that paved the way for his human follow-up act, Alan Shepherd. Another chimp named Enos was the first American in orbit. The first space travelers to make it back alive were a pair of Russian dogs named Belka and Strelka, who went up on August 19, 1960, and were successfully recovered after a day in orbit. Strelka eventually gave birth to puppies, one of which was given to American president John F. Kennedy. When that dog had puppies, JFK humorously called them "pupniks."

Makeup Moment

Does a cosmetics choice influence a presidential election?

The first year that televised presidential debates were held was 1960. Vice President Richard Nixon and Senator John F. Kennedy were running neck and neck and the debates would prove crucial.

CBS was televising the first debate from a TV station in Chicago. Wanting everything to go right, the network flew in one of television's best makeup artists, Frances Arnold, to make sure that each candidate looked his best under the hot lights.

Today it's common for men, including politicians, to wear makeup on television, but that wasn't the case in 1960. When Kennedy, tanned from a West Coast trip, said no to makeup, Nixon also refused. He apparently thought it would damage his image if it got out that he was wearing makeup and Kennedy wasn't.

MORE OF THE STORY

The director of the debate was Don Hewitt, who years later went on to become the executive producer of *60 Minutes*. Talking with Richard Nixon shortly after JFK's assassination, Hewitt said: "You know, Mr. Nixon, if you had let Franny make you up at that first debate, you might have been president now."

"Yes," said Nixon, "and I might be dead now, too."

Bad call. Back in the privacy of their dressing rooms each candidate got a hurried makeup job from an adviser. One of Nixon's assistants put something called Shave Stick on him. Kennedy's aide dabbed some Max Factor Crème Puff on the candidate's face. When they came out, Kennedy looked great. Nixon looked terrible.

People who listened to the debate on radio thought Nixon won, but the 60 million who saw it on television overwhelmingly considered JFK the victor. He went on to win one of the closest elections in history with Max Factor being a critical factor in his victory.

Jack Kennedy's on-screen charisma helped win him the election.

Pandora's Box

Here's the most bizarre assassination attempt in American history.

It was a few minutes after seven at Baltimore-Washington International Airport and passengers were lining up to get on an early-morning Delta flight for Atlanta. Suddenly a burly man ran up to the gate, shot the security guard dead, and ran down the ramp to the waiting plane.

More than 25 years before al-Qaeda got the idea, Samuel Byck (right) was carrying out his plan to hijack a jetliner and crash it into the White House.

The 44-year-old Philadelphia man had convinced himself that President Nixon was the cause of all his problems. Turning suicidal, he concocted a plan he called "Project Pandora's Box." He recorded the details on hours of audiotapes that he made beforehand. "When the plane is in this position I will shoot the pilot and then in the last few minutes try to steer the plane into the target, which is the White House."

Byck's plan never got off the ground. Once aboard the plane he killed the copilot and wounded the pilot, then was himself wounded by policemen firing through the window. He killed himself before he was captured.

Byck viewed himself as a political terrorist and said on one of his tapes: "It's very unfortunate that

Byck was arrested twice for demonstrating in front of the White House without a permit.

a good, wholesome guy like me has to kill himself or get killed to make a point."

But exactly what that point was, nobody was ever sure.

"One man's terrorist is another man's patriot…it all depends on which side of the fence you happen to be on at the time."

—SAMUEL BYCK, IN AN AUDIOTAPE HE MADE BEFORE THE ASSASSINATION ATTEMPT

Old Man's Vote

It's never too late to vote for the first time.

The old man had never voted. He was 75 years old and had never voted in any of his country's elections. Not for president, mayor, or anything.

He had been very involved in public service during his long life. He founded youth groups, worked in community organizations and did some writing. He had lots of friends and many children and grandchildren. But he had never voted in an election.

Then, in his 76th year, he cast his ballot for the first time ever. If the story ended here, it would be a simple, heartwarming tale of a man who late in life discovered what a wonderful feeling it is to exercise

Mandela spent 28 years in prison. Released in 1990, he was elected president of South Africa four years later.

the right to vote. But this story is much more than that—for two reasons.

The old man lived in South Africa. And the reason he had never exercised the right to vote was that he was black and his country had never given him that right. Now, at long last, for the first time in his life, he was allowed to vote.

What a powerful feeling it must have been.

Perhaps even more powerful than we can imagine. Because when the old man voted for the very first time, he voted for himself. For president. In the knowledge that millions of others, also voting for the first time, would do the same—thus making this old man, Nelson Mandela, the first black president of South Africa, a country that had never allowed blacks to vote until that day.

OTHER PLAYERS, OTHER PLACES

Another prisoner who became president was Václav Havel. The Czech playwright was imprisoned numerous times for his political activities, once serving four years in jail. After leading the "Velvet Revolution" that ended Communist rule of Czechoslovakia in 1989, he became the last president of Czechoslovakia and the first president of the Czech Republic.

Space 2.0

The future is born on this day.

On October 4, 1957, the launch of Sputnik gave birth to the space age. Forty-seven years later to the day another launch paved the way for a revolution in space travel.

That's the day that Burt Rutan's SpaceShipOne won the $10 million Ansari X-Prize for becoming the first privately funded spaceship to make two journeys into space within two weeks. The X-prize was modeled on the Orteig Prize, which inspired Lindbergh's famous flight to Paris.

Rutan's vessel was the size of a small biplane with a rocket engine that ran on laughing gas and rubber. After being launched, pilot Brian Binnie fired its single rocket engine for 84 seconds. The burn propelled SpaceShipOne into a suborbital flight more than 70 miles into space before it glided back to earth.

That flight marked the beginning of a new space race between businesses instead of governments. And the competition promises to advance space exploration at warp speed.

Rutan is building a fleet of 12 planes for Virgin Galactic. Each will be able to carry a pilot and five passengers 80 miles up, where they will experience four minutes of weightlessness. The anticipated price tag: $200,000 per person.

Meanwhile other visionaries are working on space taxies, space hotels and a new generation of space liners. More than seven private spaceports are under way and the state of New Mexico has established a Spaceport Authority, hoping to become America's launching pad of the future.

Space travel has come along way from the beeping ball in the sky that was Sputnik. And at last the final frontier may be opening to ordinary people, not just astronauts.

SpaceShipOne lands at the Mojave Airport Civilian Aerospace Test Center after its first mission.

It's not just guns, tools, and medical breakthroughs—inventing can be fun!

Chapter 4

Inventions and Discoveries

Human Creativity Knows No Bounds

Since the dawn of recorded history, mankind has struggled to understand and control his world in myriad ways: a weapon to end war forever, a delicious new food, a tool for instantaneous communication, a medicine that saves millions, a toy beloved by children—these are the creations of active minds and nimble hands. Whether it's the result of decades of struggle or a moment of brilliance, whether the outcome is fantastic, practical or just plain fun, the stories behind the inventions are always compelling.

Archimedes' Secret Weapon

One old man holds off a Roman fleet with amazing creations.

In 213 BC, a Roman fleet under the command of Marcus Claudius Marcellus attacked the Greek city-state of Syracuse. Marcellus was confident he could take Syracuse in five days. Instead it took more than a year, thanks to the incredible ingenuity of one old man: Archimedes.

Archimedes is best remembered for shouting "Eureka!" in his bath and running through the streets naked. But there was much more to the man than that. He was Einstein and Edison combined, the greatest scientist of the ancient world, and also a brilliant inventor. As the military adviser to the king of Syracuse he spent years devising mysterious

"Archimedes uses my ships to ladle seawater into his wine cups."

—ROMAN GENERAL MARCUS CLAUDIUS MARCELLUS

"engines" to protect the city. When the Romans came, Syracuse put Archimedes' machines to work.

There were large catapults capable of hurling rocks the size of wagons and small catapults called "scorpions" that shot darts at the Romans. A giant grappling claw lifted Roman ships by the bow and smashed them against the rocks. Mousetrap-like mechanisms levered giant weights down upon Roman siege ladders.

Then there were the mirrors. Archimedes, according to several chroniclers, created a series of mirrors that could focus the sun's energy on ships and cause them to burst into flame—a death ray in the ancient world.

Marcellus had to admit he could not take the city by storm. He was forced to lay siege to it for many months before he finally found a way in. Archimedes was killed in the eventual sack of the city, but not before demonstrating that the genius of one man could prove equal to all the military might in Rome.

Archimedes destroys a navy with mirrors?

Arms Race

A load of manure proves more valuable that you might think.

It began as a "fire drug" developed by Chinese alchemists. It eventually exploded into a fuel for killing that is now nearly 1,000 years old. What's the enduring item? Gunpowder.

The first known Chinese recipe for gunpowder dates back to 1044. Cannons appeared in China a century or so later but gun technology didn't really take off until the weapons made their way to Europe some 200 years after that. It didn't take long for the Europeans to turn primitive "bombards," as early cannons were known, into wonder-weapons that helped them extend their power over much of the globe.

If the Chinese had cannons first, how was it that the Europeans won that early arms race?

The most effective gunpowder is about three-quarters saltpeter mixed with charcoal and sulfur. And the most common source then for saltpeter was animal dung. But the Chinese had fewer domesticated animals than the Europeans, so saltpeter was harder to come by in China. Made with less saltpeter, Chinese gunpowder was less powerful. During the 1300s, Chinese engineers focused their energies not so much on guns as on bombs. These were launched by catapults and given fantastic and evocative names such as "Dropping from

Guns such as these were employed in 1331 at the siege of Civalde, in Italy, the earliest known use of cannons in a European battle.

> *"A child's toy of sound and fire."*

—ROGER BACON IN 1267, THE FIRST KNOWN EUROPEAN REFERENCE TO GUNPOWDER

Heaven Bomb," and "Bandit Burning Vision-Confusing Magic Fire-ball."

Being comparatively richer in farm animals and thus, in saltpeter, the Europeans were able to make more-potent gunpowder, which paved the way for better and more-effective weapons. And that's no bull.

Weapons Wizard

The machinations of a military maestro make mayhem.

Leonardo da Vinci (below) was a painter, a sculptor, a scientist and an engineer. He was also a one-man military industrial complex. Although he described himself as a pacifist and called war "the most bestial madness," da Vinci had a lifelong fascination with all things military. He designed an astonishing number of weapons and combat devices in the mid-to-late 1400s, many of them centuries ahead of their time.

In his notebooks can be found designs for a giant mechanical crossbow, a machine gun, a helicopter and a self-propelled armored tank. Da Vinci's design was armored with heavy wooden beams and propelled by men inside operating hand cranks. It was designed to make quick penetrations into enemy lines that could be followed up by infantry, which is exactly how motor-driven tanks were first used more than four centuries later in World War I. He sketched out a grenade with tail fins to be launched by a bowman and a

"Whatever the situation, I can invent an infinite variety of machines for both attack and defense."

—LEONARDO DA VINCI, IN A LETTER TO THE DUKE OF MILAN

prefabricated portable bridge that armies could use to cross small steams. Da Vinci even designed a steam-powered cannon, which he said could fire a 60-pound ball a distance of two-thirds of a mile.

Many of Da Vinci's ideas never got off the drawing board. For example, when the leaders of Florence sought his advice in attacking Pisa, he came up with a scheme to divert the river Arno, which would deprive the Pisans of water and cut off their access to the harbor. Breathtaking in conception, it was, like many of da Vinci's ideas, a wonderful concept that was just too difficult to execute. The effort was ultimately abandoned. But other ideas were highly practical. During his career da Vinci served as a military engineer to several European warlords including the notorious Cesare Borgia. He designed fortifications so advanced that nothing like them was seen again for centuries. He created mortars that rained down a shower of stones on enemy heads.

Had da Vinci pushed his concepts harder, he might have dramatically changed the face of Renaissance warfare. But he was notorious for leaving a project unfinished and moving on to the next grand idea.

Da Vinci is best known today as the great artistic genius who painted the world-renowned and enigmatic Mona Lisa. But it may be in the military arts that his creative genius and foresight showed through the most.

JUST A TALE?

There exists a popular myth that Leonardo da Vinci invented the bicycle. An alleged 500-year-old diagram showing a two-wheeled, pedal-powered vehicle was "discovered" during the 1974 restoration of his papers. The idea persisted for two decades until the 1997 International Conference on Cycling History, when a scientist presented research showing that the sketch was not done by da Vinci's hand. Historians now disagree on the origin of the fake draft. Some say it was made by da Vinci's assistant, Salai, who copied the design from his teacher's original. Others believe the forgery had a more sinister source—modern, nationalistic Italians seeking to further promote their countryman. But whatever the provenance of the bicycle drawing, one thing is certain: da Vinci did visualize and design other gear-and-chain mechanisms. So while a 10-speed bike of today may not be a direct descendent of da Vinci's imagination it was, in part inspired by the radical ideas and forward-thinking creations of the most famous of all Renaissance men.

These geared mechanisms were designed by da Vinci but he never got around to building them.

Siege of Bread and Butter

A famous scientist, a tasty spread and a wartime outbreak of disease lead to a gastronomic pairing.

To Polish astronomer Nicolaus Copernicus we owe our understanding that the earth moves around the sun, not the sun around the earth. It was a discovery that revolutionized science. Do we also owe to him the custom of putting butter on our bread?

In 1519, Copernicus was called upon to command Polish forces besieged in the fortified town of Allenstein, a Polish town on the Prussian border. During the siege the town was struck by plague. Copernicus isolated the town's bread as being the source of the disease. But he suspected that it wasn't the bread itself, rather the fact that something was contaminating it. Sanitary conditions in the beleaguered town were marginal at best and the coarse black loaves could be dropped in the dirty streets, or otherwise contaminated, without even showing it.

That's when a fellow by the name of Gerhard Glickselig suggested to Copernicus that the bread loaves be colored with a thin layer of light-colored spread. That would make it obvious if the bread was dropped or if debris fell on it, and people could avoid eating it. Copernicus ordered it be done and the plague soon ended. True to form, Copernicus employed the scientific method to discover the source of the disease. He divided the town's residents into four groups and fed them different things. The group that got no bread was the only one that remained plague-free. Thus were married bread and butter, at least for the first time that we know of. It didn't become common in Europe until the following century. And so we honor Copernicus as a man ahead of his time in matters of cuisine as well as the cosmos.

Copernicus' revolutionary theory about the earth revolving around the sun was published on his deathbed, sparing him conflict with the Vatican.

Up with *Uppowoc*

An herbal cure from the colonies ignites world interest and sparks a die-hard habit.

In 1585, Sir Walter Raleigh organized a British expedition to establish a new colony in Virginia. He sent along 25-year-old Thomas Hariot as a historian and surveyor. Hariot spent a year at the Roanoke Colony and wrote a report detailing his experiences—the first book in English about the New World. In his book, which enjoyed much popularity in England, Hariot claimed that *uppowoc* was so esteemed by the native people that sometimes they would throw it upon an open fire as a sacrifice to their gods.

In his account, Hariot told of discovering an astonishing herbal remedy, called *uppowoc,* cultivated by the local tribes. It "openeth all the pores and passages," Hariot marveled, "whereby their bodies are notably preserved in health and know not many grievous diseases, wherewithal we in England are often times afflicted." Intrigued, the colonists tried this herbal concoction themselves and had so many "rare and wonderful" experiences with it that they brought a load back to England.

Uppowoc created a lasting sensation upon reaching the shores of Britain. It is still with us, but now we take a different view of its medicinal qualities. We also call it by a different name, its Spanish name: tobacco.

Once it reached England the addictive habit of smoking tobacco quickly spread throughout Europe.

Coffee and the Pope

When you drink your morning coffee tomorrow, say thanks to the pope who made it all possible.

A coffee craze first gripped the world about 600 years ago, traveling from Ethiopia through Yemen to the Middle East. With a Starbucks on nearly every corner today you might think coffee has never been more popular, but that's nothing compared to the popularity it enjoyed in the Middle East during the 1500s. Some of the earliest coffee fanatics were Muslim mystics trying to stay awake for nighttime worship

As the beverage became popular, it also became controversial. Early coffeehouses began popping up all over and were such brewing grounds for radical ideas that authorities in Mecca and Cairo tried to outlaw the drink. The prohibitions proved ineffective.

When coffee hit Europe in the late 1500s, priests at the Vatican argued that it was a satanic concoction of Islamic infidels. Accordingly, they thought it should be banned. That's when Pope Clement VIII stepped in and, after tasting the beverage, gave coffee his blessing.

"This Satan's drink is so delicious," he supposedly said, "it would be a pity to let the infidels have exclusive use of it. We shall fool Satan by baptizing it."

"This is the beverage of the friends of God."

— "IN PRAISE OF COFFEE," ARABIC POEM, 1511

A young courtier carries a cup of coffee in this portrait housed in Topkapi Museum, Istanbul.

In Turkey in the 1500s, a woman could divorce a man who did not provide her with enough coffee.

With this papal blessing, coffee soon began to conquer Europe and became the morning necessity it remains for many people today. But it wasn't popular everywhere. In 1610 British poet Sir George Sandys described the bitter brew this way: "Black as soote and tasting not much unlike it." Is it any wonder the people of Great Britain became such big fans of tea?

MORE OF THE STORY

During the Middle Ages the Pope had a lot to say about what could and could not be eaten, particularly during the 40 days of Lent, which is the period leading up to Easter. Meat and fowl were forbidden on all days but Sundays. But a modern biologist wouldn't recognize many of the definitions from those days. For example, the Barnacle Goose, a common seabird and definitely a fowl, was thought of as being born of a barnacle and thus fair game.

The Seige That Gave Birth to the Croissant

A Turkish army provides the inspiration for a breakfast delicacy.

The croissant is not French—it was first baked in Austria. And its shape is anything but an accident. The popular pastry dates back to 1683. In that year an army of more than 100,000 Ottoman Turks was storming the city of Vienna. They surrounded it for months and residents inside the stout walls began to wonder if each day would be their last.

When the Turks tried tunneling under the walls bakers working through the night heard the digging sounds and raised the alarm. This early warning prevented the Turks from breaching Vienna's walls and helped save the city. Eventually an army under Polish King John III reached Vienna and drove away the Turks.

JUST A TALE?

The siege of Vienna is also believed by some to be the birthplace of the bagel. King John of Poland was widely known as a skilled horseman, and a baker supposedly created a roll in the shape of a stirrup to honor him. The Austrian word for "stirrup" is bügel—eventually Americanized to "bagel." Can it be true that one battle did so much for so many breakfasts?

The bakers celebrated the end of the siege in a remarkable way. They copied the crescent moon from their enemy's flag and turned it into a commemorative pastry. It was called a kipfel (German for "crescent") and it honored a victory that might not have happened but for the bakers themselves.

Kipfels turned into croissants in 1770, when 15-year-old Austrian Princess Marie Antoinette arrived in France to marry the future King Louis XVI. Parisian bakers started turning out kipfels in her honor and the French found themselves in love with a breakfast treat that they soon made their very own.

Paper Trail

A world-changing idea is born of a walk in the woods.

Beginning in the 1600s, Europe was hit with a crippling shortage. People had to deal with the fact that a valuable commodity was in increasingly short supply. What was it?

Rags. They were used to make paper which was in great demand. Publishers of books, newspapers

and political pamphlets all clamored for more paper. But there just weren't enough rags. Advertisements appeared asking women to save their rags. In 1666, England banned the use of cotton and linen for the burial of the dead, decreeing they must be saved for making paper. One entrepreneur even suggested using the cloth from Egyptian mummies. The scarcity of rags led to fearful paper shortages in Europe and America.

Then a French scientist took a walk in the woods. René-Antoine Ferchault de Réaumur was an accomplished physicist and chemist. He was also a man who loved bugs. Walking in the woods one day he came upon an abandoned wasps' nest. Delighted, he began to examine it in detail, and an astounding fact dawned on him: the nest was made of paper, paper made by wasps, paper made without the use of rags. How?

By chewing wood and plant fibers. And what wasps could do, he argued, man could find a way to do also. It took decades, but his discovery was the spark that inspired inventors to discover methods for making paper from wood pulp. Thanks to Réaumur's nature walk we can now do what would have once been considered almost criminal: crumple up a piece of paper and throw it out.

Thanks to Ferchault's discovery, books, such at those on his table, became much less expensive to produce.

The Mechanical Internet

Think email is cutting edge? Here's the network that linked Europe more than 200 years ago.

In the 1790s, dozens of odd-looking towers sprouted up across France. They composed the backbone of a new, state-of-the-art communications network.

The towers were the brainchild of a French inventor named Claude Chappe. Each one had mechanical arms that could be rotated into 90 different positions and were visible 10 miles away. An operator would set the arms in a certain position, then the operator in the next tower would see that through a telescope and set his arms in the same position. Messages rippled down the line at more than 100 miles an hour, astonishing for that day and age.

When Napoleon seized power in 1799, he was quick to grasp the military advantage of high-speed communications. He ordered new lines built from Paris in every direction. Soon more than 500 towers connected France's major cities. Other countries followed and lines of towers that snaked across Europe, Russia and northern Africa.

Chappe wanted to call his new invention the tachygraph, which meant "fast writer." A friend convinced him to

Chappe (left, standing) began his experiments during the French Revolution, which caused him no end of trouble with those who suspected he was trying to communicate with jailed royalty.

give it a different name, meaning "far writer." And so he called it the telegraph.

The invention of the electrical telegraph eventually made the Chappe telegraph obsolete. Today only a very few of the hundreds of towers remain—silent monuments to the world's first high-speed network and the inventive man who wouldn't stop until they were built.

OTHER PLAYERS, OTHER PLACES

He was a man of many passions. He was talented enough to become one of the foremost artists of the early 1800s. He painted Lafayette, President Monroe and the halls of Congress. He was also America's first camera buff. He fell in love with photography after meeting Louis Daguerre and was instrumental in introducing the camera to the United States when it was still brand-new. But we remember him today for quite a different passion. While painting Lafayette, he got word his wife was ill. By the time he reached Massachusetts, she was dead and he had missed her funeral. This brought home the need for quick communication. For more than a dozen years, suffering ridicule and poverty, he labored on a tool that would solve this problem. His invention finally captured the attention of the world in 1844 and helped launch an age of instant information. Samuel Finley Breese Morse: painter, photographer—and inventor of the electric telegraph. Truly an artist with a message.

"What hath God wrought?"

—MORSE'S FIRST OFFICIAL MESSAGE OVER HIS TELEGRAPH, IN 1844

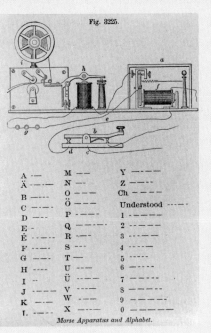

Fig. 3225.

Morse Apparatus and Alphabet.

Morse (above) and the code (left)

Revolutionary Pencil

The solution to a wartime crisis transforms the way we write.

In 1794, just five years after the French Revolution, France was at war with just about everyone else in Europe: England, Spain, Prussia and Austria. Worse still, the beleaguered French were in short supply of a precious weapon: Pencils.

Quill pens were messy and hard to use, especially for an army on the move. If you wanted to jot down a message or sketch enemy fortifications, a pencil was invaluable. But the graphite needed to make pencil lead was found mostly in England and Prussia—now France's enemies. With a dwindling supply of graphite and no way to get more, France faced a paucity of pencils.

The French minister of war decided to draw on the expertise of a highly talented inventor named Nicolas-Jacques Conté.

Conté's idea was to make a little graphite go a long way by grinding it into a fine powder and mixing it with something else. But what? Other inventors had tried glue, gum, shellac, even whale oil—but none worked.

The inventor experimented for eight days and nights without stopping. Finally he discovered the answer. He combined the graphite with clay, pressed the mixture into molds, then fired them inside a kiln. The result: dozens of pencils from a very small amount of graphite. Conté discovered that using more clay created a harder pencil, less clay a softer pencil. Conté's new method was a stunning success. It is still the way pencils are made today.

In January 1795, Conté obtained French patent number 32. And thus the modern pencil was born.

Conte designed four grades of pencil—the origin of the schoolchild's No. 2.

Ba-Bump Goes the Stethoscope

Who would ever think modesty could be the mother of invention?

In September 1816, a buxom young woman paid a visit to a French physician named Dr. René Laënnec. He felt certain that she had heart problems. But the morals of the day prevented him (a bachelor) from listening to her heart in the normal fashion of putting his ear to her chest. Besides, trying to hear a heart through such an ample bosom would be a trifle difficult.

The doctor was also a musician. He rolled a tube from paper—like a flute—and he touched this to his patient. "I was surprised and gratified," he wrote, "at being able to hear the beating of the heart with greater clearness than ever before." Soon after, he fashioned a hollow cylinder out of wood with a funnel at one end. René Laënnec thought his invention was such a simple device that it didn't need a name. But when others pushed him

"The very size of [the] breasts was a physical obstacle."

—RENÈ LAÈNNEC, DESCRIBING THE CATALYST FOR HIS INVENTION

for a name he suggested "stethoscope"—from the Greek word stethos, meaning "chest," and skopos, meaning "observer"—the stethoscope.

Many doctors were quick to adapt to this new technology. But some resisted. One American doctor put it this way: "He that hath ears to hear, let him use his ears and not a stethoscope."

But the new device allowed doctors to diagnose problems of the heart and lungs they had never before been able to uncover. A new window on illness was opened—thanks to modesty.

From a paper tube, Laënnec progressed to wood; today's versions are composed of rubber, plastic and metal.

Spearheading a Revolution

A warrior's simple idea has remarkable consequences for a whole continent.

When you throw a spear—and miss—you not only disarm yourself, you give a weapon to your enemy. This radical thought entered the mind of a Zulu warrior sometime shortly after 1800 and his response changed the face of Africa.

The warrior, named Shaka, concluded that the age-old tactic of lofting lightweight spears at enemy formations was next to useless. Instead, he devised a new kind of stabbing spear, shorter and heavier, with a bigger blade, which he used to draw close to his enemy and kill them in hand-to-hand combat.

It became known as the *iklwa*—for the sucking sound it made when it was plunged into and pulled out of a human body.

Shaka Zulu also taught his warriors how to hook the left edge of their shield behind an opponent's shield and spin him around with a backhand sweep, making him vulnerable to a stabbing thrust. He used this new combination of fighting methods to become Africa's most famous and feared conqueror, as well as one of the great commanding generals of all time. Starting with just a few men under his command, he ended up ruling an empire and commanding an army of more than 50,000. He revolutionized warfare on the African continent, introducing bold new tactics and the

Shaka also instituted encirclement tactics rather than the more traditional frontal assault.

concept of total war as opposed to the seasonal raids that had beeen common among the tribes throughout the area.

The result was the death of more than 2 million Africans, depopulating a wide swath of southern Africa just as white settlers were beginning to colonize the region.

MORE OF THE STORY

Shaka was chief of the Zulus from 1816 until 1828, when he was assassinated by his half-brother. As a boy Shaka was exiled from his village with his mother and he remained very close to her. When she died, he ordered thousands of Zulus killed so their families might mourn along with him. In his deranged grief he ordered that no crops be planted and all pregnant women slain; even cows were killed so that their calves might know what it was like to lose a mother. His assassination came shortly after this period, when many of his supporters had abandoned him.

Night Writing

This artillery captain makes it possible for the blind to read—in spite of himself.

Imagine being a frontline soldier and getting a message at night. There's no way to read that message without lighting a lamp that will expose you to enemy fire. In the early 1800s this dilemma inspired a French artillery officer, Captain Charles Barbier, to create "night writing." It was a code consisting of raised dots poked onto a piece of paper. The code used combinations of 12 dots to stand for different sounds.

"If I cannot discover a way to read and write...then I shall kill myself."

—LOUIS BRAILLE, IN HIS DIARY

Eventually Barbier introduced his concept to the blind. A 13-year-old boy at the Royal Institute for the Blind was one of the first to learn the new system. He had been blind since the age of three, when he accidentally put out one of his eyes with an awl. Infection had set in and soon spread to his other eye, leaving him completely sightless. He was excited by the opportunities the dot system offered but thought it might be too complex, so he offered Barbier some ideas on how to simplify and improve it. The haughty Barbier did not welcome his suggestions—in fact, he was insulted that a mere boy could imagine he had something to offer. When the boy tried haltingly to explain Barbier stalked out of the

French soldiers on the artillery line light a fire, which acts as a target for their enemies.

room. He angrily refused to even consider making the slightest change.

The boy, of course, was Louis Braille. Instead of losing heart, he became determined to develop his ideas on his own. He labored tirelessly for two years to transform night writing into a far simpler system that cut the number of dots in half. He also decided to make them stand for letters instead of sounds. He was just 15 years old when he completed his system of writing for the blind. And a new world was revealed to those without sight.

Braille (right) had spent hours every day using a sharp stylus to punch raised dots while he labored to improve Barbier's idea. A talented cellist and organist, he soon expanded his system to include symbols for mathematics and music. Ironically the stylus he used was very similar to the awl that had punctured one of his eyes, causing an infection that quickly left him blind in both. Braille was an extremely unusual young man. Despite Barbier's refusal to work with him, Braille was always quick to credit him for his role in developing the system that came to be used worldwide. But it took a while. Even at the very school where Braille studied and eventually became an instructor, his method was not taught until after his death.

This press from the 1920s printed pages in Braille.

Patent President

A country lawyer relies on his ingenuity to solve a problem.

Many people consider Thomas Jefferson to be the greatest inventor to live in the White House. Among Jefferson's many inventions were a more efficient wooden plow and a revolving bookstand that could hold five open books at once. But Jefferson never patented any of his ideas. Only one president has obtained a patent—someone who is not normally associated with the cutting edge of technology: Abraham Lincoln.

In the late 1840s, Lincoln served as a congressman from Illinois. He made part of the journey to and from Washington aboard a Great Lakes steamship. On one occasion the steamer got stuck on a sandbar. All the passengers and cargo had to be unloaded to float the ship over the sandbar. It was a long and tedious process.

This gave Lincoln an idea: what if there was a way to float the boat over the sandbar without having to empty it out and reload it? Lincoln's idea was to add "adjustable buoyant air changers" below the waterline. When the ship was stuck, these could be filled with air to float it off. When he got back to his law office in Illinois he began working on a device that would do just that. He whittled the model between court appearances. The result: patent 6469, "Manner of Buoying Vessels."

Lincoln's invention was never manufactured. But it did prove that this up-and-coming prairie lawyer possessed a creative mind willing to embrace and act on new ideas—a mind that would be sorely needed by the country in the turbulent years to come.

Jefferson's famous book stand was never patented.

Telephone Tale

Being first with a new idea doesn't always mean being famous.

Reis demonstrates his invention.

Alexander Graham Bell invented the telephone in 1876—right? Well, actually, a German schoolteacher managed to do it 15 years before Bell, but he didn't have very good PR.

In 1860, Philip Reis rigged up what he described as an "artificial ear." This crude instrument was built from an improbable assortment of items: a violin, a knitting needle, an ear carved in wood, even a piece of sausage. "I succeeded in inventing an apparatus by which…one can reproduce sounds of all kinds at any desired distance…I named the instrument [the] 'telephone.'"

It worked—but poorly. So Reis kept tinkering with it. He hooked up a wire between his workshop and the school, which convinced his students that he was using the telephone to eavesdrop on them. He worked on his telephone for several years and his models became more sophisticated.

Eventually Reis sent some improved models of his telephone to scientists around the world. They could transmit music fairly well, but speech came out garbled at best. "Single words…were perceptible indistinctly," said one listener. Nobody seemed very impressed.

Most scientists at the time regarded the Reis telephone as little more than a toy. Crushed, he abandoned work on it and died of tuberculosis in 1874. Two years later Alexander Graham Bell filed the patent that earned him the glory and financial rewards of telephone invention.

MORE OF THE STORY

Bell's great competitor in telephone invention was Elisha Gray, whose application for a telephone patent was filed just hours after Bell's. At the time Gray didn't seem to understand what he'd lost out on. "The talking telegraph is a beautiful thing from a scientific point of view," he wrote in 1876. "But if you look at in a business light, it is of no importance." For Bell the story was different. He didn't set out to invent a telephone. He was trying to build a telegraph that could send multiple messages down one wire. But once he realized he could make a telephone it consumed his every thought.

The Gun Meant to Save Lives

A Civil War doctor tries to save lives with an unusual invention, not a medical advance.

In the opening year of the War Between the States an Ohio doctor named Richard Gatling found himself horrified at the growing number of young men whose lives were being snuffed out. He noted that more men were falling from disease than from enemy bullets. That gave him an idea.

"It occurred to me," he wrote later, "that if I could invent a machine—a gun—which could, by its rapidity of fire, enable one man do as much battle duty as 100, that it would supercede the necessity of large armies and, consequently, exposure to battle and disease [would] be greatly diminished." In other words, he hoped that by inventing a better gun, he could save lives.

The Gatling gun could be mounted on a tripod, on wheels or, in an 1874 version, on camelback.

He tied six gun barrels around a revolving shaft and built a device to fire and reload them automatically. His machine gun could spit out 350 bullets per minute, more than 100 times what a standard-issue rifle could. By late 1862, his weapon was ready for action and if it had gone into production then, it could have had a dramatic impact on the war, ending the conflict much sooner and actually saving lives as Gatling hoped. But a fire burned down the factory and all his plans, forcing him to start over.

His gun finally saw battle late in the war and proved devastating when Union soldiers turned it on the enemy. After the war, the U.S. Army ordered 100 of the new guns, and soon armies all around the world were buying them. Machine guns have gone on to become a most efficient means of killing. And the thought they might actually save lives? Long since buried—along with Dr. Gatling.

The Cutting Edge

A presidential assassination inspires a medical breakthrough.

It was about 9:15 on a June evening in 1894, when Italian anarchist Cesare Santo darted out of the crowd and plunged his dagger into the abdomen of French president François Sadi Carnot. President Carnot slumped over in his carriage as the crowd set upon the assassin.

The dagger severed an artery leading to the president's liver and he began to bleed profusely. The best surgeons in Paris were summoned but they could do nothing. Carnot died within hours.

A young medical student in Lyons, Alexis Carrel, was struck by the fact that if doctors had known how to repair the artery, it might have saved the president's life. Carrel promptly began to search for a way to do it. The son of a silk manufacturer, he sought out one of the leading silk embroiderers in Lyons, Madame Leroudier, to tutor him in the use of tiny needles and fine thread. His efforts turned him into one of the finest surgeons in France. He also developed techniques to avoid clotting and fight off infection.

Within five years he had successfully developed a ground-breaking technique to sew severed blood vessels back together.

Carrel's work won him the 1912 Nobel Prize. More than that, it became the foundation for all organ-transplant work, first pioneered by him and later by others. President Carnot could not know that the lives of many would be saved by his own unfortunate death.

Carnot had been president of France for nearly seven years at the time of his assassination, pictured here in a popular weekly.

The Ice Cream Cone Cometh

The century-old controversy about the cook behind the cone is (perhaps) settled.

It happened on a stifling summer's day at the 1904 St. Louis World's Fair. Ernest Hamwi, an immigrant from Syria, was having no luck selling hot Persian waffles to the sweltering crowds. But at the next booth, Arno Fornachau was dishing out ice cream that was selling like, well, hotcakes. Suddenly Arnold ran out of plates. *Sacré bleu!* What to do? Suddenly, Ernest had a flash of inspiration. He

A waffle iron and a wooden fig such as these may have been used to make the first cones.

rolled a cone out of a warm and flexible waffle and offered it as a substitute for the plates. *Voilà!* The ice cream cone was born.

Well, that's the version backed by the International Ice Cream Association. But here's where the story gets sticky. At least half a dozen vendors at the fair claimed they actually deserved the credit. For example, the family of Charles Menches, another food vendor at the fair, said he invented the ice cream cone when he wrapped a homemade waffle around a wooden fig used to split tent rope. Their descendants still carry on a spirited argument about it with those who make other claims.

So what's the real scoop? It's safe to say that the World's Fair Cornucopia, as it was first known, was born at the fair one day and quickly copied by dozens of others eager to get in on a good thing. When the fair was over people took the idea back home and it became a coast-to-coast hit. Today one-third of all ice cream is licked off cones. They are one of America's favorite summer treats—no argument about that.

Fair-goers of all ages in St. Louis are delighted by America's newest taste treat.

Diamond in the Rough

The world's largest diamond breaks records—and heals a war wound.

In 1905, the superintendent of a South African diamond mine was conducting a routine inspection when he stumbled upon a stone as large as his fist. It was so big that at first he assumed it was a piece of glass planted as a joke.

But this was no joke. In fact it was the largest diamond ever discovered, weighing 3,106 carats.

Because one side of the diamond was smooth, experts believe it was only part of what was once a much larger diamond, broken up by natural forces. Named the Cullinan diamond (after the chairman of the company), it was purchased by the Transvaal Colony, which decided to give it to Britain's King Edward VII (left) as a token of loyalty.

Transvaal was home to many still bitter over their recent defeat in the Boer War and the colonial parliament split over whether to give the king the diamond. As a result the king thought his dignity might require him to refuse it. A rising young politician named Winston Churchil (above), himself a veteran of the Boer War, convinced the king to accept the jewel.

When it came time for the stone to leave the country, armed guards carried a package aboard a steamer, deposited it in the captain's safe and stood watch over it day and night. What they didn't know was that they were guarding a decoy!

Amazingly, the real diamond was sent by registered mail and arrived in the mailroom at Buckingham Palace a month later.

Joseph Asscher, the foremost diamond-cutter of his day, spent months studying the stone from every angle to determine where he should make the first cut. A mistake could ruin everything. When he was finally ready, he inserted a blade and struck it with a mallet. The blade shattered! After he succeeded in making the first cut with a new blade, his nerves got the better of him and he fell into a dead faint. Once he revived, it took him 38 days to cut it into nine major stones and nearly 100 smaller ones.

All the stones remain in the possession of Britain's royal family. The largest of them, known as the Greater Star of Africa, today adorns the royal scepter. It is the largest cut diamond in the world—weighing 530 carats.

OTHER PLAYERS, OTHER PLACES

Britain's Crown Jewels, including the Greater Star of Africa, are kept at the Tower of London behind

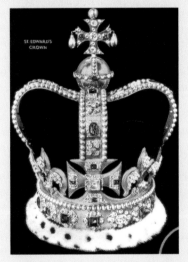

bullet-proof glass, protected by armed guards. But the monarch's gems weren't always so safe. After the execution of Charles I in 1649 Oliver Cromwell ordered the King's medals to be melted down and the stones to be sold off. The monarchy managed to rebuild their collection for the coronation of Charles II in 1661. But 10 years later an Irish-born colonel, Thomas Blood, made an audacious attempt to steal the Crown Jewels. In a planned heist, Blood befriended the jewel keeper. He then visited him one night, hit him over the head with a mallet, put the crown in a bag and shoved the orb down his own pants. He was stopped and arrested by Tower guards. But during World War II the royal family feared for the safety of the jewels again, so they were wrapped in newspaper and hidden in the Windsor Castle dungeon. It would be very difficult to replace the Crown Jewels these days. They are not insured against loss, because their value is truly impossible to calculate.

Wired Wireless

This aviation trailblazer leaves a legacy that is music to our ears.

His name is not widely known today, but George Owen Squier(below) was a true aviation pioneer. As a major in the Army Signal Corps he supervised testing of the Wright Brothers' plane in 1908. His flight with Orville Wright made him one of the first passengers ever to ride in an airplane. Squier was instrumental in convincing the Army to buy the Wright Flyer, thereby launching the age of military aviation. During World War I, he rose to command of the Army Air Corps.

As if that wasn't enough Squier was also a prolific inventor, with more than 60 patents to his name. In 1911, he patented a technology that allowed many radio signals to travel over a single wire. He called it "wired wireless."

After Squier retired from the Army, he launched a company to bring wired wireless to America. For $2 a month, consumers could have radio programs piped into their home over the electrical wires. It was an idea way ahead of its

One of Squier's more unusual but very successful innovations was his use of trees as radio antennae.

time—an early forerunner of cable TV. But people proved unwilling to pay for radio when they could get it for free. So Squier's company began targeting businesses and commissioning studies to show how piped-in music increased employee efficiency.

Squier's company was called Wired Radio, but in 1934 he came up with a catchier moniker, merging the word "music" with the name of his favorite hi-tech company, Kodak.

You may not know the name of the creative George Owen Squier, but surely you know the name he gave his company: Muzak, now heard in stores, restaurants, malls and offices by more than 100 million people daily.

Carbine Williams

A prison inmate helps outfit the U.S. Army with his invention.

In July 1921, a sheriff's posse swooped down on a moonshiner's still in North Carolina. Shots rang out and a deputy was killed. Although he always swore that he never fired a shot, moonshiner David Marshall Williams was convicted of murder. Many called for the death penalty, but instead he was sentenced to 30 years' hard labor.

In prison Williams secretly designed a gun. Working on a gun doesn't sound like the ideal activity for a prisoner, but when Williams showed the designs to Warden H.T. Peoples, the warden allowed him to build the weapon. When word got out about Williams's gun-building, Warden Peoples found

Williams, with a machine gun and an automatic weapon he designed

himself called on the carpet but he realized he was dealing with a mechanical genius who deserved encouragement. Peoples told the prison superintendent that he trusted Williams so much that if the prisoner ever used one of his guns in an escape, he would serve out the remainder of Williams' time. During his years in prison, Williams built six guns and invented the short-stroke piston, a device that captures the explosive force from the firing bullet and uses it to load the next one.

After eight years in prison Williams received a pardon from the governor. He started building weapons for the government and patenting his ideas. In 1941, Williams was working with Winchester Repeating Arms Company when the Army announced a competition for a new lightweight semiautomatic rifle. The winner was a model designed by Williams that featured his innovative short-stroke piston.

The new weapon was called the M1 carbine. Over 6 million were manufactured between 1940 and 1945, which made it the most-produced service weapon of the war.

"One of the strongest contributing factors in our victory in the Pacific."

—GENERAL DOUGLAS MACARTHUR ON THE M1 CARBINE

The Mold That Saved Millions

How did a messy research lab lead to the development of a wonder drug?

There was nothing unusual about the fact that Scottish biologist Alexander Fleming failed to clean up his lab before going on holiday in the summer of 1928. Friends often teased Fleming for being disorderly. The truth is that he was very hesitant to throw out his old bacteria cultures until absolutely sure that there was nothing more to learn from them.

He came back from vacation to find that some petri dishes had grown moldy. Sorting through them prior to throwing them out he discovered that the mold in one dish had destroyed the bacteria culture he was growing there. The mold was a kind of fungus, penicillium, that grows on bread. Fleming wrote a scientific paper on his discovery, but never really followed up on its practical applications.

During World War II a team of scientists searching for a way to treat infected wounds came across Fleming's discovery and began to experiment with a form of the mold. Its powers proved almost miraculous. Soon it was being manufactured in unbelievable quantities and rushed to the front. More than 21 chemical companies participated in a crash program to manufacture lifesaving penicillin. By war's end they were manufacturing 650 billion units per month.

Fleming, seated here in his famously messy lab, shared in a Nobel Prize for his discovery.

> *"One sometimes finds what one
> is not looking for."*
>
> —ALEXANDER FLEMING ON HIS FORTUITOUS DISCOVERY

More than 50 years later, penicillin remains the world's most used antibiotic—thanks to a scientist who didn't like to clean up.

OTHER PLAYERS, OTHER PLACES

Antibiotics, which arose from Fleming's fortuitous discovery that penicillium destroys bacteria, help cure disease. Edward Jenner pioneered something that helps prevent it: vaccines. He realized that dairy maids who had been infected with cow pox, a relatively mild disease, gained immunity from the much more dangerous small pox disease. He proved the same immunity could be artificially produced by infecting a boy with the virus from a dairy maid, then later repeatedly trying to infect the same child with the more virulent small pox. Not the most humane method, but it did prove his point when he published his findings in his *Inquiry* in 1789.

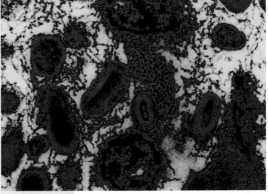

Smallpox was the scourge of Europe.

The Search for Planet X

This farmhand shows diligence can lead to great discoveries.

In 1928, Clyde Tombaugh (right) was working on his father's farm in Kansas. In love with the night sky, he built a telescope using parts he rummaged from a cream separator and his dad's 1910 Buick. He made drawings of the planets and sent them to the Lowell Observatory in Arizona. Even though he had only a high school diploma, the observatory offered him a job.

There, he was put to work searching for a planet that might not even exist. The founder of the observatory, Percival Lowell, had spent years searching for an unseen Planet X that he believed was affecting the orbit of Neptune. After he died, he left money for the search to continue. Many astronomers were skeptical. "If there were any more planets to be found," said one, "they would have been found by now."

Tombaugh had to photograph the sky quadrant by quadrant, then compare the photographs two at a time, in search of movement that might suggest a planet. Thousands of photographs, each containing thousands of stars. It was grinding work.

On February 18, 1930, he saw a dim speck move slightly as he switched between two photographs. The farm boy from Kansas became the first American to discover a planet. All over the world

Inside the Lowell Observatory

people suggested names for the new planet. An 11-year-old girl in Oxford, England, named Venetia Burney proposed Pluto, after the mythological god of the underworld. The name had another thing going for it: its first two letters are the initials of Percival Lowell.

But that's not the end of the story. On August 24, 2006, Pluto was downgraded from a planet to a dwarf planet by the International Astronomical Union because it hasn't cleared all the debris from its orbital path—one of the key elements for being a planet.

Don't feel bad for Tombaugh, though. He certainly lived out his dreams. He went on to get a Ph.D. and work for the space program. When he was in his eighties the Smithsonian asked him if it could have his original telescope. Tombaugh's answer: "I told them I was still using it."

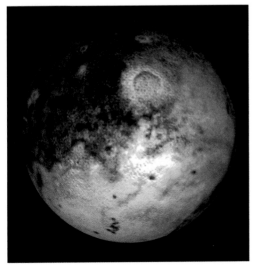

The dwarf planet, Pluto

OTHER PLAYERS, OTHER PLACES

Percival Lowell was proved right in his belief that there was something else out there beyond Neptune. He was somewhat less correct in his ideas about Mars.

Lowell, a Harvard grad and former member of the first US mission to Korea, was initially drawn into the study of Mars upon hearing that famed Italian astronomer Schaparelli, the first to identify the Martian canals, was losing his eyesight and would no longer be able to study the planet.

After an extensive search for a suitable location, he established his observatory in Flagstaff, Arizona. In his books *Mars and Its Canals* and *Mars As the Abode of Life*, he theorized that the canals, or channels, on Mars were built by intelligent beings. Their purpose was to carry water from the melting polar caps to the central, desert portion of the planet.

Even during Lowell's life, this notion was refuted by other astronomers who proved water could not exist on Mars. However, the final word on the subject didn't come until 1965, when space probe *Mariner 4* passed close enough to photograph Mars' barren surface.

The War-Winning Businessman

He's not a soldier, but Ike credits him as "the man who won the war for us."

D-Day. June 6, 1944. More than 150,000 soldiers stormed the beaches of Normandy. They made it ashore successfully due in large part to one man: Andrew Jackson Higgins.

This hot-tempered New Orleans boat-builder specialized in shallow draft boats perfect for prospectors and trappers in the Louisiana swamps. He was convinced he could build better landing craft than the Navy and was determined to prove it. Navy experts didn't think much of Higgins, though, or his crazy notion that landing craft should be built out of wood.

Higgins launched a one-man crusade to get the Navy brass to admit his boats were better. He browbeat admirals and built prototypes with his own money. He once gave a tongue-lashing to a roomful of high-ranking officers, shouting "the Navy doesn't know a goddamn thing about small boats. But I do, by God." The tough-talking Higgins became a wartime celebrity. His complaints about red tape became widely known as "bellows from the bayou." Even Hitler took notice, calling Higgins "the American Noah." Finally, when Senator Harry Truman forced a head-to-head competition, Higgins beat the Navy boat, hands down.

But that's only half the story. Higgins also turned out to be a mass-production genius, manufacturing more than 20,000 landing craft and torpedo boats over the course of the war. In 1939 Higgins had less than 100 employees. By 1944 he had more than 25,000 working at eight plants. When he ran out of room in one factory he closed off a city street and started a production line right there. Desperate on another occasion for raw materials, he stole them from an oil refinery in Texas. "This man certainly is a wonder," said the commandant of the marines. More GIs hit the beaches in Higgins's boats than in all other landing craft combined. Without them, said General Eisenhower, D-Day might never have been possible.

Higgins (far right) outside his Louisiana factory discusses his boat with Col. E.A. Wimmer (far left).

Cooking with Radar

This modern kitchen essential is essentially an accident.

In the summer of 1945, engineer Percy Spencer was conducting tests on a magnetron. That's the powerful tube at the heart of every radar set. When he reached into his pocket for a chocolate bar he found instead a gooey mess. He wondered if the magnetron could be responsible.

Spencer was an engineering genius who had already helped win World War II by devising an improved magnetron tube that was easy to mass-produce, making possible the manufacture of tens of thousands of radar sets. Now he was ready to make his contribution to postwar America. Curious to see just what was going on, he put a bag of corn kernels in front of the magnetron. Soon the first batch of microwave popcorn was popped.

Spencer, who had only a third-grade education, patented the new method of cooking. His employer, the Raytheon Company, transformed his discovery into the Radarange. Raytheon's first Radarange was so big and expensive it made sense only in places like hotel kitchens and railroad dining cars. The earliest model weighed 750 pounds and had a price tag of $3,000, so sales were limited. It took more than 20 years for this big daddy of all microwaves to spawn the new generation that today graces kitchens everywhere. Today nine out of 10 American homes have a microwave—albeit a good deal smaller than the original.

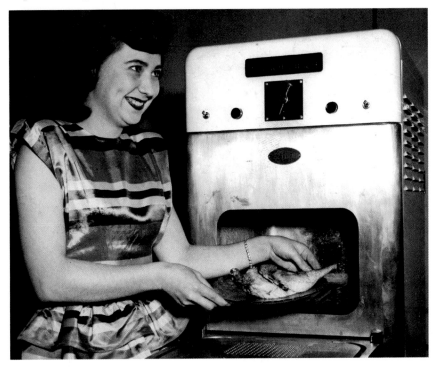

A model demonstrates the radar range's ability to cook or reheat food in just minutes.

American Pie

What do UFOs and good old American pie have in common?

In the summer of 1947, the United States went UFO crazy. After an object that many believed to be a flying saucer crashed near Roswell, New Mexico, there was a frenzy of sightings of unidentified flying objects around the country.

California inventor Walter Frederick Morrison, hoping to cash in on America's sudden UFO obsession, created a toy that flew like a saucer. He and a partner started selling these Flyin' Saucers in California, but sales were hardly out of this world.

The Frisbee was hit on college campuses.

Morrison and one of the first plastic disks

Morrison went back to the drawing board and devised a vastly improved model that he named the Pluto Platter. It became a big hit with California college kids, which is how it came to the attention of the brand-new Wham-O toy company. Morrison would do almost anything to market his Pluto Platters. He was selling them out of his trunk on a street corner when the young founders of Wham-O—Rich Knerr and A.K.

MORE OF THE STORY

With a postwar baby boom, a vigorous economy and increased leisure time for most Americans, the 1950s and 1960s are considered the golden age of toys by many in the industry. Mr. Potato Head, in 1952, became the first toy advertised on television and grossed $4 million in its first year. Twister, first released in 1966, sold more than 3 million units in its debut year, with more than 22 million more sold since then. And the Frisbee certainly wasn't Wham-O's only hit: 100 million Hula Hoops were sold in the first two years after they were introduced in 1958.

Melin—first approached him to buy the rights to the product.

In 1957, Wham-O started distributing Pluto Platters across the country, promoting them heavily on college campuses. When one of the Wham-O founders visited Yale University he found students there had been playing a lawn game for over 30 years in which they tossed around metal pie tins. Just as golfers shout "Fore," the students throwing the pie tins shouted out the name of the pie company that was emblazoned on them: "Frisbie!"

Wham-O, already wondering if "Pluto" was passé, adopted the name Frisbee (altering the spelling in the process) instead. And a national craze was launched.

In its prime, the Frisbie Pie Company boasted a fleet of 200 trucks that delivered 80,000 pies each day.

The Frisbie pie tin was the original flyng disk.

G.I. Joe

An all-American fighting man is born.

The president of the Hasbro toy company wanted to make a splash at the 1964 New York Toy Fair. The question was: Which product to go with? It was a choice between a miniature grocery store for girls and a doll for boys.

Hasbro president Merrill Hassenfeld decided to go with the doll.

Of course no one wanted to call the new toy a doll. What red-blooded American boy would want to play with dolls? So the design team coined a new phrase for their product. They called it an "action figure," and it was put into production right away.

That's how it came about that G.I. Joe reported for duty on February 9, 1964. His body was inspired by a 12-inch-tall wooden sculptor's mannequin that could bend at every joint. His rugged face had a scar on the right cheek so that he looked a lot tougher and more appealing to boys than Barbie's boyfriend, Ken. (It also made him easier to copyright!)

The U.S. was still mourning President Kennedy's death, the Beatles were

taking the country by storm, and Vietnam was not yet part of the national consciousness. G.I. Joe was the right toy at the right time. Soon an army of Joes began to invade American homes.

Joe was retired from active duty in 1978, a victim of the nation's disillusionment over the Vietnam conflict and the OPEC oil embargo, which sent the price of the plastic used to make him through the roof. A three-and-three-quarter-inch version of Joe came out in the 1980s, but the original foot-high soldier didn't return to service until his 30th anniversary, in 1994. He's been going strong since. Sales skyrocketed after September 11, 2001, and it looks like this is one soldier with a long career ahead of him.

Webmaster

Meet the man who brings the world to our fingertips.

Burners-Lee and a screen grab of the original program

The Internet was created by many people over many years—and yes, Al Gore did play a role. The World Wide Web, on the other hand, was the product of one man's imagination.

In 1980, software consultant Tim Berners-Lee was having trouble keeping track of all his notes. So he designed a piece of software to access everything on his computer through random links. He called this system "Enquire."

Then he got another idea: what if he could link information on many computers all over the globe? After years of thinking about this he sat down at a

"I got into a lot of trouble when somebody called me the creator of the World Wide Web. I got an angry call from somebody who said that was preposterous because I couldn't have written all that stuff."

—TIM BERNERS-LEE

computer in December 1990, and in a few weeks created the first browser and server. "It was really not a whole lot of work," he claims.

The hard part was still to come: convincing people he was onto something. Part of that involved coming up with a name for it. Colleagues referred to it as "that hypertext thing," but Berners-Lee knew he needed something inspiring.

His first thought was to call it "the Mesh," but it sounded too much like "mess." He considered "the Information Mine," but decided that the abbreviation—TIM—sounded too egotistical. "Having people talk about finding it on the TIM would be awful," he says. Of course, he finally settled on "World Wide Web."

"It will never take off," friends told him. It did, at least in part because Berners-Lee renounced patent rights on the Web to ensure its growth. Patenting it, he says, "would have scuppered the whole thing. It never would have taken off."

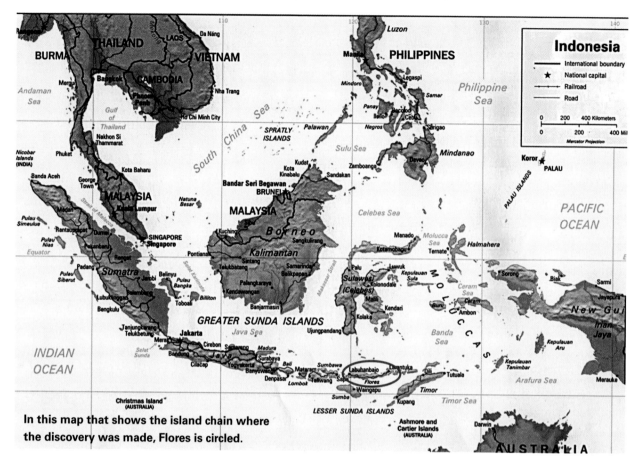

In this map that shows the island chain where the discovery was made, Flores is circled.

Enter the Hobbits

These little people may change our understanding of ourselves.

Imagine a world where three-foot-tall hobbit-like humans do battle with dwarf elephants, ROUS (Rodents of Unusual Size) and dragon-like lizards. Though it sounds like something out of fantasy fiction, such a world actually existed 20,000 years ago.

In 2004, an expedition to the island of Flores, 370 miles to the east of Bali, discovered the remains of a woman who was about three feet tall and weighed 55 pounds. Tests on her skull showed her brain was about one-third the size of the modern brain but capable of a high degree of intelligence. Partial remains of seven other, similar skeletons were also unearthed.

MORE OF THE STORY

Some scientists argue that the remains are not of a distinct species but are pygmies stunted by developmental disorders. Most scientists, however, support the new-species designation. Researchers are now trying to conduct DNA testing to see exactly where *Homo floresiensis* fits into our family tree.

Many scientists believe the little people are a separate human species previously unknown to science. They gave this new species the scientific name of *Homo floresiensis*. Workers at the dig called them hobbits, and the nickname has stuck. They also found evidence that the hobbit-like people had mastered fire and used tools to hunt dwarf elephants weighing up to 2,000 pounds—quite an effort for creatures about the size of a modern five-year-old child.

No one is sure why they were so small. It may be that it was a way of

An artist's rendition of what *Homo floresiensis* might have looked like

adapting to limited resources. Scientists believe they were killed off by a volcanic eruption 18,000 years ago, although local tales speak of "little people" living on the island as recently as a few hundred years ago. There is even speculation that surviving members of the species may live in the jungles of Indonesia today.

Before the discovery of *Homo floresiensis* the most recent thinking was that once humans became distinctly separate from other primates, they developed in a relatively straight line, with little or no overlap between species. This discovery may end up rewriting the story of human evolution—suggesting that in the recent past there may have been many different species of humans walking the earth at the same time. And it offers the tantalizing possibility that tales of leprechauns and other seemingly mythical beings may indeed have a basis in reality.

"Given that Homo floresiensis *is the smallest human species ever discovered, they out-punch every known human intellectually, pound for pound."*

—RICHARD ROBERTS, GEOCHRONOLOGIST AT THE UNIVERSITY OF WOLLONGOG, AUSTRALIA

For a while, throwing folks from windows was all the rage in Prague.

V. BROZIK. PARIS.

Chapter 5

Just Plain Strange

Stories Too Odd to Be Untrue

The history we know is full of tales of horrible or heroic people, amazing feats of derring-do and acts of terrible cruelty, incredible scientific breakthroughs and powerful forces of nature. But how about the lesser-known oddities? Those times gone by are full of strange behaviors of otherwise normal people, odd acts in the name of barely thought-out philosophies and happy results of unplanned actions. A skinny-dipping head of state? A hard-wired cat? A pizza predictor? Yes, they're all here and they're all simply too weird to have been made up!

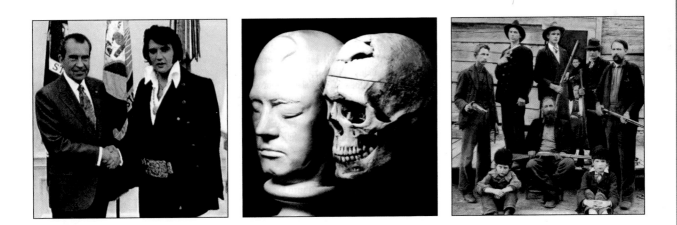

The Swallows of Volohai

How did cat whiskers and bird wings help Genghis Kahn conquer an empire?

Genghis Khan (below) was a brilliant military leader who united the Mongol tribes and created a fearsome army. In 1207, his men swept across the Gobi Desert and began to attack China. But they were halted at the walled city of Volohai, their dreams of conquest stalled. Here the hard-riding Mongols discovered that their cavalry tactics were virtually useless in attacking a heavily fortified city.

MORE OF THE STORY

His experience at Volohai persuaded Genghis Khan to adopt some of his enemy's tactics. He began to use siege engines—catapults, towers, and explosives—manned by captured Chinese engineers. These gave his army the ability to attack the fortified walls of Chinese cities. Another strategy of Khan was to march newly captured locals at the front of his ranks. Inhabitants of the area under attack would be hesitant to hurt their neighbors, shielding the Mongols until they got close enough to attack.

It was time for some outside-the-box thinking, and the great Khan was up to the challenge. He offered to end the siege in exchange for an unusual tribute: 1,000 cats and 10,000 swallows. One can imagine the puzzlement of the town's defenders upon receiving this message, but they decided to comply with it.

That was the wrong decision. When they delivered the tribute, Kahn ordered his men to tie puffs of cotton to the animals' tails, and then set the cotton on fire. The frightened creatures fled back to their city. A thousand fires seemed to break out everywhere at the same time, and the citizens of Volohai rushed to fight them.

At that moment, the Mongols attacked! Volohai fell. And though it would take decades, all of China would follow.

Not only fearless, Khan was also clever and devised ever-new ways of conquering his enemies.

Dangerous Games

There was a day when soccer and golf were a threat to national security.

In 1314, England's King Edward II issued a royal edict banning the game of soccer. It wasn't because he was morally opposed to the game, but rather because he believed that its very popularity was a threat to his realm. He decreed harsh prison terms for anyone found playing the game.

Other British kings followed suit. Edward III, Richard II and Henry IV issued their own bans. In 1457, King James II of Scotland banned soccer and golf. In 1491, Scottish king James IV issued this decree: "It is statute and ordained that in no place of the Realme there be used Fute-ball, Golf, or uther unprofitable sports."

So what was it about soccer and golf and "uther" sports that was such a huge threat? The kings considered these activities "unprofitable" because they were distracting men from archery practice, which was essential to the defense of their countries. Without a populace of trained archers, neither England nor Scotland could raise effective armies in times of crisis.

But kings' edicts ultimately proved no match for men's passion for sport. The laws were ignored and eventually forgotten. Soccer and golf continued to thrive, despite the kings who saw them as a national-security nightmare.

> *"We command and forbid on behalf of the King, on pain of imprisonment, such game to be used."*
>
> —EDWARD II, BANNING SOCCER IN 1314

A Falling-Out in Prague

It might have been downright funny—if it hadn't started a war.

In May 1618, three men were hurled out a high window of Hradcany Castle in Prague. Instead of being killed or badly hurt, they landed in a dung heap that cushioned their fall. They took to their heels and scampered off, their pride being the only thing seriously injured.

The event sounds almost comical, but it proved to have tragic results. The men were official representatives of the Roman Catholic Hapsburg emperor. An enraged crowd of Protestant nobles had thrown them out of the window to protest the closing of several Protestant churches. This act of rebellion outraged the emperor and triggered a war.

It began as a struggle between Catholics and Protestants in Bohemia. Soon Austria got involved, then Denmark and Sweden. Shortly thereafter Poland, France and the Netherlands joined in. The scandal in Bohemia had exploded into a seemingly endless conflict that engulfed much of Europe: the Thirty Years' War.

Ten million people would die in the war, which was more than a quarter of the population of cen-

The Protestant nobles prepare to toss out the Catholic emissaries.

Hradcany Castle, scene of the window-tossing, still stands in Prague today.

tral Europe. When a peace conference was finally called to end the war, it required six months of negotiations just to agree on where everyone would sit. After another year of discussions, the Treaty of Westphalia was signed. When the war was finally over, the authority of the Roman Catholic Church was dealt a major blow. What emerged from the war was a Europe filled with sovereign states that could choose their own religions—the Europe we still know today.

Beer and the Mayflower

Did the pilgrims really come to Plymouth on a beer run?

The *Mayflower* was headed for Virginia when storms blew it off course. It ended up hitting the shore of Massachusetts. Rather than heading south to find a better location for their colony the Pilgrims put ashore at Plymouth Rock.

One Pilgrim's journal explains: "We could not take time for further search or consideration, our victuals being much spent, especially our beere."

Yes, the Pilgrims made port because they ran out of beer. In those days beer was considered an essential and healthy part of everyone's daily diet—water, on the other hand, was usually considered suspect, because it easily became contaminated with disease. The *Mayflower* had set out from England loaded with beer barrels that were now nearly running out.

Once ashore the Pilgrims promptly erected a brew house and got to work brewing up a new batch to slake their thirst. So Plymouth, Massachusetts, became the historic home of the Pilgrims—because they needed to make a beer run.

The Pilgrims came ashore at Plymouth Rock.

OTHER PLAYERS, OTHER PLACES

One of the Pilgrims who came ashore that day was a young man there strictly for the beer—in a manner of speaking. John Alden was hired for the journey as a cooper, primarily to make beer barrels. British law required that "whosoever shall carry Beer beyond the sea" had to bring a cooper along to make replacement barrels, since barrels back in England were always in short supply. Otherwise Alden never would have had a chance to romance Priscilla Mullins and have at least 10 children. Their descendants include John Adams and the poet Henry Wadsworth Longfellow.

Tulipomania

These fast-growing investments are quick to wilt.

In the fall of 1636, it wasn't the Dow or the NASDAQ that investors in the Netherlands were watching but rather the price of the tulip. The flower had become a passion in this nation of gardeners with demand far outstripping supply.

The Netherlands had recently come out of a depression and its citizens had money to burn. The buying and selling of bulbs turned to a frenzied speculation on bulb futures. As prices shot up—sometimes doubling in a week—bricklayers, tradesmen, clergymen and lawyers all became day traders trying to cash in on the market.

Prices quickly rose to irrational levels. Toward the end of the craze some of the rarest tulip bulbs were being sold at a price that is equivalent to about $100,000 today.

Then, in February 1637, the bottom suddenly dropped out of the market. Dealers panicked and the price of bulbs fell to one percent of their previous value—sometimes less. Paper profits were wiped out, and tulipomania was over almost as quickly as it began.

The cultivation of tulip bulbs is still a major industry in Holland.

JUST A TALE?

The most prized varieties of tulips were ones that were almost entirely yellow or white, with brilliant streaks of violet or red. It is a delicious irony to note that these tulips were in fact diseased, infected by a virus unique to tulips. But would anyone really pay such a high price for a flower? A price of 3,000 guilders was not uncommon for a prized bulb. A writer in 1637 pointed out that this extraordinary sum could also purchase all of the following:

8 pigs	4 barrels of beer
4 oxen	2 tons of butter
12 sheep	1 ship
24 tons of wheat	48 tons of rye
1 silver cup	2 hogshead of wine
new clothes	1,000 pounds of cheese
1 bed	

Washington arrives at his swearing-in in lower Manhattan.

Bible Blunder

The first inauguration hinges on finding the right book.

The very first inauguration of a U.S. president took place not in Washington (which didn't exist yet) or Philadelphia, but at Federal Hall in New York City. The date was April 30, 1789. Organizers had planned every detail—or so they thought. Crowds had gathered and George Washington's carriage was already on the way before it occurred to them that there was something amiss.

Nobody had thought to bring a Bible the new president could use to take his oath of office.

A quick search of Federal Hall failed to turn up a copy of the good book. That's when New York chancellor Robert Livingston, who was to administer the oath, took matters into hand. Like Washington, Livingston was a high-ranking Freemason. He knew there would be a Bible at the nearby Saint John's Masonic Lodge and dispatched parade marshal Jacob Morton—who was the master of the lodge—to fetch the Bible and rush it back for the swearing-in. The Masonic Bible was opened to a random page from Genesis and Washington placed his hand on it as Livingston administered the oath.

After reciting the oath of office, President Washington added the unscripted words "so help me God," a practice that has been followed by almost every president since.

The Bible, now known as the Washington Bible, has been used by four other presidents for their inaugurations: Warren Harding, Dwight Eisenhower, Jimmy Carter, and George H.W. Bush. A fifth president, George W. Bush, had to scrap plans to use it because of bad weather. The book was also used at Washington's funeral, the dedication of the Washington Monument in 1885, and the rededication of the U.S. Capitol cornerstone in 1959.

OTHER PLAYERS, OTHER PLACES

Only one elected president has not used a Bible at his inauguration. Franklin Pierce placed his hand on a law book instead. Pierce was suffering from a crisis of faith after the death of his 11-year-old son in a train accident on the way to Washington for the inaugural. And he didn't "swear" to the oath; instead, he "affirmed" it, as is his right according to the Constitution. He was, perhaps, referring to his heartbreaking loss in the opening words of his inaugural address given on March 4, 1853, "No heart but my own can know the personal regret and bitter sorrow over which I have been borne to a position so suitable for others rather than desirable for myself."

The Washington Bible is still in the possession of Saint John's Lodge. When it travels to an inauguration or some other exhibition it is accompanied by three members of the lodge.

The Naked President

At least one chief executive enjoys clothing-optional adventures.

In looks as well as personality, John Quincy Adams (right) was one of the most straitlaced presidents ever to live in the White House. He was also the only one who liked to stroll down to the Potomac River every morning to go skinny-dipping.

Many in official Washington were unofficially aware of the president's buff-bathing habit. New York political leader Thurlow Weed wanted to see for himself one of the sunrise swims. He secretly observed the president leaving the White House one morning before daybreak. Adams began to shed his clothes before he even got to the river, tied them in a bundle, and jumped in. Thurlow added: "He seemed as much at ease in that element as on *Terra Firma*."

Another memorable morning Adams varied the routine. He had a servant named Antoine row him across the Potomac in an old boat, planning to swim back. When a sudden squall blew up, the leaky boat capsized in the middle of the river, dumping both men overboard. They managed to swim to the opposite bank, but Antoine had lost all of his clothes, and the 58-year-old president was exhausted by the ordeal. Adams gave his clothes to Antoine and sent him to fetch a carriage. Meantime, according to his diary, the president got in some "naked basking on the bank."

Adams always referred to the incident as "a humiliating lesson." His wife called it "altogether ridiculous." And while the skinny-dipping continued the president never tried to swim the entire river again.

JUST A TALE?

A crusading female journalist named Anne Royal supposedly bearded Adams during one of his swims. As the story goes, she sat on his clothes and refused to leave until he gave her an interview. But neither Adams nor Royal ever mentioned the incident, so while it could have happened, there's no evidence that it did.

> *"While struggling for Life, and groping for breath, [I] had ample leisure to reflect upon my own discretion."*
>
> –JOHN QUINCY ADAMS, COMMENTING ON THE NEAR-DROWNING IN HIS DIARY

Dead Broke

All men are created equal—but some can't balance a checkbook.

Thomas Jefferson (right) was a man of amazing brilliance and wide-ranging achievement. Not only was he the author of the Declaration of Independence and president of the United States, he was also a philosopher, diplomat, inventor, architect and musician. Some say he was the most brilliant man ever to reside in the White House. Was there anything this genius couldn't do?

The answer is yes. He was absolutely awful at managing his money.

For his whole life, Jefferson spent more than he took in—even while making a salary as president and earning income from his plantation.

It got him into deep trouble. After his presidency his debts piled up to astronomic heights. He didn't have enough money to pay for household items. Things got so desperate that Jefferson persuaded the state of Virginia to pass a special law allowing him to hold a lottery to raise money. He called it "almost a matter of life and death." But few people bought tickets in the Jefferson lottery, and his friends started secretly raising money for the former president. Even so, they failed to pay half his debts.

When Jefferson died, on the 50th anniversary of Independence Day, his debts exceeded $1 million in today's money. His heirs had to sell his beloved home, Monticello, to pay them off. The man who seemed to be good at everything had actually died broke.

MORE OF THE STORY

When British invaders burned down the Library of Congress in 1814, Jefferson offered his 6,487-volume library as a replacement. Widely seen as a generous gesture it was actually an attempt to raise some much-needed cash. After a bitter and divisive debate Congress voted to pay a generous $23,950 to buy Jefferson's books. Recently discovered documents suggest most of the books in the Library of Congress were actually saved from British destruction. Jefferson's friends apparently suppressed that fact so they could distribute a little political pork to the strapped Virginian. And his friends' generosity didn't end with Jefferson's death. After his daughter Martha was left penniless, she she contemplated opening a school to support herself. However, the states of Virginia and South Carolina each came to her aid, offering her financial support.

The Petticoat Affair

This is how a woman brought down the president's cabinet.

Peggy O'Neale (left) was a notable beauty with a flirtatious gleam in her eye. The daughter of a Washington tavern keeper, she had many suitors. She eventually married a ship's purser named John Timberlake.

While Timberlake spent a lot of time at sea, Peggy spent a lot of time on the arm of Tennessee senator John Eaton (right), a boarder at the tavern. Their 10-year "friendship" caused tongues to wag. In 1828, Timberlake died at sea—some say he committed suicide over his wife's affairs—and

Eaton married O'Neale. Washington insiders were indignant. "Eaton has just married his mistress," wrote one politician, "and the mistress of eleven doz. others."

When Andrew Jackson became president he appointed John Eaton secretary of war. The ladies of Washington were scandalized that O'Neale would suddenly have a prominent role in Washington society. The wives

A cartoon mocking the influence of women over Andrew Jackson's cabinet

> *"Do you suppose that I have been sent here by the people to consult the ladies of Washington as to the proper persons to compose my cabinet?"*
>
> –PRESIDENT ANDREW JACKSON, DISCUSSING THE APPOINTMENT OF JOHN EATON TO SECRETARY OF WAR

of cabinet members refused to socialize with the Eatons. Other Washington women followed suit. Soon the Eatons were completely ostracized.

President Jackson was outraged. He hired investigators to refute charges against O'Neale, and called a cabinet meeting to defend her. "She is chaste as a virgin," he argued. But members of his cabinet told him they could not force their wives to socialize with O'Neale.

Silly as it sounds, the issue polarized Washington and brought business to a standstill. One hundred congressmen threatened to abandon Jackson if it wasn't resolved. Eventually the entire cabinet—including Eaton—had to resign so Jackson could appoint a new cabinet and business could go forward.

That broke the ridiculous impasse at last—and led to this memorable toast: "To the next cabinet: May they all be bachelors—or leave their wives at home."

MORE OF THE STORY

During the Eaton affair, when Jackson found he could no longer rely on his cabinet as a whole, he turned to other advisors—friends and colleagues from earlier days—to assist him. This led to what's become known as the "kitchen cabinet" as opposed to the formal and official "parlor cabinet." Jackson may have been the first to form such as a group, but he certainly wasn't the last. Kennedy and Johnson were both said to have a kitchen cabinet. But it may have been Ronald Reagan who made the most use of this tool in the modern era. He packed his unofficial cabinet with long-time supporters from his California days such as Charles Cook, who encouraged him to get into politics; investment counselor William Wilson who was later rewarded by being made a representative to the Vatican; Tuttle Holmes, a wealthy car dealer who supported Reagan's run for governor; and most famously, Joseph Coors, the conservative beer mogul. All were relied upon by Reagan to unofficially assist him in forming policy.

State Funeral

One leader finds a novel way of getting a leg up on the opposition.

Antonio López de Santa Anna's funeral was magnificent. A glittering military procession paraded through the streets of Mexico City to the cemetery of Santa Paula. As a large crowd looked on, a crystal urn containing the remains of the Mexican president was placed atop a gilded column. Full military honors were observed. Moving speeches were given. All in all it was quite a day. Especially given the fact that Santa Anna was alive and well, and managing the entire event. The funeral was only for his leg.

After losing the Texas War of Independence in 1835, Santa Anna returned to Mexico in disgrace. Three years later a French fleet attacked Mexico, and Santa Anna leaped into the fray. While rallying the citizens of Vera Cruz he was struck by a cannonball that took off much of his left leg.

Santa Anna milked his loss for everything it was worth and won back the allegiance of the people. It wasn't long before he was again president of Mexico. When his popularity started to wane, he ordered the state funeral for his leg.

In the end its effect was only temporary. Santa Anna soon fell from power, though he would one day be back. As for the leg? Stolen by vandals.

JUST A TALE?

The war in which Santa Anna lost his leg is known as the "Pastry War." And the story behind it is incredible but true. A French pastry cook in Mexico claimed his shop had been looted by Mexican soldiers and appealed to the king of France for help. When Mexico refused to pay damages to the chef, the French used that as an excuse to go to war against Mexico.

Santa Anna leading Mexican soldiers to battle against France

Lincoln's Duel

The mighty pen proves a precursor to the sword.

Imagine Abraham Lincoln standing in shirtsleeves, waving a broadsword through the air in preparation for a duel to the death. That was the scene along the Mississippi River on September 22, 1842.

It began when a series of letters appeared in a Springfield, Illinois, newspaper ridiculing state auditor James Shields. The anonymous letters called Shields "a conceity dunce" and "a fool as well as a liar." They mocked a recent state proclamation he had issued, and heaped insults upon him: "If I were deaf and blind I could tell him by the smell."

The hot-tempered Shields confronted the editor of the paper and demanded to know who had written the letters. The editor quickly pointed the finger at Lincoln. Many historians today believe

that Mary Todd wrote several of the letters, and that the normally amicable Lincoln felt he had to stand up for her. (He married her six weeks later.)

Shields demanded satisfaction. When Lincoln refused to retract the letters, Shields challenged him to a duel. Lincoln had choice of weapons. "I did not want to kill Shields," he later told a friend, "and I did not want the damned fellow to kill me."

Since he towered over Shields, he chose cavalry broadswords, which gave him a huge advantage and underlined the ludicrous nature of the affair.

The antagonists traveled to the dueling ground and were preparing to fight when their seconds managed to make peace. And what Lincoln referred to as his "scrape with Shields" ended with a handshake.

The Curious Case of Phineas Gage

This man's misfortune opens the brain to greater understanding.

On the afternoon of September 13, 1848 Phineas Gage, a railroad foreman in Cavendish, Vermont, was placing high explosives inside a hole drilled in the rock to prepare a bed for the Rutland and Burlington Railroad. But he mistakenly dropped a three-foot-long tamping iron into the hole. It set off an explosion that shot the heavy, inch-thick pole

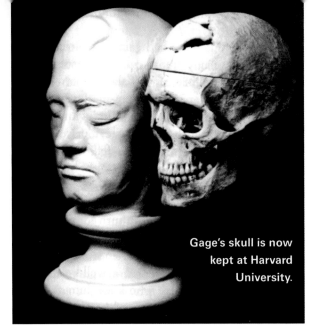

Gage's skull is now kept at Harvard University.

The site of Gage's accident

back out the hole and straight through Gage's own head. It entered under his cheekbone and exited through the top of his skull, flying though the air to land yards away. Gage fell back and went into convulsions.

Everyone was sure that Gage was a goner. But moments later he was up and talking. Expected to die, he was quickly loaded on an cart and taken to Dr. John Harlow (right). He confounded everyone by largely recovering within 10 short weeks of the accident. It seemed like a miracle. Something, however, was amiss: Gage had undergone a complete personality change. Gone was the honest, trustworthy, hardworking man that friends and coworkers had known. The new Gage was vulgar,

> *"The most singular circumstance connected with this melancholy affair is that he was alive at two o'clock this afternoon, and in full possession of his reason."*
>
> — *BOSTON POST,* SEPTEMBER 14, THE DAY AFTER THE ACCIDENT

irresponsible and prone to bouts of profanity. Fired from his job, he ended up on display in the Barnum & Bailey Circus.

Gage died 13 years after the accident, penniless and suffering from epilepsy. After his burial doctors exhumed his remains, and his skull was donated to medical research. In time, his much-studied case helped change the way science looked at how the brain works—providing the first evidence that different regions of the brain control different things. The brain had begun to disclose its secrets—though at great cost to Phineas Gage.

The tamping iron that blew through Gage's skull

MORE OF THE STORY

In the early 1990s, a neurobiology team at the University of Iowa, led by Dr. Hannah Damasio, used computer graphics and neural imaging techniques to plot the course of the tamping iron as it passed through Gage's skull. They confirmed that it damaged the ventromedial region of the frontal lobes but completely missed that part of the frontal lobes responsible for intellectual ability, speech and motor function. The ventromedial region does at least two things: It receives and processes information about the outside world and it communicates with the parts of the brain that regulate heart rate, breathing, blood pressure and sweating. It's thought that damaging that region negatively affects social behavior—that being "nice" is learned behavior and thus is actually work for the brain and that being "selfish" is the default. And so, more than 100 years after the accident, Gage's skull was yielding its secrets.

Short-Term Solution

Meet the president-for-a-day.

The history books say that President James K. Polk was succeeded by President Zachary Taylor. But there are some who say that there was another president between them who served as chief executive for exactly one day.

The date in question was Sunday, March 4, 1849. President Polk's term of office officially ended at noon. But because it was a Sunday, Zachary Taylor refused to take the oath of office until the next day.

So who was president from the time Polk's term expired to the time Taylor was sworn in?

Missouri senator David Rice Atchison (right) was serving as president pro tempore of the Senate, which made him next in line after the president and vice president. Therefore, the argument goes, he served as our nation's 12th president until Taylor's swearing-in.

Historians and legal scholars have quibbled about this for more than a century. Atchison himself chose to embrace the suggestion with good humor, describing his presidency as "the most honest administration this country ever had." Asked what he did on the day of his supposed presidency, Atchison replied: "I went to bed." He had presided over the Senate in a late-night session the day before.

Perhaps he can also lay claim to being the only president who never made a mistake in office.

The president-for-a-day is also memorialized in the name of one of the most famous railroads of all time, the Atchison, Topeka and Santa Fe.

Twenty-Four Notes

This Civil War general whistles his way into history.

Dan Butterfield was a New York businessman turned Union general. People seemed to love him or hate him. He was awarded the Medal of Honor for rallying his brigade under withering fire, but he had a bad temper that irritated fellow officers. One wrote that he was a man of "blemished character."

Perhaps so. But he was also a man who had poetry in his soul. One night in July 1862, he called the brigade bugler to his tent. Butterfield wasn't happy with the regulation bugle call played at the end of the day to signal "lights out." It wasn't sufficiently musical, he said.

The general had something different in mind. Since by his own admission he couldn't write a note of music, he whistled it for bugler Oliver Norton. When Norton played it back, the result wasn't quite what Butterfield wanted, and they went back and forth for a while—the general whistling, the bugler blowing—until they had something Butterfield was satisfied with. Norton used the new call that night. Buglers from other brigades camped nearby were so struck by it that they began using it as well. Soon the call spread throughout the Army and to the Confederate Army as well. And so a collaboration between a general and a bugler on a warm July evening led to 24 notes known as "Taps" that have gone down in history: a haunting melody known to all that announces the end of day for soldiers and graces the air at military funerals and Memorial Day observances.

The Actor and the Son

One brother saves a life and the other takes one—from the same families.

One of America's most famous actors stood on a train platform in Jersey City, New Jersey. He was among a crowd of people about to board a train. As the crowd pressed forward to enter one of the coaches the train unexpectedly started with a jolt, rolling a few feet before it stopped. The actor saw a young man lose his balance and begin to fall helplessly between the platform and the moving car.

Thinking quickly the actor reached down and grabbed the young fellow by the collar, pulling him to safety. The grateful young man recognized his celebrity savior, "whose face was of course well known to me, and I expressed my gratitude to him, and in doing so, called him by name."

> *"It was just as if I was struck on the forehead by a hammer."*
>
> —EDWIN BOOTH, ON HEARING THAT HIS BROTHER HAD SHOT THE PRESIDENT

It was only later that the two men recognized the haunting irony. The actor was Edwin Booth (left). His younger brother, John Wilkes Booth, assassinated President Lincoln the following spring. And the young man whose life he saved? It was Robert Todd Lincoln—Abraham Lincoln's son.

Robert Lincoln (far right) and his younger brother, Tad, with their parents.

What Dreams May Come

The shocking visions of a sleeping president foretell doom.

Abraham Lincoln had many vivid dreams that he shared with his friends. In April 1865, he told his wife and a few companions, including Ward Hill Lamon, who wrote down the words of a particularly powerful one from the night before.

Lincoln heard sobs, as if many people were weeping. In his dream, he left his bed and walked through the White House. The halls were empty, but he could still hear the same mournful sounds of distress.

He recalled, "I was puzzled and alarmed. What could be the meaning of all this? Determined to find the cause of a state of things so mysterious and so shocking, I kept on until I arrived at the East Room, which I entered.

There I met with a sickening surprise. Before me was a catafalque, on which rested a corpse wrapped in funeral vestments. Around it were sta-

"Although it was only a dream, I have been strangely annoyed by it ever since."

—ABRAHAM LINCOLN, THREE DAYS BEFORE HIS DEATH

tioned soldiers who were acting as guards; and there was a throng of people, gazing mournfully upon the corpse, whose face was covered, others weeping pitifully.

'Who is dead in the White House?' I demanded of one of the soldiers, 'The President,' was his answer; 'he was killed by an assassin.'"

Three days later, Lincoln was shot by John Wilkes Booth. On Easter Sunday, he lay in state in the East Room, on a catafalque surrounded by soldiers, just as he had dreamed.

John Booth shoots Lincoln at a performance at Ford's Theater.

The Day the Irish Invaded Canada

A Fenian fiasco proves the law of unintended consequences.

They came across the border the night of June 1, 1866: an army of Irish-American nationalists—Fenians, as they called themselves—ready to fight and die to free Ireland from British rule.

So what they heck were they doing in Canada?

Their goal was to seize the British territory's major cities and use them as bargaining chips to negotiate with Britain for Ireland's independence. Clearer thinkers among them understood this was far-fetched, but they hoped that an invasion launched from American soil would start a war between the U.S. and Britain that would result in British troops being pulled out of Ireland.

And so 800 Irish-American soldiers, most of them Civil War veterans, crossed over from Buffalo, New York, and invaded Ontario. There was the 13th Tennessee Fenian Regiment, the 7th New York, the 18th Ohio and others. They raised the Fenian banner and hoped for the best.

A regiment of Canadian volunteers confronted the Irishmen the next day in the Battle of Ridgeway.

At the Battle of Ridgeway, the Canadian troops suffered 10 dead and 38 wounded. The Fenians lost only a handful of men.

It was more of a glorified skirmish, really, which ended when the Fenians routed the Canadian volunteers with a bayonet charge. It would be their first and only victory. When Canadian reinforcements began to appear, the Fenians skedaddled back to the United States, where they were all promptly arrested by U.S. authorities. Another group of Fenians who crossed over from Vermont into Quebec were similarly unsuccessful.

The bizarre invasion had more impact on Canada than Ireland: It sparked an unexpected surge in Canadian nationalism that helped unify the provinces and lead to the creation of the modern Dominion of Canada.

Irish Independence, however, would have to wait another 50 years.

OTHER PLAYERS, OTHER PLACES

The first time Canada was invaded from its southern neighbor wasn't in 1866. In 1775, General Richard Montgomery invaded and actually captured Montreal. As part of the same campaign, Benedict Arnold mounted a second invasion with the intention of capturing Quebec City. He was wounded during the battle and Montgomery, who had brought troops to aid him, was killed. That invasion was a failure. But it didn't kill the idea entirely. During the War of 1812, several forays into Canada were made. The first was led by general William Hull from Detroit, in July 1812. But he had to fall fall back when his supply lines proved unwieldy. A second invasion, led by William Henry Harrison, was more successful. Indian leader and British supporter Tecumseh was killed at the resulting Battle of the Thames in 1813, which led to the end of the alliance between Britain and various American Indian tribes. Ultimately, however, the war came to an end with no territorial changes on either side. All that invading for nothing!

Montgomery prepares for his invasion of Canada.

Speed Demon

"Mr. President, may I see your license, please?"

It was on a summer evening that the Washington, D.C., policeman saw the one-horse carriage careening down the street at high speed. The policeman, one of the capital's new black officers, flagged down the driver and berated him for zooming down the city street. It simply wasn't safe, he said. It was only when the policeman began writing out a citation that he realized just who the driver was: President Ulysses S. Grant.

Grant fell in love with horses as a boy and had a lifelong reputation as an exceptional horseman. When he became president he brought his favorite horses with him to the White House. In the evening he often went for a buggy ride to let off steam, and he liked to drive the buggies the way he had always liked to drive horses—as fast as he possibly could.

Upon recognizing Grant the policeman tried to back off. But the president calmly told him that he was right in doing the job and to finish writing the ticket. The president paid the $20 fine on the spot, which was quite a sum at that time. According

to some accounts, his horse was impounded, and Grant had to walk home.

He remains the only president ever to receive a speeding ticket, whether for a carriage or a car. It's a distinction he is unlikely to lose anytime soon!

Grant's most famous horse was probably Cincinnati, which he supposedly rode to the surrender meeting with Robert E. Lee. He also had a horse named Jeff Davis.

Grant seemed to have a need for speed. In 1866, he was part of a presidential party traveling through New York City in two carriages, each led by a team of stunning horses. Grant took the reins of his carriage and with a twinkle in his eye challenged President Johnson's carriage to a race. In a flash the two carriages were flying through Central Park. Grant pulled ahead. and according to the *New York Times*, "the non-driving gentlemen of Mr. Grant's coach began to consider with some anxiety the probability of a safe arrival." Grant easily won the wild half-mile race. It is worth noting that one of the anxious gentlemen in his carriage was an impetuous cavalry officer named George Custer. He needn't have worried; his number wouldn't be called for another 10 years.

"Horses seem to understand Ulysses."

—GRANT'S MOTHER HANNAH

The Buffalo Hangman

It's a dirty job, but somebody has to do it.

Numerous men who became president engaged in surprising occupations earlier in their careers. Theodore Roosevelt was a cowboy, Harry S. Truman was a haberdasher and George W. Bush owned a baseball team. But no president has had a job that is quite like the one for which Grover Cleveland reluctantly volunteered.

He served his county as an executioner.

Cleveland was elected sheriff of Erie County, New York, in 1870. The law called for the sheriff to handle all executions. A deputy named Jake Emerick had handled the job for many years, but he had officiated at so many hangings that he was becoming known as

The last public hanging in the U.S. was carried out in 1936 in Kentucky.

"Hangman Emerick," a source of great consternation to him and his family.

In 1872, Jack Morrissey was sentenced to die for executing his mother. The circumstances of the case generated a lot of sympathy for Morrissey, but he failed in his attempt to obtain a pardon. Cleveland announced that he would handle the execution himself, because he didn't feel he had the moral right to impose that burden on someone else, even if it was part of that person's job.

MORE OF THE STORY

Describing why he took the job, Cleveland said: "Jake and his family have as much right to enjoy public respect as I have, and I am not going to add to the weight that already brought him closer to pubic execration." The following year he presided at a second execution, that of Jack Gaffney, a well-known gambler who had been found guilty of shooting a man over a card game. Cleveland's opponents in the 1884 presidential election mocked him as "The Buffalo Hangman," but his supporters cited the incident as an example of his moral fiber.

Cleveland's moral compass probably came from his father, a Presbyterian minister.

On the appointed day, Sheriff Cleveland stood behind a screen some 20 feet from the gallows and pulled the lever that opened the trapdoor. Friends said he was sick at heart for days afterward. But in refusing to duck the ugly job he started building a record of service and public integrity that would one day lead him to the White House.

The Battle of the Luxury Liners

A saga of the high seas has an amazing twist.

There's never been a naval engagement quite like it: two top-of-the-line ocean liners duking it out on the high seas. What made it even stranger was this: each ship was disguised as the other.

The *Carmania* was a British ocean liner, the *Cap Trafalgar*, a German vessel. At the start of World War I each ship was commandeered by its respective government and converted into an armed merchant cruiser. Sandbags were stacked up in lieu of armor, and guns were bolted to the deck. Two weeks after war was declared both were ready for military service.

The *Carmania* set out on its first war mission from Liverpool, England; the *Cap Trafalgar* from Buenos Aires, Argentina. Each captain knew that his vessel was no match for heavily armored warships and in the interest of self-preservation each hit upon the idea of disguising his ship to make it look like an enemy vessel.

Some strange fate must have been at work, because the two captains each decided to disguise his ship as the other. They made the alterations as they sailed on toward a destiny that must have seemed unimaginably improbable. For as luck would have it, the two vessels happened upon each

The *Carmania* had only two funnels, so the crew had to add a dummy third funnel to make it look like the *Cap Trafalgar*. The German ship, meanwhile, dismantled one of its 40-foot funnels and repainted the remaining funnels the same color as the *Carmania's*.

other off the Caribbean island of Trinidad. Each ship saw through the other's disguise immediately and the battle commenced. The giant ships dueled for an hour, until the *Carmania* sent the *Cap Trafalgar* to the bottom. And the strange battle of the luxury liners was over.

Acoustic Kitty

These high-tech cats were designed to fight the Cold War.

In the 1960s, the Cold War pitted intelligence agents of East against West—KGB versus CIA—in a high-stakes game of espionage cat-and-mouse. Then somebody decided that an actual cat might be an effective weapon.

During the 1960s, the CIA's Directorate of Science and Technology tried to turn cats into bugs—walking eavesdropping devices for listening in on Soviet diplomats in public places. "Project Acoustic Kitty" reportedly involved five years of design and the expenditure of millions of dollars.

OTHER PLAYERS, OTHER PLACES

Another animal almost drafted for service in the Cold War was the gerbil. The furry creatures can smell fear—or, more accurately, the increased adrenaline in a fearful person's sweat. Spy-catchers in various countries considered using the rodents in the 1970s. But when airport-security experts in Israel put them to work, they found that the little fur balls couldn't tell the difference between a wrong-doer scared of being caught and a passenger afraid of flying.

Miniaturized transmitting devices were surgically implanted inside the body of a cat. "They slit the cat open," says one former CIA operative, "put batteries in him, wired him up. The tail was used as an antenna."

Problems were many. The CIA apparently discovered what cat owners have always known: cats are hard to train. They tended to walk off the job when they got hungry or distracted, which was distressingly often. Still, the CIA persisted. One document, parts of which are still classified today, praises the patience of those who worked with the feisty felines: "The work done on this project over the years reflects great credit on the personnel who guided it."

When the wired-up cat was deemed ready for a full-scale test, it was taken to a park and let out of a van. Then disaster struck—in the form of a taxi, which promptly ran over the feline operative. "There they were," said the former agent, "sitting in the van with all those dials, and the cat was dead." And so was the rather silly Project Acoustic Kitty.

The Soccer War

We've all heard of tough soccer matches but how about one that started a war?

In June 1969, Honduras and El Salvador faced off in a soccer game, the first in a series of qualifying matches for the World Cup. The two countries were bitter rivals and the fans in Honduras made sure the visiting Salvadoran team wouldn't be able to sleep the night before the game by setting off firecrackers and honking horns outside their hotel. Not surprisingly, Honduras won 1–0.

Fans in El Salvador were beside themselves. Eighteen-year-old Amelia Bolanios was so distraught she shot herself after Honduras scored the winning goal. Her death was mourned as a national tragedy. "The young girl could not bear to see her fatherland brought to its knees," wrote the Salvadoran newspaper El Nacional. An army honor guard led her funeral procession, and the president of El Salvador walked behind the casket.

With emotions running high the Honduran team came to El Salvador for a second match a few weeks later. Salvadoran troops and tanks ringed the field. After El Salvador won, 3–0, vicious riots broke out among the fans, and several people were killed.

It wasn't only in the stadium where things got out of hand. The game's outcome pushed a simmering century-old border dispute to the boiling point, and war broke out on July 14. Although the fighting lasted only 100 hours before a cease-fire was agreed upon the casualties were

Victor Hugo Merino of El Savador (left) and Emilio Izaguirre of Honduras compete in a more peaceful match in 2007.

significant: 5,000 people were killed and more than 10,000 wounded.

It became known as "La Guerra del Fútbol": The Soccer War. It started on the playing field and ended up on the battlefield.

It wasn't until 1980 that Honduras and El Salvador ironed out their border issues and signed a peace treaty.

The King and I

This has to be one of the most bizarre White House meetings.

It was just another 1970 Monday morning at the White House when an unannounced visitor walked up to the gate and said he wanted to meet with President Nixon. Normally such people are given the brush-off, but this one was treated differently.

This visitor was "The King." Elvis Presley. The famous singer dropped off a six-page handwritten letter requesting a meeting. Nixon adviser H. R. Haldeman decided to give him an appointment with the president the very same day.

Their brief get-together in the Oval Office may be one of the oddest moments in the Nixon presidency. Presley told the president earnestly that he had been studying Communist brainwashing and the drug culture for over a decade. He asked Nixon to make him a "Federal Agent at Large" to help fight the spread of drugs (especially ironic given that Presley was a chronic drug abuser who eventually died of an overdose). Ultimately the White House arranged for him to get a Bureau of Narcotics badge with his name on it.

He also offered the observation that the Beatles were a source of anti-American spirit, and that their music was filled with anti-American themes.

As the meeting drew to a close, Presley seemed gripped by emotion as he told the president that he was "on your side." He surprised the normally aloof Nixon by giving him a bear hug. The next thing you know, Elvis had left the building.

JUST A TALE?

Was Elvis a patriot or a nut? While he did have his problems later in life, he served his country faithfully when he was drafted into the Army in 1958. He could have applied for the Special Services, but instead chose to serve in the regular army, doing his tour without any unusual privileges. So when he met with Nixon, was he really trying to help out his government or was it a just a crazy stunt? No one knows for sure.

Presidential Pardon

There's a pardon President Ford isn't famous for.

Gerald Ford created a national controversy with his pardon of President Richard Nixon in September 1974. But that didn't stop him from signing another pardon a year later. This one was given to someone who had applied for it 110 years before.

The applicant was Civil War general Robert E. Lee (right). After the war had ended any Confederate soldier could apply for pardon and have his citizenship restored. General Lee decided to do just that. He sent his application to General Grant who recommended to President Andrew Johnson that it be approved.

For that to happen Lee had to take a notarized oath of allegiance to the Union. Such a move was considered controversial in a South still not reconciled to its defeat. But Lee went ahead and did it, wanting to set an example that others would follow to help heal the wounds of war.

Lee's oath of allegiance was forwarded to the secretary of state. But instead of passing it on to the president, he gave it to a friend as a souvenir—perhaps purposely wanting to derail Lee's application. General Lee died in 1870 without ever receiving a pardon or having his U.S. citizenship restored.

One hundred years after his death, Lee's oath turned up in the National Archives. Congress voted to pardon Lee and restore his citizenship. President Ford signed the bill into law. And an oversight 110 years old was corrected at last

MORE OF THE STORY

The pardon of General Lee was not without controversy, though it was on a far smaller scale than Nixon's pardon. John Conyers, an African-American representative from Michigan, called it "neither healing nor charitable." Other congressmen suggested that Vietnam draft-dodgers should be pardoned before Lee. Despite the complaints, Ford signed Lee's pardon at Arlington House, the prewar home of Lee that is now part of Arlington Cemetery. Robert E. Lee IV and Robert E. Lee V were present for the signing.

Scrap Metal War

This reclaiming operation triggered quite a scrap.

Britain calls them the Falklands. Argentina knows them as Las Malvinas. In 1982 the centuries-old dispute between the two countries over the remote South Atlantic islands was heating up. Argentina's ruling junta hoped to regain control of the British-occupied islands to help restore its rapidly fading popularity. But the possibility of war still seemed very remote.

Then a wealthy Buenos Aires scrap dealer named Constantino Davidoff sent a group of workmen to salvage scrap metal from an abandoned whaling station on one of the southernmost of the contested islands. He had a contract with the owner as well as permission from the British embassy to be at the site.

But when Davidoff's men raised an Argentine flag on the island it caught the attention of scientists from the British Arctic Survey Team. They reported to British authorities that there had been an Argentine landing.

The suspicious British sent a note of protest to Argentina and dispatched the warship *Endurance* to watch over the scrap dealers. Argentina sent a warship of its own. The British landed marines. The Argentines sent more ships.

Perhaps this was just the pretext Argentina was looking for. Perhaps it inflamed passions beyond the point of no return. In any case, less than a week later, Argentina invaded the islands. The junta saw the invasion as a

British soldiers come ashore on the Falklands.

> *"If I had never been born, Argentina and Great Britain would not be fighting."*
>
> —CONSTANTINO DAVIDOFF, SIX WEEKS INTO THE WAR

way to appeal to patriotic pride and distract people's attention away from 600-percent inflation and other economic problems. They did not expect the British would be willing or able to conduct a major military effort 8,000 miles from London, over a little group of windswept islands inhabited by only 2,000 people.

They were wrong. Britain eventually retook the islands at a cost of 256 of their men killed. Nearly 700 Argentine troops were killed in the war. They are the only Argentines who have been allowed to stay on the windswept islands, which are still the subject of an ongoing and extremely bitter disagreement between the two nations.

The most well-known warrior in the British invasion force was HRH Prince Andrew, son of Queen Elizabeth II, brother of Prince Charles, and known to his fellow helicopter pilots simply as "H."

The Domino's Theory

Who knew there's a connection between war and pizza?

At 5 a.m. on Wednesday, January 16, 1991, the word flashed out from Washington: war with Iraq was

imminent, likely to begin within hours. Sure enough, later that day, the bombs began to fall. The Persian Gulf War was under way.

The early warning came not from a high-placed presidential aide or a ranking military officer, but from a more unlikely source: A pizza man.

Frank Meeks owned 60 Domino's Pizza franchises in the D.C. area. Meeks was famous for keeping a close eye on pizza orders, and the night before the war began he noticed a sharp uptick in the number of late-night pizza orders coming from the White House, the Pentagon and the State Department. White House pizza orders went through the roof with more than 50 pies ordered between 10 p.m. and 2 a.m.

Meeks had seen the same thing happen the night before the invasions of Grenada and Panama. He was sure this meant war, so he called the news media and put out the word. The rest is history.

The number-one pizza at the Pentagon was pepperoni.

Will this slice of history prove the ultimate undoing of the republic? Is fast food the soft underbelly of American military might? Will foreign agents start infiltrating Washington pizza joints to see what's baking in government offices? Are counterintelligence agents ready to swing into action with a "Pizza Interdiction Effort" (PIE) to order up a little Domino's deception?

Deliver us!

> *"I don't think they're sitting around watching Redskins reruns."*
>
> —FRANK MEEKS, ANALYZING A SURGE IN LATE-NIGHT PIZZA ORDERS FROM THE PENTAGON

Feuding Finale

The final chapter of this famous family saga closes peacefully.

The violence had been over for more than 100 years. Yet thousands of people showed up to witness the signing of a truce between two of American history's most famous adversaries: The Hatfields and the McCoys.

The Hatfields lived on the West Virginia side of a meandering stream called the Tug Fork. The McCoys hailed from the Kentucky side. The origins of their feud date back to the Civil War when the families were on opposite sides. A stolen pig and a Romeo and Juliet-style romance (which left an unmarried McCoy woman pregnant with a Hatfield man's baby) and a series of perceived slights exacerbated the smoldering hostility between the two clans.

The men of the Hatfield family in a hand-colored photo taken in 1899

Violence broke out in 1882 when three sons of Rand'l McCoy stabbed to death Ellison Hatfield during an election-day brawl. William "Devil Anse" Hatfield, Ellison's brother, retaliated by kidnapping the McCoy brothers, tying them to trees, and having them shot to death.

Violence escalated over the next nine years. There were raids and counter-raids. Houses burned, women were whipped, people were shot from ambush. The death toll mounted. Things got so out of hand that it took the governors of both states and a case that went all the way to the Supreme Court to bring the feud to a halt.

The feud essentially ended in 1891 and the families began holding joint reunions in 1976. But there was still the occasional flare-up, including a dispute in 2000 over access to a cemetery. In 2003 Reo Hatfield and Bo McCoy decided it was time to lay to rest the bad feelings for once and for all. History's most famous family feud was finished.

JUST A TALE?

Did disease keep the bitter feud alive so long? Many of the McCoys then and now suffer from Von Hippel-Lindau disease, which causes tumors in the adrenal gland. That can cause people to suffer from high blood pressure and make them testy and prone to violence.

Photographer Joe Rosenthal's bad day results in a much-loved political image.

Chapter 6

Politics in Action
Government, Rules, and Law Gone Awry

Next time you're on line for hours to renew your driver's license or endlessly put on hold when calling the passport agency, take heart from these tales! Here are the stories of the powers-that-be who went a little power mad. To be sure, sometimes being headstrong led to good results—like the general who disobeyed orders to burn Paris and the cooler heads who didn't go to war over a pig. Often, though, the results were more predictable: the Olympic committee that banned a women's race or the president who made breaking-and-entering a habit. And we've included a few honorable mentions: a government employee who went that extra mile, a political figure with perhaps one too many wives, and an editor who turned the tide of an election.

The Sacred Band

Ancient leaders devise an elite fighting unit like no other.

The Spartans of ancient Greece were among the most famous and fearsome warriors of all time. Never have there been a people more single-mindedly devoted to the military arts. Spartan boys were taken from home to attend military school at age seven, and every male between 20 and 60 had to serve in the armed forces. The result was that Sparta fielded the most powerful military force in Greece.

Nevertheless the vaunted Spartan army was defeated by Thebes at the battle of Leuctra in 371 BC. The turning point in the battle came when an elite Theban military unit

"Perish any man who suspects that these men either did or suffered anything that was base."

—PHILIP II OF MACEDON, VIEWING THE BODIES OF THE SACRED BAND SLAIN IN BATTLE BY HIS ARMY

Spartan training was so tough—it even included sleeping outdoors with no blanket or shoes for one year—war was a rest.

Spartans could retire at 60—if they made it that long.

known as the Sacred Band led a breakthrough against the Spartan right wing. Famed for both its fighting ability and its unusual makeup, the Sacred Band consisted of 300 soldiers who all had something in common that's somewhat unusual for soldiers. They were gay.

This one-of-a-kind unit consisted of 150 homosexual couples. The idea was that every man in the force would be motivated to fight to his maximum ability both to protect his lover and to avoid shaming himself in front of his lover. In modern military jargon it was thought that this Theban "band of lovers" would enjoy a high degree of unit cohesion.

It worked. The Sacred Band was undefeated for more than 30 years. When it was finally overcome by the Macedonians, the unit was so unwilling to yield that every man fought to the death.

MORE OF THE STORY

The Spartans were the original men of few words. Sparta was part of a larger area known as Laconia, which is where the word "laconic" comes from. The story is told that Philip II sent a threatening message to the Spartans, warning, "If I enter Laconia, I will level it to the ground." The Spartans' one-word reply: "If…"

The Men Who Stole Time

We've all heard of public corruption. But stealing time itself?

The early Romans used the moon as a measure of the months. That led to a 12-month year that came up short, with only 355 days. To keep the seasons straight the custom of occasionally adding extra weeks and months began. But the potential for mischief was too great a temptation. Corrupt public officials began to manipulate the calendar to prolong their terms in office and shorten the terms of hated rivals. In essence they were stealing time to further their own political purposes.

By 46 BC, the Roman year was more than two months off. That's when Julius Caesar took charge. He mandated a new solar calendar, making the year 365 days long. He changed New Year's Day from March 1 to January 1 and added an extra day every four years. Opponents grumbled that Caesar, not content with ruling the earth, was now trying to command the heavens above.

To bring the calendar back on track, Caesar added two extra months

to the year 46 BC—sticking them in between November and December. He also squeezed in an extra three weeks between February and March. The result was a year such as no one had ever seen before—445 days long. In Rome this forever became known as the "year of confusion," even though, as Caesar himself was very quick to point out, it was actually the year the confusion came to an end.

Julius Caesar (right) was introduced to Sosigenes by Cleopatra.

At least for a while. By 1582, the spring equinox had drifted from March to winter because the calendar instituted 1,628 years before was just the tiniest bit off. So the world had lost 11 minutes per year, for 1,600 years. Things were a mess.

Pope Gregory XIII took matters in hand. He appointed a committee of calendar experts to examine the problem, and they suggested a more scientifically correct model. The pope accepted their recommendations and issued a papal bull mandating the changes.

But to get things back on schedule, 10 days had to be slashed. So on October 4, 1582, much of western Europe went to sleep and woke up the next morning on October 15. Reaction was mixed. The citizens of Frankfurt, Germany, rioted against the pope, who they thought was trying to steal days from their lives. On the other hand, peasants living in isolated rural villages barely noticed at all.

Some countries didn't accept the change for years, creating massive confusion. But eventually everyone let go of the missing days and adopted the Gregorian calendar that is still in use today, which is only off by one day every 3,000 years.

A Roman farmer's calendar

MORE OF THE STORY

In the Roman calendar, days were divided into 12 hours of light and 12 hours of darkness. So a daytime "hour" on a long summer day might be the equivalent of an hour and 15 minutes today, whereas an hour on a dark winter day might be as short as 45 minutes.

Even so, Caesar might never have gotten around to cleaning up the calendar if it hadn't been for his most famous lover: the beguiling Cleopatra. She introduced Caesar to the Egyptian astronomer Sosigenes, who explained the idea of a calendar based on the sun, then traveled to Rome to help Caesar put it into effect.

More than 1,500 years later, Pope Gregory formed an advisory committee to get a consensus on the project and come up with the right solution. Even so, Protestant England rejected the new calendar and didn't adopt it for another 170 years. When it finally did so, protesters took to the streets shouting, "Give us back our 11 days," or chanting this antireform, anti-Catholic ditty:

In seventeen hundred and fifty-three
The style it was changed to popery.

Were the Olympics Banned?

A zealous ruler shuts down the Games—or so he thinks.

In ancient Greece the Olympic Games were held every four years in tribute to the god Zeus. They began in 776 BC and continued for more than 1,000 years. They were male-only affairs—women weren't allowed to compete or even to watch. These competitions were considered so important that when the Games were held, trade was suspended and wars were postponed. Even after the Romans conquered Greece, the Games continued.

But in 394 AD, the Roman emperor Theodosius put a stop to the Games. Why? After converting to Christianity a decade before, Theodosius had become a religious zealot determined to stamp out all pagan worship. He considered the Games to be a scandalous glorification of the ancient Greek gods. So he ended them for all time—or so he thought.

For the next 1,500 years, the Olympics were but a distant memory. In 1892, a 27-year-old French baron named Pierre de Coubertin proposed reviving the Olympic ideal. The initial response from

A poster promoting the first modern Olympic Games

athletic officials: a big yawn. But Coubertin's single-minded devotion eventually carried the day. So it was that in 1896 the modern Olympics were born, and after a span of more than a millennium, once again brought the world together in sport.

One Sweet Deal

Two countries engage in a spicy swap unlike anything in history.

In the early 1600s, Great Britain and Holland were vying for control over the valuable Spice Islands in the East Indies. All but forgotten today, these tiny islands were at one time considered prize possessions because of the nutmeg and cloves that could be found there and nowhere else. The British and the Dutch spent years battling for control of the lucrative trade.

In 1616, British captain Nathaniel Courthope staked a claim on the island of Run, which contained one of the world's only known nutmeg forests. With only a ragtag band of sailors and natives, Courthope fended off Dutch attacks for nearly four years. But there was a spy among his men who eventually betrayed him to the Dutch. They murdered Courthope and finally took the island in 1620.

When it was still a Dutch possession, Manhattan was inhabited by just a handful of people.

The British, however, steadfastly maintained that Run was rightfully theirs and continued to wage war with the Dutch. Years later, when the two nations were finally ready to sign a peace treaty, the island was still a bone of contention. So to sweeten the deal, the Dutch offered to hand over another island in return. That island's name? Manhattan. A forest of nutmeg for the Big Apple—not a bad deal.

Nutmeg was especially valued, not just because of its taste but also because it was believed to cure the plague.

Pivotal Vote

This presidential election comes down to one man.

It isn't often that a single person gets to decide a presidential election. But James Bayard had the chance to do exactly that.

The bitter election of 1800 pitted incumbent John Adams against Thomas Jefferson. When the voting was done, Jefferson had defeated Adams. But due to a quirk in the way the Electoral College operated at the time, he was tied with his own vice presidential candidate, Aaron Burr.

That's when things really started to get out of hand. The election went to the House of Representatives. Federalists, who had supported Adams, so hated Jefferson that they decided to throw their support to his vice presidential candidate. And once Aaron Burr realized he had a shot at the top office, ambition took over and he began to maneuver for votes.

The rules required the House to vote by state. On the first ballot Jefferson had eight states—one short of what he needed. Six states went for Burr and two were tied. Over the next few days the House went through 32 more ballots. The vote totals remained unchanged.

Tensions were rising. Jefferson supporters threatened to take up arms if he wasn't elected. The threat of violence was so real that the governor of

Jefferson on his way to his presidential inauguration

Aaron Burr was a divisive figure. One Federalist who refused to support him under any circumstances was Alexander Hamilton, who called Burr "the most unfit man in the U.S. for the office of President." Oddly enough, although Burr did not gain the presidency, he still became the vice president and was serving in that capacity when, in 1804, he challenged former Treasury Secretary Hamilton to a duel on the banks of the Hudson River in Weehawken, New Jersey. There, on July 11, he fatally wounded Hamilton and, amazingly,

later returned to Washington to serve out the rest of his term. But his political career was over. He eventually went west and was even tried (but acquitted) for treason for trying to carve a new country out of the Louisiana Territory.

Burr shoots Hamilton at their now-famous duel.

Virginia placed guards around a supply of 4,000 arms so that the Federalists would not be able to get their hands on them. As President Adams later wrote, "a civil war was expected."

The Federalists had been supporting Burr, but after three days of voting, the sole congressman from Delaware, John Bayard, announced that he was going to abstain, which would give the election to Jefferson. Other Federalists stood up and shouted, "Traitor, traitor," at him, but Bayard said he acted to save the country. The deadlock was broken—and Thomas Jefferson became president.

Jefferson's Handshake

A radical gesture may be Jefferson's greatest gift to politicians.

Thomas Jefferson, the revolutionary genius who wrote the Declaration of Independence, was one of the United States' most gifted presidents. But his passion for equality may best be revealed by a simple gesture. With it, the leader who helped create a democracy in the era of kings and aristocrats set an example for all presidents to follow.

When President George Washington greeted guests at official functions he bowed stiffly to them and they bowed in return. The second president, John Adams, continued the custom which was widespread among nobility and high-ranking officials at that time. It's a custom that still persists in some countries and in certain formal situations.

But on the Fourth of July 1801, President Jefferson shocked guests at a White House reception by doing something that was almost unthinkable. Rather than bow to his visitors, he shook their hands, signaling their status was equal to his. Furthermore he introduced the practice of treating every guest the same way regardless of social stand-

The handshake pioneered by Jefferson telegraphs equality. It's also a symbol of peace, as when President Buchanan encouraged the Pawnees and Pocas (below) to shake hands and end their fighting.

ing—no one was treated differently than anyone else. Even high-ranking diplomats who felt their social position demanded a formal bow had to settle for a simple grasping and shaking of the right hand. Scandalous!

From that day forth, presidents have seized the egalitarian gesture of shaking hands as their own, pressing the flesh at every opportunity. Where would presidential politics be without it?

Presidents Franklin D. Roosevelt (top) and John F. Kennedy (right) press the flesh.

OTHER PLAYERS, OTHER PLACES

On New Year's Day 1907, a whopping 8,150 people lined up at the White House to shake Theodore Roosevelt's hand. That's a presidential record that stands to this day. TR's powerful handshake was legendary. "It is a very full and firm grip," wrote one person who shook hands with Roosevelt, "that might bring a woman to her knees."

Jackson and Benton

This presidential adviser has a most unusual résumé.

One of President Andrew Jackson's most trusted advisers was Missouri senator Thomas Hart Benton (opposite, right). Pretty extraordinary considering that 20 years earlier, Benton and his brother had put a bullet in Jackson!

Benton was an aide to General Jackson during the War of 1812, but the two men quarreled over an obscure point of honor. Jackson was fiercely jealous of his reputation and had already killed one man who had insulted him. One day in Nashville in 1813 he saw Benton and his brother and went after them with his pistol. But it was Jackson who ended up being shot in the shoulder and the left arm and nearly dying from the wounds.

Benton shoots his rival, Jackson.

From that moment Benton knew that if he stayed in Tennessee, Jackson's friends would exact revenge. "I am in the middle of hell, and see no alternative but to kill or be killed," he wrote. But he did find an alternative—he lit out for Missouri.

By the time Jackson came to Washington in the 1820s, Benton had become a powerful senator from the Show Me State. In fact, Benton is considered one of the great figures in the history of the U.S. Senate, where he eventually served for 30 years.

Some thought Old Hickory might shoot Benton on sight. But instead he made peace and gained an ally.

Together Jackson and Benton men fought attempts to split the Union asunder. They also both advocated "hard currency" or money backed by gold. Both men thought this would be critical as the country expanded westward, which they both also supported. It seemed they had a lot more in common than just a quick trigger finger.

Twenty years after the shooting, doctors finally removed the bullet. Jackson supposedly offered it to Benton saying the bullet was his property. Benton, however, declined to accept it, saying that by carrying it for nearly 20 years, Jackson had earned the right to keep it.

MORE OF THE STORY

Andrew Jackson (below) clearly had a fierce temper and tangling with him could be fatal. In May 1806, Charles Dickinson published a statement in a Nashville newspaper calling Jackson a "worthless scoundrel...a poltroon and a coward." Jackson challenged Dickinson to a duel, even though Dickinson was known as one of the best shots in Tennessee. When the two men met, Dickinson fired the first shot, which broke two of Jackson's ribs and lodged near his heart. Some say that Dickson didn't kill Jackson because he misjudged the position of Jackson's heart: his clothes were very baggy because he was so skinny. Thin though he may have been, he was very tough. The wounded Jackson coolly took aim and fired back, killing Dickinson outright. It was a controversial move; many felt dueling custom required Jackson to fire into the air rather than shooting to kill.

Masons, Morgan, and Murder

This kidnapping changes presidential history.

In 1826, a disgruntled Freemason in Batavia, New York, named William Morgan announced that he was going to write a book disclosing the most sacred secrets of the Freemasons. Local Masons, incensed by Morgan's actions, published advertisements denouncing him and got a friendly sheriff to arrest him for a $2 debt.

On the night of September 12 a group of men descended on the jail and spirited Morgan out. "Murder! Murder!" shouted the struggling Morgan as he was thrown into a waiting carriage.

The carriage went clattering into the night, and Morgan was never seen again. Theories vary on what happened to him. Some believe he was murdered, others that he was driven off to Canada, and still others that the whole thing was a publicity stunt for his book, which wasn't published until after his disappearance.

The kidnapping and alleged murder of Morgan triggered a ferocious anti-Mason movement. Clergymen decried the Masons' secret oaths, claiming from the pulpit that Masons were part of an international conspiracy. Hundreds of lodges across the country closed, and the fraternal order's respected position in American society was very nearly completely destroyed.

Out of the emotional protests emerged a new political party, the Anti-Mason Party. It was America's first real third-party movement and had great success in the Northeast. The

A contemporary illustration of Morgan's supposed murder

MORE OF THE STORY

Before Morgan's kidnapping, Freemasonry had achieved a high degree of public prominence in America. George Washington and Ben Franklin were only two of numerous early American leaders who were Freemasons. But as the order grew in power and influence people became more suspicious of it. The Anti-Masons nominated William Wirt (himself a former Mason) as their candidate for president and presented a platform condemning Masonry for its secrecy and exclusivity. Wirt

managed to win one state: Vermont. But demonstrating just how influential Freemasonry was, the victors in the election were two past Masonic grand masters: Andrew Jackson and Henry Clay. The tradition extends to modern times, too. Both Roosevelts, Truman and Ford were all Masons of one level or another.

Anti-Masons decided to mount a presidential campaign. They gathered in Baltimore to pick a candidate for the 1832 election. In so doing, they became

the first political party to hold a national nominating convention. Other parties quickly picked up on the idea, and a new tradition in presidential politics was born.

Morgan is forced into the waiting carriage.

One Man, One Vote

A single vote can sometimes make all the difference.

On a sweltering summer afternoon in 1842, Henry Shoemaker was toiling as a hired hand on a farm in Indiana. Suddenly he remembered it was election day, and he had forgotten to vote. He had personally promised his vote to one of the candidates running for state representative, a Democrat named Madison Marsh.

Shoemaker might be forgiven if he had ducked out on his civic duty and broken that promise. But he didn't. He saddled his horse, rode to the polling place and cast his ballot. As a result, Madison Marsh was elected—by one vote.

At that time, state legislators elected U.S. senators. In January 1843, Marsh and his fellow Indiana lawmakers convened for just such an election. After much maneuvering, Marsh changed his vote on the sixth ballot, electing Democrat Edward Hannegan to the United States Senate—by just one vote.

Fast-forward to 1846. A sharply divided U.S. Senate was debating whether or not to declare war on Mexico. A caucus vote was deadlocked until the absent Senator Hannegan was called. He cast his vote in favor of war. One of the results of that war was that California changed hands from Mexico to the United States.

Henry Shoemaker had no idea what he was setting in motion that day he went to the polls, never thinking that his one vote would make the difference between peace and war. But now that you know, never assume that your one vote doesn't count.

Casting a ballot in the 1840s was, of course, a males-only affair.

The Pig War

Can a shot swine really bring the United States and Great Britain to the brink of war?

In 1859, the last bit of territory in dispute by the U.S. and Great Britain was the San Juan Island chain, in the waters between Canada and the Oregon Territory. Both countries claimed the islands, and both had settlers there who eyed each other with suspicion and some hostility.

That was the status quo the day Lyman Cutler, an American living on San Juan Island, shot a pig that was rooting around in his potato patch. But it was not just any pig. It was a British pig.

British authorities threatened to arrest Cutler if he didn't make restitution. After Americans on the island turned to the U.S. Army for help, a hotheaded general named William Harney responded by sending a company of men from the Ninth Infantry. The governor of British Columbia in turn ordered a warship to the scene. Both sides escalated. Soon 400 American soldiers were dug in on the island while a fleet of British ships carrying thousands of armed men waited just offshore.

The possibility of war seemed very real. Fortunately at this point cooler heads prevailed. British naval officers refused orders to land Royal Marines on the island thus avoiding a confrontation. The

The pig shot by Lyman Cutler was actually a Berkshire boar, such as the black one above.

U.S. government, horrified that the actions of one irate farmer could precipitate a war, sent General Winfield Scott, Commander of the U.S. Army, to calm things down. Both parties eventually agreed to a joint occupation of the islands, bringing an end to a military confrontation in which the only casualty was a pig.

Ten years after the events of the "Pig War," the U.S. and Britain referred their dispute over the islands to a neutral third party: Kaiser Wilhelm I of Germany. He eventually ruled in favor of the United States, and today the islands are part of Washington State.

And Tyler, Too?

This president turns his back on his own country.

John Tyler (opposite, bottom) is the only American president to commit a public act of treason against the government of the United States.

Tyler had been out of the White House for 15 years when the Southern states began to secede, in 1860. A lifelong slave owner and states' rights advocate, he led an effort to find a compromise plan that could bring North and South together. He chaired a Peace Convention that convened in Washington in February 1861. He avowed that his only goal was "to preserve the Government and to renew and invigorate the Constitution."

At the very same time, however, he was engaged in

Banner of the Secession Convention in Charleston, South Carolina, 1861

Slave quarters on Jefferson Davis' cotton plantation

secret correspondence with Jefferson Davis, president of the Confederacy. When the Peace Convention's efforts failed, Tyler took up the Southern cause with gusto. Shockingly for a former president he encouraged his native Virginia to join the other Southern states in rebellion. After Virginia seceded from the Union, Tyler was elected from there to the Confederate Congress. At this time four other ex-presidents were alive: Van Buren, Fillmore, Pierce, and Buchanan. All lived in the North and supported the Union to varying degrees. Tyler died shortly after his election, an elected member of a rebel government that was at war with the country he had once faithfully served as president.

MORE OF THE STORY

The Peace Convention brought together 131 delegates from 21 states to the Willard Hotel in Washington. They represented a last-gasp effort to avoid bloodshed between the states. But none of the states that had already seceded from the Union were represented, and the recommendations of the Peace Convention were rejected by Congress and incoming president Abraham Lincoln.

Native Guards

This unit serves on both sides in the Civil War but gains kudos from neither.

The Louisiana Native Guard was a militia regiment formed by eager volunteers in the early days of the Civil War to fight for the South. What made it unique among Confederate military units was the origin of its men.

They were all free blacks living in and around New Orleans.

Why were they willing to fight for the South? Some saw it as a way to gain equality. Others owned property they were afraid of losing if they refused to fight. Many were mulattoes who identified more with Southern whites than with slaves.

The South didn't permit the Native Guards to go into battle and used it more for favorable propaganda than anything else. This treatment quickly dampened the unit's enthusiasm for the Confederate cause.

But the men of the Native Guards still desperately wanted to prove themselves. After New Orleans was occupied by the Union many of the officers and men volunteered to fight for the Union. They were joined by runaway slaves also anxious to take up arms.

And so the Native Guards, reconstituted as three Union regiments, became the only unit to serve both the South and the North during the Civil War. In the North they were also called the *Corps d'Afrique* or Africa Corps.

They were the first black units in the Union Army, and they fought bravely at the Battle of Port

A studio portrait of an unidentified Native Guard

> *"They fought splendidly! Splendidly! Everybody is delighted that they did so well."*
>
> —GENERAL NATHANIEL P. BANKS ON THE NATIVE GUARDS AT PORT HUDSON

Hudson. In spite of their performance, they were not treated well by the Army. The black officers were replaced with whites, and the men were used primarily for guard duty and manual labor.

Despite their willingness to work and fight the Native Guards were orphaned by two armies. As one of their officers observed: "Nobody really desires our success." But at least one member of the Guard went on to success. P.B.S. Pinchbeck, who was one-quarter African-American (the son of wealthy white planter and his mulatto mistress), served as a governor of Louisiana, making him that state's first and only black governor to date.

Northern newspapers celebrated the Guards.

OTHER PLAYERS, OTHER PLACES

Once the war was over, many adventurous men stayed in the Army to participate in the western movement. Among these men were black war veterans, former slaves and free black men who didn't feel they had a place in the North or the South. They became known as Buffalo Soldiers, a name thought to have been given them by the Comanche. They were the first black solders to serve in the armed forces in the U.S. during peacetime. As cavalry divisions primarily stationed in the Southwest, they did everything to help claim the West by building roads, mapping water sources and escorting the mail. When the Indian Wars heated up, they fought bravely and did so in the Spanish-American War as well, including the Battle of San Juan Hill. Although their numbers grew, they remained segregated until the Army was integrated a half century later, in 1951.

The Editor and the Election

Is there any doubt the press can influence an election?

Telegrams were sent by Reid to Republicans in key states.

Republican presidential candidate Rutherford B. Hayes went to bed on election night convinced that he had lost the election to Democrat Samuel Tilden. That's the story most of the nation's newspapers printed, too.

But *The New York Times* managing editor John Reid wasn't convinced that Hayes had lost. He made sure that the headline in the *Times* reflected an election still in doubt. Then, being a dyed-in-the-wool Republican, he set out to do what he could to swing things for Hayes.

In the hours before dawn Reid walked over to the Fifth Avenue Hotel, the headquarters of the Republican National Committee. He woke up party chairman Zachariah Chandler to argue that the election was not lost. "If you will only keep your heads there is no question of the election of President Hayes."

In this political cartoon Miss U.S. prefers to dance with Mr. Hayes instead of Mr. Tilden.

> ## *"The presidential election depends on the vote of Florida."*
>
> —REID TELEGRAM TO REPUBLICANS IN FLORIDA. IN AN EERIE REPLAY 124 YEARS LATER, THE BUSH-GORE ELECTION ALSO CAME DOWN TO THE VOTES IN FLORIDA

Chandler authorized Reid to do what he thought was needed. Reid promptly dictated telegrams to Republican leaders in Florida, Louisiana, South Carolina and Oregon, advising them that the election was still in doubt and to fight for every vote. Reid rushed them to the telegraph office, and when the clerk told him that the Republicans didn't have an account, he charged the telegrams to the *Times.*

Reid's telegrams helped inspire Republicans to contest the results in those key battleground states. After months of bitter partisan wrangling that divided the country, a special electoral commission voted along party lines to give the election to Hayes—thanks in part to the newspaper editor who just wouldn't concede defeat.

The electoral commission announces their results, which favored Hayes over Tilden.

OTHER PLAYERS, OTHER PLACES

The news media has been known to make a few mistakes regarding elections, too. Take, for example, the election of 1948. Although early returns and the numbers throughout the night accurately predicted a win for Truman, he had done so poorly in the polls leading up to the election that radio announcers such as CBS's H.V. Kaltenborn predicted a win by Dewey. The *Chicago Tribune* even printed a few hundred copies of its early edition with the headline, "Dewey defeats Truman."

Labor Day

This workers' holiday is born of political strife.

President Grover Cleveland signed a law making Labor Day a national holiday. It was already a holiday in 23 states. In creating a special day to honor workers he handed organized labor a huge victory. President Cleveland also sent soldiers to battle striking workers in Chicago. In using the Army to violently crush the strike he handed organized labor a stunning defeat.

Now for the amazing part: he did both those things within four days of each other.

In May 1894, workers at the Pullman Palace Car Company in Chicago went on strike after receiving a 25-percent pay cut. When the company balked at submitting to arbitration 50,000 railroad workers across the country refused to work on any train with a Pullman car. Rail traffic was slowed to a crawl, and violence was in the air.

> ### "If it takes the entire Army and Navy of the United States to deliver a postcard in Chicago, that card will be delivered."
>
> —PRESIDENT GROVER CLEVELAND

The Pullman strike of 1894 erupts into violence.

By June 28, one newspaper reported that the strike had "assumed the proportions of the greatest battle between labor and capital that has ever been waged in the United States." That very same day, President Grover Cleveland signed into law a bill making the first Monday of every September a national holiday: Labor Day.

The timing may seem odd, but the bill was probably intended to calm labor unrest. What the president did four days later was not.

In response to reports of violence Cleveland declared that the strikers were disrupting the U.S. mail and sent soldiers to establish martial law. Within days soldiers and strikers clashed, and seven men were killed. Union leaders were jailed and the strike was brutally put down. The action crippled the labor movement in America for decades. Yet the holiday endured. Who doesn't love a long summer weekend?

The Female Lawrence of Arabia

An audacious British woman is tapped to draw the borders of modern Iraq.

Gertrude Bell (below) was a Victorian woman who did things women just weren't supposed to do.

Eschewing the idea of a proper marriage and quiet life in England she made the Middle East her passion. It was among the Bedouin that she truly felt at home.

In the years before World War I, Bell traveled extensively throughout the Middle East. Crisscrossing the Syrian and Arabian deserts she developed an encyclopedic knowledge of the tribes and their chieftains and wrote of her travels in widely acclaimed books.

When war broke out she was recruited by British intelligence to obtain the loyalty of Arab sheiks throughout the Middle East. Bell boldly ventured behind enemy lines to gather information. When T. E. Lawrence set out to spark an Arab revolt he relied on invaluable research and intelligence supplied by the indefatigable Bell. It was remarked that she was the brains behind Lawrence's brawn.

The headstrong Bell sometimes found herself frozen out by British military officers resentful that a woman was telling them what to do. But her knowledge of the Arab world was too great to ignore. She proved indispensable to military and diplomatic efforts in the Middle East.

After the war, in 1921, British colonial secretary Winston Churchill asked Bell to create the borders of modern Iraq. She pushed to unite Shiites, Sunnis and Kurds all in one country despite their mutual hostility. This decision set the scene for much of the turmoil that has since plagued that troubled land. Gertrude Bell: a woman determined to make her mark in a man's world—which she did.

The Race to End All Races

A governing body sets back women's sports for more than 30 years.

The crowd was cheering wildly as the runners rounded the final curve in the women's 800 meters at the 1928 Olympic Games. This was the first year women were allowed to run such a long distance, and it was an exciting race. In the final moments, Germany's Lina Radke pulled ahead to win gold and set a new world record that would stand for more than a decade.

After the race several women fell to the ground in exhaustion, and some had to be given aid. That sort of thing happened all the time to male athletes. But critics pounced on this as proof that women shouldn't be running at all. The London *Daily Mail* quoted a doctor who said that such "feats of endurance" could make women "old too soon." The president of the International Olympic Committee called for eliminating all women's sports from the Olympics and returning to the custom of the ancient Greeks, who allowed only men to compete.

It sounds silly to our modern ears, but the results were anything but. Women were banned from Olympic races longer than 200 meters for 32 years. It was 1960 before female Olympians could compete in longer events, their race for equality slowed to a crawl. But U.S. runner Wilma Rudolph, a polio victim who couldn't walk without crutches until the age of seven, showed the world how strong a woman could be when she won gold in the women's 200-, 100- and 400-meter relays. Did someone say anything about the weaker sex?

Wilma Rudolph sprints to the finish in the women's 200-meter race at the 1960 Rome Olympics.

Don't Mess with Thanksgiving!

One president admits to a real turkey of a political mistake.

In 1939, Thanksgiving was scheduled to fall on the last day of November. Retailers lobbied President Franklin Roosevelt to move it one week earlier in order to lengthen the Christmas shopping season.

FDR wanted to do anything he could to help a still-shaky economy, so he agreed. In the middle of August he casually announced to reporters that Thanksgiving would come a week early that year, and the next as well.

The decision quickly became front-page news, and it sparked a firestorm of controversy. The White House was flooded with letters, and cartoonists had a field day. Especially aggrieved were calendar makers, whose products were suddenly inaccurate, and high-school football coaches, who were upset to find that the big Thanksgiving game was no longer on the right day.

> ## *"The Protestants will raise hell."*
>
> —ROOSEVELT AIDE STEVE EARLY, IN A MEMO TO THE PRESIDENT ON CHANGING THANKSGIVING

A Roosevelt-style family Thanksgiving

The issue divided the country. Twenty-three states decided to celebrate on the original date, while 23 others went along with the new date proclaimed by Roosevelt. Texas and Colorado, unable to decide, celebrated both.

The following year Roosevelt sheepishly admitted that the whole thing was a big mistake and returned Thanksgiving to its original date. Congress then passed a law setting that date in stone, so that no president could ever again mess with the tradition of Thanksgiving.

Is Paris Burning?

One man, seeing how the war is going, disobeys orders and saves the Eternal City.

Allied armies were rolling through France in August 1944, but Adolf Hitler was determined they would never get to Paris. He handpicked General Dietrich von Choltitz to take command of the city. Von Choltitz was a hero of the Russian front, but he had never had an assignment like this one. "I received orders," he said, "to turn Paris into a mass of ruins and to fight and die amidst its wreckage."

Von Choltitz prepared to do his duty. He ordered explosives planted in landmarks such as Notre-Dame Cathedral and Les Invalides. He told his superiors that he was ready to blow up the Arc de Triomphe and the Eiffel Tower.

Hitler had chosen von Choltitz because of his unswerving loyalty. But the monocled general was troubled by his orders. He couldn't bear to go down in history as the man who destroyed Paris.

So he made a decision that could have earned him an

"Paris must not fall into the hands of the enemy, or if it does, he must find there nothing but a field of ruins."

—HITLER'S ORDERS TO VON CHOLTITZ, AUGUST 23, 1944

The führer himself spent only a few hours in Paris in June 1940 and never returned.

execution. As pressure grew on him to begin destruction of the city he secretly agreed to a truce with the Resistance and got a message to the Allies begging them to invade—and quickly. They needed to enter Paris within 48 hours; otherwise, he would be forced to carry out his orders.

The Allies had been planning to bypass Paris but when General Omer Bradley got the message, he acted fast. "Have the French Division hurry the hell in there," he ordered.

As he awaited the Allies, von Choltitz feared he would be deprived of his command for disobeying destruction orders. But the German ambassador, Otto Abetz, agreed to help by sending a telegram to Berlin protesting von Choltitz's "brutality." That convinced Berlin he was being tough and bought him the extra few days he needed.

In his Berlin bunker, Hitler screamed: "Is Paris burning?" But thanks to the courage of von Choltitz, the City of Light and her people were saved from utter destruction.

OTHER PLAYERS, OTHER PLACES

The Germans weren't the only ones to consider burning a city to the ground. In fact, the Allies actually did it. In the closing days of the war, Royal Air Force and U.S. Air Force bombers commenced raids over the medieval city of Dresden, which had not been previously bombed. The seventh-largest city in Germany, its population had swelled with refugees fleeing the advance of the Red Army. Over a three-day period in February, hundreds of planes dropped incendiary bombs on the city, creating firestorms that resembled burning tornadoes. Estimates vary, but it is thought that 35,000 people were killed during the attacks. The city, and its famous cathedral, the Frauenkirche, was essentially destroyed. The city rose again: The rebuilding and restoration of the landmark church was finally completed in 2005.

Flag Day

In military and political propaganda, the second time may be the charm.

Associated Press photographer Joe Rosenthal was having a bad day. Coming ashore on Iwo Jima to cover the fighting there, he slipped on a ladder and fell from the boat into the ocean. Once ashore he heard about a flag-raising on Mount Suribachi—a great opportunity for a picture—but was frustrated to learn he was probably too late to catch it.

Still he joined some soldiers hiking up the mountain. They came under heavy fire. When they were halfway up, soldiers coming down brought Rosenthal the disappointing news that the flag was already flying. He thought about heading back, but decided to keep going. Good call.

At the top he saw that a flag had already been raised. But he also saw a group of Marines getting ready to raise another. A Marine colonel had ordered a second flag-raising so that the first flag could be kept for posterity.

Rosenthal almost missed the shot. He was trying to get his bulky camera set up on a pile of rocks as the flag started going up, and he wasn't even looking in the viewfinder when he pressed the

Dedicated on November 10, 1954—the 179th anniversary of the founding of the Marines—the United States Marine Corps War Monument, better known as the Iwo Jima Monument, was based on Rosenthal's award-winning photo.

button. He had no idea if he had snapped a decent picture. When the film was developed, it turned out that frames 9 and 11 were ruined by light leaks.

But all the film wasn't damaged. Frame 10 turned out bold and beautiful. "Here's one for all time," said the photo editor who first saw it. Printed on front pages across the country, it won a Pulitzer Prize and soon became one of the most famous war photographs in history. Pretty good work for a bad day.

Jack's First Wife

Is there a political cover-up of JFK's first marriage?

In January 1947, Massachusetts congressman Jack Kennedy was a swinging bachelor vacationing in Florida. He was spending a lot of time with a twice-divorced Palm Beach socialite named Durie Malcolm. "The two were inseparable," according to the *New York World Telegram's* society writer. Early one morning Kennedy and Durie were married by a justice of the peace.

Or so the story goes. The tale first surfaced in 1961. Many dismissed it as mere rumor. There was, however, a piece of documentary proof: the so-called Blauvelt genealogy, a carefully compiled private history of one of America's oldest families, which reported the marriage as fact.

Once the story broke in the media the White House issued firm denials. Kennedy leaned on his friend Ben Bradlee, then an editor at *Newsweek,* to help discredit the tale. Durie Malcolm stoutly denied it then and ever afterward.

But after more than 50 years of silence, Kennedy family friend Charles Spalding told investigative reporter Seymour Hersh that it did indeed happen. "You must be nuts," he says he told his friend at the time. According to Spalding, family patriarch Joe Kennedy demanded that the whole thing be hushed up for fear that marriage outside the Catholic Church to a divorcée would kill his son's career in politics. Spalding said he and an attorney removed the pertinent records from the courthouse and destroyed them.

Many Kennedy intimates believe there was such a marriage and that he really loved her. Did it really happen? It all depends on whom you believe.

Was Jack's marriage to Jackie actually his second?

A Piece of Tape

A sticky situation topples a popular president.

Security guard Frank Wills was making his nightly rounds when he found a piece of tape covering a latch on a basement door. He assumed some worker in the office complex had left it there to make it easier to get in and out. Shaking his head, he removed it.

An hour or so later he found the latch re-taped. This time he called the police. They locked all the doors, shut off the elevators, and

"Next time there may be no watchman in the night."

–REPRESENTATIVE JAMES MANN OF SOUTH CAROLINA, VOTING FOR A BILL OF IMPEACHMENT

started searching the building. When they reached the sixth floor they caught five burglars hiding behind desks in one of the offices.

Pretty routine case, except that the burglars were bugging the offices of the Democratic National Committee at the Washington, D.C., Watergate complex. Two *Washington Post* reporters, Robert Woodward and Carl Bernstein, tirelessly pursued the incredible story. The ensuing scandal consumed the presidency of Richard Nixon and eventually forced his resignation.

Had the president's men pulled off their burglary in secret, Watergate might have been the scandal that never happened. But everything came unstuck—because of one piece of tape.

Carl Bernstein (left) and Bob Woodward broke the story for *The Washington Post*.

Nixon's resignation was headline material all around the world—making the national nightmare very public indeed.

MORE OF THE STORY

The three Duke Law School students were all near the top of their class. Exams were over, and they were dying to see their final grades, which hadn't been made public yet. In the hall outside the dean's office, two of the students hoisted the third up on their shoulders. He climbed through an open transom over the locked door. Once inside, he opened the door to his friends. Quickly they located keys to the dean's locked file drawer, got a peek at the grades and the final class rank, then slipped away as quietly as they came, regarding their adventure as a harmless prank. But for one of the students the break-in was an ironic foreshadowing of things to come. While Richard Nixon got away with the schoolboy shenanigans at the dean's office, the Watergate break-in would prove the complete undoing of his presidency.

Legacy Lost

This infamous man is the father the Internet never had.

Nowhere in the history of the Internet is the name H. R. Haldeman mentioned. But if not for Watergate, things might have been very different. And the Internet might have burst upon us years earlier.

Way back in 1973 Haldenman, the chief of staff to President Nixon, was planning a major initiative for what he referred to as the "Wired Nation." He hoped it would be the jewel of Nixon's second term. But Watergate soon consumed the Nixon White House, and the idea came to nothing. Haldeman talked about what might have been shortly after Nixon resigned in 1974.

"Through computer you could order whatever you wanted. The morning paper, entertainment services, shopping services, coverage of sporting events and public events. Technologically it can be done." It was going to happen anyway, Haldeman predicted. "But if I had stayed on for the second term, I believe it would have come much faster."

Haldeman's words showed great foresight, since the Internet lay a decade or two in the future. With federal backing in the 1970s, it might have materialized more quickly. And instead of being reviled as the architects of the Watergate cover-up, Richard Nixon and H. R. Haldeman might be hailed as the visionaries who helped create the Net.

Al Gore (left) and Bill Clinton participate in "Net Day" in 1997.

OTHER PLAYERS, OTHER PLACES

The politician most associated with the Internet is Al Gore, who endured national ridicule for telling an interviewer in 1999, "I took the initiative in creating the Internet." Gore did help pass legislation in the late 1980s that moved the Internet dramatically forward. But its birth was much earlier. The man who had the first computer on the Internet was Dr. Len Keinrock. IMP 1 was installed in his laboratory in UCLA in September 1969. Another computer was installed in a lab at Stanford a month later. On October 29 of that year, technicians got the two machines talking to each other and ARPANET, the immediate predecessor to the Internet, was born.

Seeing Red (and Blue)

Political color-coding becomes part of our self-image.

The 2000 election was ultimately decided by Florida voters.

It's become a form of shorthand: red states and blue states. Red states, of course, vote Republican. Blue states go Democratic. But the expression also conjures up a cultural and geographic divide. Red-staters, according to the stereotype, dwell in the heartland and love NASCAR and country music. Blue-staters inhabit the coasts and big cities, sipping lattes and reading *The New York Times*. Where, oh where, did it all begin?

In the 1870s, Texas color-coded its ballots to help Spanish-speaking voters make sense of them.

The Democrats were the blues and the Republicans were the reds.

In 1972, NBC News executive Gordon Manning introduced the color-coded electoral map to election-night coverage. Other networks followed, but there was randomness to it. One network might use blue for Democrats, another red.

By 1996, the major networks had informally agreed to use red for the Republicans and blue for the Democrats. Then came the 2000 presidential election between George Bush and Al Gore. The nation stared at those electoral maps not just for a day or two, but for week after week as the two sides argued over who had won. The maps suggested a regional and cultural divide as well as a political one, and the color-coding began to imprint itself on the national consciousness. Soon the whole nation was seeing red—and blue

A week later, talk-show host David Letterman offered a compromise: "Let's make George W. Bush president of the red states and Al Gore head of the blue ones."

OTHER PLAYERS, OTHER PLACES

One of the first uses of the color code in a cultural sense came from NBC anchor Brian Williams, writing in *Time* about the death of Dale Earnhardt in March 2001. "Millions of Americans, mostly in the red states, if you recall your election charts, lost a hero the instant the black car veered violently into the wall." He was referring to NBC's 2000 election map with red states for Bush and blue for Gore.

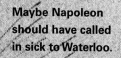

Maybe Napoleon should have called in sick to Waterloo.

Chapter 7

Twists of Fate
The Course of History Altered in a Moment

Consider the chance encounter that blossoms into a lifelong love affair, the barely avoided car accident, the job that was turned down. We've all experienced those unexpected but memorable events that have shaped our lives. Now consider history. While a great leader can change the world, how much of what has happened through time would have been different on just a turn of a dime? Consider the monarch whose driver took a wrong turn directly to an assassin, a custody battle that resulted in a president being a U.S. citizen, a rebellion caused by the use of animal fat, a storm destroying the warships of opposing armies. Any of these seemingly pedestrian events could have gone another way. Read what happens when fate steps in.

An Islamic Europe?

But for one pivotal battle, Notre Dame Cathedral might have been a mosque.

In the year 610, the angel Gabriel came to the Prophet Muhammad in a dream. Thus Islam was born, and it soon spread like wildfire. By the year 732, just 100 years after Muhammad's death, an Arab empire with 30 million Muslim subjects stretched from India all the way to Spain. It seemed only a matter of time before all of Europe fell under Islam's sway.

Some of the most ardent converts were nomadic Moors in North Africa. They were determined to spread the word with their swords. In 732, a mighty army of 80,000 Moors roared through Spain, crossed the Pyrenees Mountains, and rode into what is now France. "Everything gave way to their scimitars," wrote one Arab chronicler. The Moors swept away everything in their path, and came within 100 miles of Paris.

But fate intervened in the form of Charles, king of the Franks. He led his army south from Paris and met the Moors near the town of Tours. In a desperate battle, his foot soldiers beat off attack after attack from the Moorish horsemen, and finally routed the enemy.

The Battle of Tours may have been one of the most important in history. Had the Moors been victorious there, much of Europe might have been dominated by Islam instead of Christianity— and the world would be a very different place.

The Moors of northern Africa had conquered all of the Iberian peninsula.

The Battle of Tours earned Charles the nickname
Martel, or Hammer, for the way he beat his enemies.

*"The two great hosts of the
two languages and the two
creeds were set in array
against each other."*

—AN ARAB CHRONICLER OF THE BATTLE

OTHER PLAYERS, OTHER PLACES

When King Ferdinand and Queen Isabella united Spain under their Catholic rule in the 15th
century they were concerned about the cultural
unity of their country. They decreed that all
Jews and Moors should convert to Catholicism
or leave the country. Many did convert, but the
King and Queen doubted the sincerity of the
conversions and asked Pope Sixtus IV to
inquire into their beliefs. Thus the infamous
Spanish Inquisition was born, in part out of the
re-conquest of Spain from the Moors.

Man Overboard!

The lives of three American presidents hinge on the rescue at sea of one lucky man.

A powerful storm battered the *Mayflower* as it carried the Pilgrims across the Atlantic in 1620. The wind and waves were ferocious. When passenger John Howland came up on deck the force of the storm swept him into the sea, where he seemed sure to perish beneath the roiling waves.

Fate was kind to John Howland. He just managed to grab a rope trailing from the ship and hold on for dear life. His head disappeared below the surface, but men on deck hauled up the rope until he was alongside the ship and then fished him out with a boat hook. "Though he was something ill with it," reported another passenger, "he lived many years after."

By that slender thread hung three presidencies. Watching from the deck of the *Mayflower* was a 12-year-old girl named Elizabeth Tilley. She and John Howland eventually married. They populated the New World with 10 children, 82 grandchildren and descendants too numerous to count.

Among them were three presidents of the United States: Franklin D. Roosevelt and the two George Bushes—all of whom might never have

Also descended from John Howland: actors Humphrey Bogart and Alec Baldwin, as well as Joseph Smith, founder of the Church of Latter-day Saints.

been born if their ancestor hadn't been plucked from the death grip of a vengeful ocean.

OTHER PLAYERS, OTHER PLACES

A second rescue at sea helped preserve the Bush line. In 1944, Ensign George Bush was pulled from the Pacific Ocean by crew members of the submarine USS *Finback* after his torpedo bomber was shot down in 1944.

Custody Battle

What if the father of our country had grown up an Englishman?

George Gale married a widow from Virginia and brought her back home to London along with three children from her previous marriage. But the happy life he envisioned wasn't to be. Not long after they arrived in England, Mildred Gale died in childbirth in 1701. Her will directed her new husband to raise his stepchildren and bequeathed him the money to do so. He dutifully put the two boys, Lawrence and Augustine, into an English boarding school and applied for legal custody.

The boys were well on their way to being raised as proper Englishmen—until the family of Mildred's first husband back in Virginia decided to dispute the will. A custody battle ensued. It took years to sort out all the issues, but eventually a court ruled that the children should return to Virginia to be raised by relatives there.

That ruling would have a dramatic effect on American history.

The name of Mildred's first husband was Lawrence Washington. Her son Augustine, brought back to America from England, eventually had three sons of his own. He named one of them after his stepfather, George Gale.

That boy, of course, was George Washington. The Revolutionary War hero might easily have wound up serving on the other side, if not for a transatlantic court case.

An illustration of young George Washington, famously admitting to chopping down a cherry tree

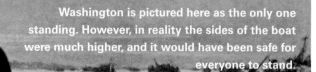

Washington is pictured here as the only one standing. However, in reality the sides of the boat were much higher, and it would have been safe for everyone to stand.

The Colonel and the Note

A bit of procrastination changes the outcome of the American Revolution.

On the cold Christmas night of 1776, General George Washington brought the tattered remnants of his army across the Delaware River. His troops were in wretched shape, decimated by previous battles, worn out and ill fed. Nonetheless Washington was leading them on a surprise attack on Hessian soldiers occupying Trenton, New Jersey.

The Hessian commander, Colonel Johann Rall, was attending a Christmas party that night. To him, an experienced commander of seasoned troops, it was inconceivable that the disorganized colonials would dare to mount an attack. Around midnight a local farmer who was also a British sympathizer, came to the door with a message. A servant took the message and gave it to Rall, but the colonel wasn't in the mood to interrupt his holiday card game. He stuffed the note in his pocket—unread.

At daybreak, in a freezing sleet, Washington and his sleep-starved troops attacked. Their powder was so wet that many of them couldn't fire their weapons, so they charged with bayonets or used their muskets as clubs. The groggy Hessians received quite a Christmas surprise—in fact, they were completely overwhelmed. Nine hundred Hessians were taken prisoner and Colonel Rall was mortally wounded. As a doctor cut away his clothes to treat his wounds, the note fell from his pocket.

It turned out to be a message warning of Washington's stealthy approach. If he'd taken the time to read it earlier Rall might have lived to see the Americans defeated and Washington as his prisoner.

Before he died the ill-fated Colonel Rall had a chance to look at the message that could have turned the tables. "If I had read this," he said mournfully, "I would not be here."

MORE OF THE STORY

Preparing to cross the Delaware, Washington stepped into a boat containing Colonel Henry Knox (below). He gave the 300-pound officer a nudge with his toe and uttered these immortal words, which gave a much-needed lift to his cold and miserable troops: "Shift that fat ass, Harry. But slowly, or you'll swamp the damn boat!" Washington wasn't the only future government leader in the boats that night. Future president James Monroe, future vice president Aaron Burr, future chief justice John Marshall, and future secretary of the treasury Alexander Hamilton also made the fateful crossing.

THE COLONEL AND THE NOTE

Miracle at Saratoga

An impetuous and unlikely hero changes the course of a key battle.

On a hillside near Saratoga, New York, a bitter battle was raging between a ragtag American army and crack British troops. One of the Americans' best officers was stewing on the sidelines. He'd been quarreling with the commanding general for days, and just hours before, he had been dismissed for insubordination.

But once the battle began the headstrong officer couldn't stay away. Damning his orders, he downed a slug of rum, leaped onto a borrowed horse and raced up to the front lines, saber flashing. Men rallied around him, and he led them into the teeth of British fire. He galloped his horse from one part of the field to another under constant fire, leading devastating attacks on enemy positions. A bullet shattered his leg and down he went—but not before helping to rout the Redcoats.

The victory at Saratoga in 1777, proving as it did that the British were not at all invincible, convinced France to enter the war on America's side. That turned out to be the key to ultimate triumph—thanks in large part to the

Benedict Arnold makes his impulsive but successful charge at Saratoga.

heroic officer who just a few years later would make his name a synonym for treachery and betrayal: Benedict Arnold.

It was just three years later that Arnold, angry at what he felt was shabby treatment by Congress, offered to hand over the American fort at West Point to the British for the sum of £20,000. Arnold was in desperate need of cash. He had married the young Philadelphian, Peggy Shippan, in 1779. It was a big step up the social ladder for Arnold and he was having great difficulty keeping up financially. That may have been part of the reason why he began the correspondence with British General Sir Henry Clinton through an intermediary—Major John André, his wife's former suitor. When the plan was found out Arnold escaped to a waiting British ship and later became a brigadier general in the British army. André should have been on the very same ship, but he was captured with the documents that incriminated Arnold in his sock. André was later hanged as a spy.

André was captured by three American soldiers, only one of whom could read the incriminating documents.

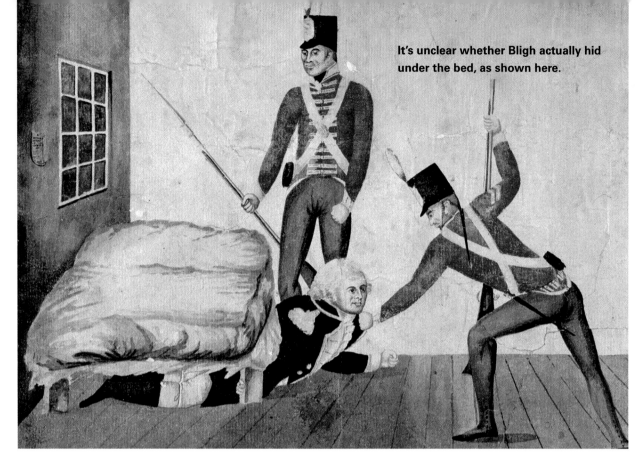

It's unclear whether Bligh actually hid under the bed, as shown here.

Rum Rebellion

For one man, this conflict is déjà vu all over again.

It was a mutiny. There simply was no other word for what went on. It happened in New South Wales, a British penal colony in Australia. A new governor, a man with a notoriously quick temper and a very keen sense of duty, had been sent from London. He soon came into conflict with the colony's officer corps.

The governor considered his officers inept and corrupt and moved to shut down the thriving rum trafficking ring that they controlled. The officers claimed he was a tyrant and was acting outside of the law. Eventually they decided to depose him. In what later become known as the "Rum Rebellion" 300 soldiers surrounded his house. The governor was at dinner when he got word that the mutineers were coming to arrest him. He hid out in a servant's room, hoping to escape. The soldiers who captured him at gunpoint claimed he was hiding under a bed. The mutineers kept him as their prisoner for more than a year, but it seems the taunting and accusations of cowardice stung the sensitive governor more deeply than the rebellion itself.

Eventually, a dramatic public court-martial in London convicted the mutineers and vindicated the abused official. It was an experience that would have tested any man, but especially one who must have felt that history was repeating itself in a twist most cruel and unusual. For the governor of New South Wales was a British naval officer who was discovering that lightning could indeed strike the same place twice. The governor was none other than William Bligh, the ship captain famously deprived of his command nearly 20 years before—in the mutiny on the *Bounty*.

MORE OF THE STORY

The mutiny on the HMS *Bounty* took place in April 1789 in the open ocean about 1,300 miles from Tahiti, where the ship had been sent to gather breadfruit trees for transport to the West Indies. Twenty-two of the men on the *Bounty* remained loyal to Bligh, but four of those were held captive by the mutineers and Bligh was set adrift in a small boat with 18 men and very limited supplies. Bligh really was an amazing sailor. He successfully navigated more than 4,000 miles to safety on the island of Timor, on the eastern edge of the Malay Archipelago. He sailed for 47 days in a 23-foot open boat, with only a pocket watch and a sextant (no charts or compass) to guide him. As for the mutineers, many of them eventually made their way to Pitcairn Island with several Tahitian men and women and burned the ship in what became known as Bounty Bay so there could be no turning back. A few of their descendents still live on the island today.

The War of Bad Timing

In an odd coincidence, this conflict starts a bit too early and ends a little too late.

The main cause of the War of 1812 was Britain's interference with American shipping, stemming from a British embargo on trade with France. The United States tried for years to get the British to change the so-called Orders in Council that regulated the hated policies, but to no avail. So finally on June 18, 1812, the United States declared war.

Bad timing, it seems. It turned out that the British government had revoked the Orders in Council just two days before the declaration of war. In other words the main reason for the war had disappeared. President James Madison later admitted that if he had known of Britain's change of heart he would have held off declaring war. But it was months before the news reached Washington and by then the die was cast.

Britain and the United States fought for more than two years. The most famous battle of the war was General Andrew Jackson's decisive defeat of the British at the Battle of New Orleans on January 8, 1815. It made Jackson a national hero and eventually led to his becoming president.

More bad timing, unfortunately. The Treaty of Ghent, which formally ended the war, was signed on December 24, 1814. The battle, in other words, was fought a full two weeks after the war between the two countries had officially ended.

General Andrew Jackson actually became president in part because of his success in the unnecessary Battle of New Orleans.

An Army of Two

Leftovers and the wits of a young girl save a Massachusetts town.

In June 1814, the British frigate HMS Bulwark, bearing 74 guns, raided the Massachusetts town of Scituate, setting fire to six ships in the harbor. The town promptly formed a militia company to protect itself. The men held their drills by the lighthouse, but as the summer went by without any more incidents, they began to let their guard down.

In September, the *Bulwark* came back for another bite. Rebecca Bates, the 18-year-old daughter of the lighthouse keeper, spotted the British ship sitting offshore. A longboat full of soldiers was setting off toward the harbor, where two merchant ships presented a juicy target.

Her father wasn't around. There was no time to get to town to warn of the attack. Then Rebecca noticed something the men had left behind, something that gave her an idea: a fife and drum.

The soldiers had taught Rebecca and her sister a few songs over the summer. Now Rebecca thought they could use one of them to fool the British. "Keep out of sight," she warned her sister. "If they see us they'll laugh us to scorn." The two girls hid out behind a dune and played "Yankee Doodle" for all they were worth.

The British heard the all-too-familiar tune wafting over the water. It could mean only one thing: American soldiers were gathering to repel their attack. A signal pennant was hoisted and the raiding party aborted their mission.

Scituate was saved from attack by Rebecca and Abigail Bates, forever known to their town as "An American Army of Two."

> *"You take the drum and I'll take the fife."*
>
> —REBECCA BATES TO HER SISTER ABIGAIL, AS THEY PREPARED TO DRIVE OFF THE BRITISH

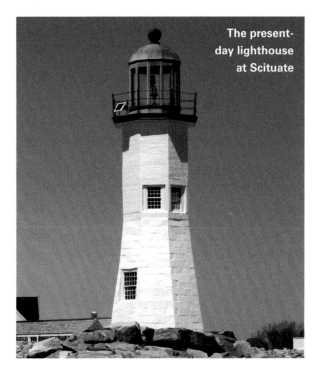

The present-day lighthouse at Scituate

Bad Day at Waterloo

One man's off day loses a mighty empire.

Napoleon Bonaparte was ready for battle. He faced a host of enemies: a mighty army composed of British, Belgian, Dutch and German units that had gathered together for the express purpose of destroying him. But Napoleon was the world's greatest general. It would take more than an army to stop him. It would take an act of nature.

The mighty emperor was sick. Hemorrhoids and a bladder infection struck him with force and fury and did what no earthly army could—render him immobile. In great pain the night before the battle he took a dose of opium that caused him to

Four days after his defeat at Waterloo, Napoleon surrendered to the British, who exiled him to the distant island of St. Helena.

JUST A TALE?

Napoleon clearly lost the Battle of Waterloo. But who won? It depends on whom you ask. The English credit the Duke of Wellington, who commanded the combined British, Dutch and Belgian forces that battled Napoleon most of the day. Bah, say German historians; they argue for Marshal Blücher, who arrived on the battlefield in the late afternoon with a Prussian army that delivered the decisive counterpunch.

sleep late and lose crucial hours that could have made all he difference.

The morning of the battle he was in such pain that he could barely mount his horse. Personal reconnaissance of the battlefield was out of the question. Some accounts say he took more opium, which may have clouded his judgment.

The emperor was not at his best, and his day went from bad to worse as he suffered an empire-ending defeat. If only he could have called in sick.

Saved by a Song

Good manners keep a president from misfortune.

In 1844, President John Tyler was one of hundreds of Washington VIPs crowded aboard the warship *Princeton*. They were there to see a demonstration of the biggest naval gun in the world. Called the Peacemaker, it had been designed under the supervision of the *Princeton's* captain, Robert Stockton. Weighing nearly 13 tons it could hurl a 228-pound cannonball five miles.

After the fearsome cannon was fired twice the delighted crowd repaired belowdecks for a sumptuous feast. Toasts were drunk and guests began to break out in impromptu song. Then came the announcement: the big gun would be fired one more time. Many hurried up to the deck to get a good view of it.

President Tyler had his foot on the ladder to climb up to the deck when he heard his son-in-law start to sing a military song. It would be rude to leave in the middle of it, so he paused.

And that's what saved his life. Before the song was done the cannon fired once again. Catastrophe! The gun's breech exploded, sending jagged chunks of hot iron flying into the crowd on the ship's deck. Secretary of State Abel Upshur and Navy Secretary Thomas Gilmer were both killed, as were four others.

Among the dead was a friend of Tyler's named David Gardiner. As the 53-year-old president consoled Gardiner's 23-year-old daughter, Julia, in the days following the incident, romance blossomed between them. They were married four months later.

The *Princeton* was the country's first steam-powered naval ship with a propeller instead of a side-wheel.

Bite the Bullet

A lack of understanding in one instance eventually fells a worldwide empire.

For 150 years the British East India Company ruled India through an army of native soldiers known as Sepoys who were commanded by British officers. In the 1850s, the officers began distributing a state-of-the-art firearm to their Indian men: the Enfield rifle. It was a decision that would soon backfire in terrible ways.

Instead of old-fashioned musket balls the Enfield fired the new conical Minie bullet, giving the rifle increased range and accuracy. Bullet and powder were contained in a paper cartridge, which was heavily greased to keep the powder dry. Loading the rifle required biting off the end of the greased cartridge to expose the gunpowder.

This was a big problem. Word spread among the troops that the grease contained fat from pigs and cows, meaning that biting the cartridge was sacrilege for both Hindus and Muslims. In May 1857, 85 Sepoys in the town of Meerut refused to use the new rifles. They were stripped of their uniforms and sentenced to 10 years of hard labor. Outraged by what they saw as religious persecution fellow soldiers rose up and killed their British officers then freed their captive comrades.

India was already seething with discontent, and this mutiny launched a full-scale rebellion. Violence quickly spread as Indian princes and

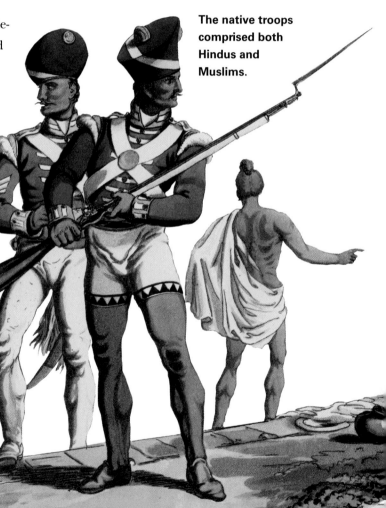

The native troops comprised both Hindus and Muslims.

oppressed peasants joined the revolution. Thousands died, with atrocities on both sides.

In the end the British government brutally suppressed the rebellion and took direct control of the country. But as costly and unsuccessful as it was, the mutiny triggered by a new kind of rifle planted the seeds of a nationalist movement that would eventually make India independent 100 years later.

The Sepoy Mutiny was marked by incredibly gruesome actions on both sides and extended beyond the battlefields to soldiers' quarters.

MORE OF THE STORY

Like so many culture clashes this one was born of ignorance and mistrust. The British believed they were showing faith in the men by giving them their newest rifle, while many Sepoys believed the greased cartridges were part of a plot to force them to become Christians by first making them outcasts from their own religions. The Sepoys became so enraged that they massacred British soldiers and their families at Cawnpore, hacking them to death even after they had surrendered. When the British retook the town, they forced their prisoners to lick the blood off the floor before taking them out and hanging them. They indulged in other cruelties too, inventing a punishment known as the "Devil's Wind" in which they would lash a man to a cannon and fire a cannonball through his body, blowing him to bits and thus demolishing his hope for an afterlife.

Where There's Smoke...

This general-turned-president is the victim of a simple, popular description.

In February 1862, a then-little-known Union general named Ulysses S. Grant (below) won a tremendous victory at Fort Donelson, Tennessee. After several days of intense fighting, an entire Confederate army surrendered to Grant. He took more than 12,000 prisoners.

Fort Donelson was the battle that made Grant famous. It was also the battle that killed him. In the wake of the victory Grant became the toast of the nation. Church bells in Northern cities rang out in celebration. Numerous articles were written about the victorious general. Several described him as smoking a cigar at the height of the battle.

Up to this time, Grant had only been a light smoker. But now people across the North began to send him boxes of the choicest brands of stogies. Unbelievably, he had soon received more than 10,000 cigars.

"I gave away all I could," Grant later wrote, "but having as such a quantity on hand I naturally smoked more than I would have done under the ordinary circumstances, and I have continued the habit ever since."

Grant, of course, went on to win the war and serve two terms as president. At the at age 63. he died of throat cancer, 23 years after the battle. Doctors agreed that the cancer was brought on by his years of heavy cigar smoking. Fort Donelson had claimed its final victim.

Grant was often pictured with one or the other of his two favorite things: horses and cigars.

Three Cigars

The South could have won the Civil War—but for three cigars.

In September 1862, Confederate general Robert E. Lee seized the initiative and invaded the North. It was a critical time in the war. If Lee could win a decisive victory European nations might recognize the Confederacy, and the war would for all intents and purposes be over—with the triumphant South an independent nation.

Chasing Lee was General George McClellan (right), one of the most overcautious officers ever to wear Union blue. His response to Lee's bold moves was slow and hesitant. As his army moved slowly through Maryland searching for Lee's troops, McClellan agonized over what he should do to turn the tide.

Fate intervened when an Indiana regiment stopped for a rest in a field occupied by Confederates a few days before. Three soldiers who were sprawled out on the ground noticed an envelope lying in the grass. Inside were three cigars wrapped in a piece of paper. Delighted, the soldiers decided to split the cigars—and then one of them thought to look at the paper.

His curiosity changed history. He had found what a Confederate officer had lost—a copy of the marching orders for Lee's army telling where the Confederates were headed and what they had planned. Galvanized by this captured information McClellan promptly went on the attack.

As a result the Confederates were turned back at the Battle of Antietam on the bloodiest single day in American history. And it was all because of three little cigars.

> *"Here is a paper with which if I cannot whip Bobby Lee I will be willing to go home."*
>
> —GENERAL GEORGE MCCLELLAN

Burial Ground

But for one man's house, a national shrine might be elsewhere.

Montgomery Meigs had reason to be angry with Robert E. Lee. Meigs and Lee had been fellow officers before the Civil War. Both were southerners, West Point graduates and engineers. They had worked closely together.

But while Lee resigned his commission to lead the armies of the Confederacy Meigs stayed loyal to the Union, becoming quartermaster general of the Union Army. He watched in anger as Lee's armies filled up Union cemeteries with dead. And every day he could see Lee's prewar mansion mocking him from a hillside high above the city of Washington.

Meigs found the perfect way to punish the Confederate commander: He recommended that Lee's longtime and much-beloved home be turned into a national cemetery.

Meigs wanted to fill the beautiful grounds with Union dead. When bodies weren't buried close enough to the house, he came out to personally supervise the burial of 26 soldiers in Mary Lee's beloved rose garden. He wanted bodies to ring the house so that the Lees could never return.

Northerners approved wholeheartedly. One Washington paper thought it "a righteous use of the estate of the rebel General Lee," and by the end of 1864 more than 7,000 soldiers were buried there. Mary Lee was devastated to find that the

Montgomery Meigs is among the dead buried at Arlington Cemetery; his son lies there too.

RAYMOND A FIERST

> *"The Romans sowed the fields of their enemies with salt; let us make it a field of honor."*
>
> —MONTGOMERY MEIGS TO ABRAHAM LINCOLN

house was now "surrounded by the graves of those who aided to bring all this ruin on the children and the country."

Today Arlington Cemetery is the closest thing there is to hallowed ground in America. It might not exist but for a soldier's anger at an old comrade.

Arlington House was originally built by a step-grandson of George Washington, George Washington Custis.

More than 300,000 people are buried at Arlington National Cemetery with an average of 28 added every day. It contains the remains of veterans of every U.S. conflict including Revolutionary War veterans who were re-interred at the cemetery after 1900. There are three soldiers buried in the Tomb of the Unknowns (below): an unknown veteran from each of World Wars I and II and a third from the Korean Conflict. A fourth unknown from the Vietnam Conflict was interred on May 28, 1984. However, that body was exhumed in 1998 and identified as Michael Joseph Blassie, who was shot down near An Loc in 1972. His body was returned to his family in St. Louis, Missouri. The crypt for the Vietnam Unknown will remain empty as the Department of Defense uses DNA testing to attempt to identify all remaining unknown Vietnam veterans.

A Bitter Harvest

Could it be that a quick action approved by Lincoln leads to his own assassination?

In 1864, President Abraham Lincoln personally approved a daring cavalry raid on Richmond, Virginia. The stated goal was to free Union prisoners held at Richmond's Libby Prison and hand out copies of President Lincoln's amnesty proclamation. The 4,000 Union cavalrymen met fierce resistance and got nowhere near Richmond. The mission that started with such high hopes turned out to be a complete fiasco.

Its aftermath proved catastrophic. During the retreat an officer commanding one wing of the raid, Colonel Ulric Dahlgren, was shot and killed by Confederates. In his pockets they found papers that suggested the raid had another, far darker purpose: to kill Confederate president Jefferson Davis and burn Richmond to the ground.

The North denied everything, but Southerners were outraged. A Richmond newspaper called it "The Last Raid of the Infernals." The discovery of the documents whipped up tremendous sentiment for taking revenge on the Union.

And so the South unleashed its own covert operations in the North. Numerous plots were hatched by angry conspirators, some with the sanction of the Confederate government, some not.

One plot to kidnap President Lincoln and hold him for ransom involved an actor named John Wilkes Booth (right). When that plan fell apart,

Libby Prison was originally built as a tobacco warehouse, then was used as a prison for Union officers and a transit station for Northern soldiers.

Booth began work on another plot—one that would come to fruition the night of April 14, 1865 at Ford's Theater.

From a president's order full circle to a president's assassination. It's a bitter harvest indeed.

JUST A TALE?

After Dahlgren's death, arguments erupted over whether the documents found on his body were real or forged. The controversy continues to this day. There is evidence to suggest that the documents may indeed be real, and that the killing of Jefferson Davis was secretly ordered by Secretary of War Edwin Stanton, most likely without Lincoln's knowledge. Stanton was famous for advocating harsh measures against the leaders of the Confederacy.

This Old House

The fate of the White House is to survive against the odds.

In 1814, an invading British army torched the White House. Only a thunderstorm prevented the building from burning to the ground. As it was, just the exterior walls were left standing. Some in Congress clamored to raze the ruins and move the capital city, but public sentiment, stirred up by the war, overruled the idea. The house was rebuilt.

In 1864, the commissioner of buildings pronounced the White House unfit for occupation. The occupant, Abraham Lincoln, kept on living there anyway.

Three years later, officials concerned about the dilapidated building drew up plans for a suburban White House to be located on hundreds of acres outside the city. It would be a dazzling presidential palace, private and secure, isolated from the hubbub of downtown Washington. Then Grant became president. He and his wife, Julia, liked living in the old White House right in the middle of things, and the plan fizzled.

In 1881, newly sworn-in president Chester A. Arthur was so horrified at the mansion's state of repair that he exclaimed: "I will not live in a house like this." Arthur proposed tearing down the White House and building a replica on the same spot. The Senate approved the idea, but the House never did.

Despite every effort, the "people's house" continued to stand, as it does today.

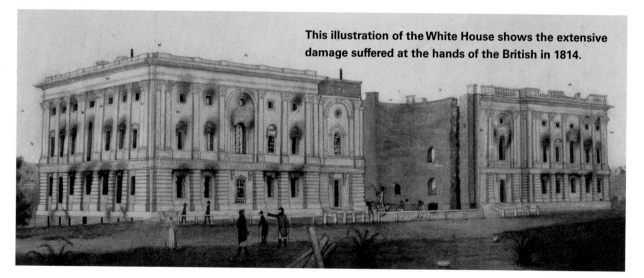

This illustration of the White House shows the extensive damage suffered at the hands of the British in 1814.

Winds of War

It's possible Mother Nature prevents a world war.

It began with a civil war in the Pacific island kingdom of Samoa in 1889. Germany decided to intervene and put troops ashore to fight for one of the factions. The United States took a dim view of this: German aggression in the Pacific was considered a threat that couldn't be ignored.

Three U.S. warships were dispatched to Samoa to keep an eye on the three German warships already there. Tensions between the two countries grew. Heated messages flashed back and forth between Washington and Berlin. America was angry, Germany defiant.

U.S. public opinion was inflamed by reports that American citizens in Samoa were being treated poorly by German soldiers and that an American flag had been torn down. When a San Francisco newspaper reported (incorrectly) that the Germans had sunk an American ship, conflict seemed imminent and unavoidable. Storm clouds were gathering, figuratively speaking.

Then they started to gather, literally. On March 19 a powerful typhoon struck the island. The fierce winds and deadly waves destroyed or severely damaged all six of the U.S. and German warships. Fifty Americans and 95 Germans perished in the storm. Many of the rest found themselves dazed and shipwrecked on shore.

But, as the expression goes, it is an ill wind that blows no good. The natural disaster eased tensions at a critical moment, and talk of war took a backseat to planning rescue and recovery efforts. Eventually Germany and the United States agreed to put Samoa under a joint protectorate. War between the two countries would come, but not for another 25 years.

Officers who had been readying for a fight found themselves attending memorial services for their dead and for those of their supposed enemy.

Annie and the Kaiser

A single gunshot could have prevented the War to End All Wars.

Annie Oakley was nervous. Just moments before, while she was performing her trick-shooting act before a crowd of thousands, a prominent local citizen had surprised her by stepping out of the audience. Gesturing emphatically he challenged Annie to shoot the ashes off his cigarette while he was smoking it.

As Annie told the story later, Wild West bravado compelled her to accept the awesome challenge. After all she had done this trick before. But his fame unnerved her. Anxiously she paced off the distance, regretting the whiskey had she consumed the night before. The man drew

Annie Oakley appears in a poster promoting her famed Wild West Show. Kaiser Wilhelm (above) at his coronation in 1890.

a cigarette from his gold case and lit it with a flourish. Hesitating only a moment Annie carefully took aim and fired.

The bullet flew to its target and knocked the ashes right off the cigarette. The crowd roared with delight.

The show was in Berlin. But who was the man with the cigarette? It was none other than the newly crowned monarch: the young Kaiser Wilhelm.

Had the bullet strayed off course just a little it might have hit the Wilhelm, not the cigarette. The belligerent ruler who played a major role in launching World War I might never have had the chance. It was a weird twist of fate and a moment Annie would never forget.

> *"If I shot the Kaiser, I might have saved the lives of several millions of soldiers."*
>
> —ANNIE OAKLEY

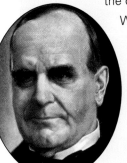

MORE OF THE STORY

In 1898, on the eve of the Spanish-American War, Annie Oakley wrote to President William McKinley (below) offering to put at his disposal "a company of 50 lady sharpshooters." Annie promised that each member of the company would provide her own rifle and ammunition. Nothing ever came of the offer. Later, during World War I, Annie's husband, Frank Butler, told reporters that he had written the Kaiser (now the hated enemy), saying Annie would like the chance to take a second shot at him. Wilhelm never replied.

The President and the Priest

Here's the story of how procrastination led to an assassination.

On October 28, 1893, Chicagoans were shocked to learn that an assassin had shot to death their mayor, Carter Harrison. One of those deeply affected by the shooting was a Polish priest named Casimir Zeglen. He became consumed with the idea of designing a practical bulletproof material that might save innocent lives in the future. Zeglen tried and discarded all sorts of material for his vest: steel shavings, moss, hair and others.

The assassination of President Mckinley

Four years later, Father Zeglen succeeded in coming up with the world's first truly practical bulletproof vest—light enough to wear under clothing but strong enough to stop a bullet. It consisted of wafer-thin steel plating sandwiched inside layers of tightly woven silk.

He first tested it on a cadaver, then on a Great Dane and finally—in several dramatic public demonstrations—on himself. It worked perfectly.

Zeglen left the priesthood to found the Zeglen Bullet Proof Cloth Company. As part of his promotional efforts he contacted the White House in 1901 to offer President William McKinley a vest. The president's personal secretary expressed an interest but said the matter couldn't be considered until after the president's trip to the Pan-American Exposition in Buffalo, New York.

He shouldn't have waited. It was in Buffalo that assassin Leon Czolgosz walked up to McKinley and shot him twice at point-blank range. Had the president been wearing the vest he would have lived and Zeglen would have become famous. Instead McKinley died eight days later, and Theodore Roosevelt became president. Zeglen never achieved the level of success he sought. And history was left with another intriguing, "What if?"

The Election That Killed

If not for a hotly contested election, the islanders would be alive.

In May 1902, election season was heating up on the Caribbean island of Martinique. So was the volcano, Mount Pelée. It was belching smoke and fire and otherwise making a nuisance of itself. In the city of Saint-Pierre residents regarded the fiery peak above them with mounting concern.

Bit the governor of Martinique, Louis Mouttet, was more worried about the upcoming election than he was about the volcano. He feared that a panic would hurt the candidates of the ruling Progressive Party. So he directed the editor of the local paper to downplay the danger of an eruption.

He set up roadblocks to prevent people from leaving the city. He suppressed telegrams warning of the danger. And in a grand gesture he paid a visit to Saint-Pierre three days before the election to assure everyone that things were really just fine.

> *"This date should be written in blood."*
> —AN EYEWITNESS TO THE DEVASTATION

The searing cloud of ash that descended on the city was hot enough to melt glass and metal.

The following morning, at 8 a.m., Pelée erupted. A cloud of gas and ash more than 1,000 degrees centigrade hurtled through the town at nearly 100 miles per hour. It didn't distinguish between political parties but killed the governor and 30,000 others in less than two minutes.

There were only two survivors. Ironically one was a prisoner in an underground cell who was scheduled for execution the next day.

Governor Mouttet said he was covering up warnings about the volcano because they "could create a state of false fear and pessimism." It apparently never occurred to him that the fear could be justified.

Auguste Ciparis, the condemned man who survived the eruption, was lucky enough to have his sentence commuted. He spent years traveling with the Barnum & Bailey Circus in a replica of his cell.

Ike throws the first ball in the 1957 season opener between Washington and Baltimore.

You're Out!

A presidential career is jeopardized by baseball games and a little white lie.

Dwight Eisenhower is the only president ever to play professional baseball. He played a couple of seasons on a minor league team in the Kansas State League. He apparently played one summer before he attended West Point and another summer between his first and second years at the military academy. "I went into baseball deliberately to make money," he said later, "with no idea of it being a career."

Ike played center field, but you won't find his name in any league records or newspaper accounts of its games. That's because he played under an assumed name: Wilson. You might say that he was engaged in his first cover-up more than 40 years before entering the White House. He took the alias because he knew that playing even a few games could disqualify him from college athletics given the strict amateur code of the time.

His deception could have had far more grave consequences. As a West Point student-athlete Eisenhower had to pledge that he had never played professional sports. Lying on that pledge was a violation of the West Point honor code. If anyone had found out, Eisenhower's military career and his storied rise to president might never have happened at all.

Eisenhower as a West Point cadet

"I told him I wanted to be a real major league baseball player. ...My friend said that he'd like to be president of the United States. Neither of us got our wish."

—DWIGHT D. EISENHOWER, RECOUNTING A CON-VERSATION WITH A FRIEND THAT HE HAD AS A BOY

MORE OF THE STORY

Like Eisenhower, legendary athlete Jim Thorpe played minor league baseball while still an amateur. It cost him his Olympic gold medals, although they were reinstated after his death. Eisenhower and Thorpe had something else in common: They played football against each other on November 9, 1912. Thorpe's Carlisle College decimated West Point, 27-6. When Ike and a team-mate tried to tackle the dazzling Thorpe late in the sec-ond half the two cadets ran into each other and were so stunned, they had to be removed from the game. Eisenhower injured his knee in a game against Tufts the following week, and his athletic career was over. However, even though he was finished with sports, he remained guarded about his baseball past. He first revealed it in a conversation with New York Giants manager Mel Ott in 1945, but offered few details. When Ott asked him what position he played, Eisen-hower said, "That's my secret." Later he instructed his staff not to answer questions about his professional baseball days because it could get "too complicated."

Christmas Truce

If only peace has a chance every day.

Christmas Day 1914 saw millions of young men facing each other in a double line of trenches several hundred yards apart that snaked hundreds of miles across Europe. These soldiers had seen some desperate fighting in the opening months of World War I, and plenty more lay ahead.

But on this particular day peace seemed to break out all over.

In violation of orders British and German soldiers climbed out of their trenches waving flags of truce and made their way into no man's land to celebrate Christmas with their enemies. Leaving the horror of war behind they shared Christmas pudding and belted out songs together. They exchanged toasts and traded cigarettes and food. "Most peculiar Christmas I've ever spent, and ever likely to," scribbled one British soldier in his diary.

In one place along the line, German soldiers from Saxony were fraternizing with Scottish Highlanders when one of the Scots brought out a soccer ball. A few minutes later a full-fledged game was under way on the frozen turf of no man's land. Men who had been trying to kill each other just the day before played enthusiastically for more than an hour.

A German lieutenant, Johannes Niemann, wrote home about the game: "We Germans really roared when a gust of wind revealed that the Scots wore no drawers under their kilts. The game finished with a score of three goals to two in favor of Fritz against Tommy."

The next day, the impromptu truce ended as quickly as it began—and the men who had celebrated together returned to the ugly job of killing one another.

> *"Fancy a German shaking your flapper…and then a few days later trying to plug you."*
>
> —HERBERT SMITH, FIFTH BATTERY, ROYAL FIELD ARTILLERY

Wrong Turn to World War I

If he'd asked for directions, a war might never have begun.

June 28, 1914. Archduke Franz Ferdinand, heir to the Austro-Hungarian throne, visited Bosnia, one of the far-flung provinces of his empire. Then, as now, the area was seething with tension. Serbian revolutionaries conspired to kill the archduke while his motorcade drove through Sarajevo. One of the would-be assassins tossed a bomb at his car, but the archduke deftly batted it away. It exploded in the street, injuring one of his aides. "So you welcome your guests with bombs!" the indignant Ferdinand spluttered to local officials.

Later, the archduke insisted on visiting the injured aide in the hospital.

Unfamiliar with the route, his driver took a wrong turn, which made all the difference. An official shouted, "That's the wrong way," and the driver stopped the car.

> *"Do you think Sarajevo is full of assassins?"*
>
> —THE GOVERNOR OF BOSNIA, REPLYING TO A REQUEST FOR BODYGUARDS FROM THE ARCHDUKE'S AIDE

The Archduke and Duchess were assassinated on their 14th wedding anniversary.

Unfortunately it did so right in front of one of the conspirators involved in the failed bombing. The surprised young man saw his opportunity, drew his pistol and fired several times.

Within minutes Ferdinand and his wife were dead. The archduke's assassination triggered World War I, which would ultimately claim more than 10 million lives. All because of a wrong turn.

Enigma

A little suspicion helps win World War II before it's even begun.

On a Saturday in January 1929, a crate shipped from Berlin arrived at the customs office in Warsaw, Poland. It was soon followed by a German official explaining that it had been shipped there by accident, and demanding it be returned to Germany before going through customs.

This aroused the suspicion of customs officers. Forcing open the crate, they took photos and made diagrams of the odd-looking device inside before returning it to the Germans.

This was Poland's first introduction to the famous Enigma coding machine.

No one had been able to break Germany's Enigma code, but the Poles were determined to try. A team of brilliant young cryptographers led by Marian Rejewski attacked Enigma with innovative mathematical techniques. By 1932, they had built a working model of the machine and were decoding German military messages. But it was a constant struggle for code breakers to keep up.

In 1938, the Germans created a new and improved Enigma machine. The Poles could no longer decipher German messages. Knowing that war was on the way they shared their information

German solders using the Enigma machine in the field

"A stunning moment."

—A FRENCH INTELLIGENCE OFFICE, DESCRIBING THE MOMENT THAT THE POLES UNVEILED THEIR RECONSTRUCT-ED ENIGMA MACHINES TO THE ALLIES IN JULY OF 1939

with the French and British. One of the machines was smuggled to London in the baggage of playwright Sacha Guitry and his wife, actress Yvonne Printemps, so as not to raise the suspicion of German spies. Two weeks later Germany stormed into Poland.

It turns out the gift was priceless. The Poles were decades ahead of other countries in breaking Enigma. Their efforts and their willingness to share their knowledge with England and France paved the way for the now-famous code-breaking effort that eventually allowed the Allies to read the Germans' most secret messages, which proved instrumental in winning the war. The role played by the massive Allied decipherment project wasn't revealed until 1974. One of those most surprised was Marian Rejewski, who never knew until then just how critical his prewar code-breaking efforts were to eventual Allied victory.

OTHER PLAYERS, OTHER PLACES

Julius Caesar is thought by many to be the first person to use encryption to secure messages. In this case it was to his army. He used a simple substitution method in which one letter of the alphabet is substituted for another. This method has since come to be called a Caesar cipher. In 1467 Leon Battista Alberti, the son of an Italian noble, developed a revolutionary new encryption method. He invented a tool consisting of two connecting metal disks, one of which rotated and one that was stationary.

One disk had 20 letters of the Latin alphabet and the numbers 1 through 4, which corresponded to words and phrases in a code book. The other disk had random letters. By lining up a mark on the inner disk with a mark on the outer disk, a key could be created for each encryption. To decipher the code, only the single key is needed. Both of these methods are forerunners of Enigma.

Both keys and disks were used in Enigma.

Einstein's Error

A single piece of correspondence may have changed the course of history.

Have you ever written a letter and wished you could take it back?

Albert Einstein wrote a letter like that in 1939. Concerned by reports that German scientists had succeeded in splitting the atom, Einstein wrote to FDR suggesting that recent nuclear research might make it possible to build "extremely powerful bombs of a new type." Einstein advised speeding up research—before the Germans got there first. He also recommended that the United States take action to secure an adequate supply of uranium.

This letter set off a chain reaction of its own, eventually resulting in the

This is the letter Einstein lived to regret.

Albert Einstein
Old Grove Rd.
Nassau Point
Peconic, Long Island
August 2nd, 1939

F.D. Roosevelt,
President of the United States,
White House
Washington, D.C.

Sir:

Some recent work by E. Fermi and L. Szilard, which has been communicated to me in manuscript, leads me to expect that the element uranium may be turned into a new and important source of energy in the immediate future. Certain aspects of the situation which has arisen seem to call for watchfulness and, if necessary, quick action on the part of the Administration. I believe therefore that it is my duty to bring to your attention the following facts and recommendations:

In the course of the last four months it has been made probable - through the work of Joliot in France as well as Fermi and Szilard in America - that it may become possible to set up a nuclear chain reaction in a large mass of uranium, by which vast amounts of power and large quantities of new radium-like elements would be generated. Now it appears almost certain that this could be achieved in the immediate future.

This new phenomenon would also lead to the construction of bombs, and it is conceivable - though much less certain - that extremely powerful bombs of a new type may thus be constructed. A single bomb of this type, carried by boat and exploded in a port, might very well destroy the whole port together with some of the surrounding territory. However, such bombs might very well prove to be too heavy for transportation by air.

A model of the bomb dropped on the Japanese city of Nagasaki

Manhattan Project—the enormous effort to create the first atomic bomb.

By 1945, many scientists were alarmed by the awesome power of this new weapon—especially since it was now clear that Germany wasn't building one of its own. Einstein wrote FDR another letter asking him to meet with scientists who opposed its use. Unfortunately, the president died before he could read it.

Einstein later said the first letter was "the single greatest mistake" of his entire life.

"Alas. Oh my God."

—EINSTEIN, ON HEARING THE NEWS OF
THE BOMBING OF HIROSHIMA

OTHER PLAYERS, OTHER PLACES

Einstein carried on a wide and varied correspondence throughout his life. Perhaps his favorite correspondent was his second wife, Elsa, to whom he wrote almost daily when away from home delivering or attending lectures. He also corresponded with children, answering their many questions with frankness and dignity.

But one of his most fascinating exchanges was with fellow German Sigmund Freud (left). In the early 1930s as the Fascist and Nazi movements were on the rise, Einstein wrote to Freud asking his opinion on the causes and cures of war. Freud pessimistically responded, "There is no likelihood of our being able to suppress humanity's aggressive tendencies."

Close Call of the Porter

This friendly fire almost changed the course of World War II.

"Torpedo! Torpedo on the starboard beam!"

—LOUDSPEAKER WARNING ON THE USS IOWA

On November 14, 1943, President Roosevelt and the country's top military brass were secretly crossing the Atlantic aboard the USS *Iowa* on their way to an Allied summit meeting in Teheran, Iran, with Joseph Stalin and Winston Churchill. Tremendous care was taken to hide the identity of the VIPs in order to assure their safety.

But suddenly a torpedo was seen heading straight for them. How could the Germans have known where Roosevelt was?

They didn't. The escort ship USS *William D. Porter* had accidentally fired the torpedo during a drill. As danger alarms went off and crewmen headed to battle stations the battleship *Iowa* maneuvered sharply and avoided the torpedo, which exploded just 100 yards off the stern. When the torpedo warning came over the loudspeaker Roosevelt told his valet: "Take me over to the starboard side, I want to watch the torpedo." The force of the explosion rocked the *Iowa* so violently that one officer aboard shouted, "My God, he hit us!" But the ship was not harmed at all.

History records a successful summit that helped secure an Allied victory. But there could have been a very different outcome—if not for a near miss.

The Big Three (left to right): Joseph Stalin, Franklin Roosevelt, and Winston Churchill

The USS Battleship *Iowa* dodged the torpedo and went on to fight in a second conflict: Korea.

MORE OF THE STORY

After the incident, the USS *Porter* was escorted to Bermuda, where the entire crew was placed under arrest. "You never saw so many people coming and going, interrogations all night long," says former crewman Bob Jones. The captain was transferred to a desk job, and the *Porter* was ordered to Alaska's Aleutian Islands. It is said that after that, other ships often hailed her with the greeting "Don't shoot—we're Republicans!" A year later the *Porter* was hit by an enemy plane off Okinawa and became the only destroyer in the war to sink without the loss of a single man.

Nearby ships were able to pluck all the survivors out of the water.

The USS *William D. Porter* sank June 10, 1945.

CLOSE CALL OF THE PORTER

One-Sided Battle

With a little investigation, the battle could have been avoided completely.

In 1942, the Japanese invaded and occupied the Aleutian islands of Attu and Kiska. It was the first time American soil had been occupied by an enemy since the War of 1812, and the United States was determined to throw them out.

The Americans retook the island of Attu in May 1943, suffering heavy casualties. Then, in August, came the invasion of Kiska.

A joint American-Canadian force of 35,000 hit the beaches, backed up by a massive naval fleet. The initial landings were unopposed, but the soldiers knew from experience that the Japanese would want to lure them in before answering their fire. The battle soon turned into a nightmare. Heavy gunfire could be heard, but thick fog made it impossible to see the enemy. Reports of casualties started filtering in, and wounded men were taken to the rear. Soldiers moved slowly forward, clambering up tough mountain ridges, firing as they went.

After two days of heavy fighting, with 32 soldiers dead and more than 50 wounded, the Allies made a stunning discovery:

There was no enemy.

The Japanese, it turned out, had staged a cunning evacuation three weeks before, pulling 6,000 men off the island without American blockaders having a clue. The battle deaths were all from friendly fire. Americans and Canadians had fought with great bravery. But as it unfortunately turned out, they were shooting at each other.

The invasion, code-named Cottage, was later referred to by *Time* magazine as a JANFU: Joint Army Navy Foul-Up.

A soldier stands guard atop Kiska, with the invasion fleet below.

About Face

Imagine saving the life of an ally—who winds up becoming your most bitter foe.

In 1945, an American intelligence team code-named "Deer" parachuted into the jungles of Asia to help a band of guerrillas fighting the Japanese. They found the leader of the guerrillas, Nguyen Ai Quoc, seriously ill from malaria and dysentery. "This man doesn't have long for this world," exclaimed the team medic, but he successfully nursed him back to health against all odds. The grateful leader agreed to provide intelligence and to rescue any downed American pilots he and his people could find in return for ammunition and weapons to continue their fight.

The team suggested that the U.S. continue to support Nguyen after the war, but the recommendation was considered too controversial, and it was ignored. The following year the guerrilla leader pleaded with President Truman to support his movement to gain independence from the French, but to no avail.

Nguyen Ai Quoc was also known by another name: "He Who Enlightens." In Vietnamese: Ho Chi Minh. Sixty thousand Americans died in the Vietnam War, battling a former ally whose life the U.S. once fought to save.

Ho Chi Minh in 1946 with General Jacques-Philippe Leclerc, commander of the French Far East Forces.

Lost in Translation

A little quick work with a dictionary could have made all the difference.

By July 1945, the war-weary Japanese government was ready to surrender. When the cabinet first received unofficial word of the surrender terms laid out by the Allied leaders meeting in Potsdam, Germany, they considered the terms lenient and were inclined to accept. But they decided to withhold comment until they received the Allied ultimatums through truly official channels.

With that in mind elderly premier Kantaro Suzuki tried to tread a careful path when questioned about the Potsdam Declaration. Unfortunately he used a word that has two meanings. He told a press conference that the cabinet was adopting a position of *mokusatsu.*

The word *mokusatsu* is made up of two characters: *moku,* meaning "silence," and *satsu* meaning "kill." Thus the translation is literally "to kill with silence." The term is generally translated in two different ways. It can mean "withhold comment for the moment" or it can mean "ignore." The Japanese News Agency mistakenly translated it the

The first atomic bomb was dropped on Hiroshima on August 6, 1945; the second on Nagasaki on August 9.

second way. Radio Tokyo flashed the erroneous translation to the world. Headlines in the United States blared that Japan was ignoring the declaration and rejecting the surrender terms.

The results were nothing short of tragic. President Truman decided that he had no choice

The survivors of the bomb blast are called Hibakusha, or "explosion affected people."

but to go ahead and drop the atomic bomb to force a capitulation. More than 100,000 people were killed and the cities of Hiroshima and Nagasaki were virtually destroyed—in part because of a poor translation.

"This was a piece of foolhardiness."

—TOSHIKAZU KASE, JAPANESE FOREIGN OFFICE

The Man Who Predicted 9/11

Two warnings that could have saved the lives of thousands are ignored.

The Statue of Liberty and the Twin Towers

When terrorists crashed airliners into the World Trade Center on September 11, 2001, Rick Rescorla may have been the only person in the buildings who wasn't surprised. They had done exactly as he had predicted.

Rescorla was the head of security for the Morgan Stanley Dean Witter offices occupying 44 floors in the WTC's south tower. A native Brit and naturalized American who had fought for both the British and American armies, he was a natural-born warrior who had also studied law and literature. Rescorla mastered the towers' vulnerabilities as few others did.

In the early 1990s, he concluded that the biggest threat would be a truck bomb driven into the underground garage. He shared his concerns with the Port Authority, which operated the complex. They told him it was none of his business. In 1993 terrorists struck just the way he predicted.

He was convinced they would try again. Next time, he theorized, they might fly a cargo plane filled with explosives or chemical weapons into the towers. Again he shared his thinking with the Port Authority. Again no one seemed interested.

So Rescorla focused on training his charges for the disaster he sensed was coming. He staged

This photo, taken by a security camera in the World Trade Center, shows Rescorla directing the evacuation of his charges on September 11, 2001.

evacuation drills twice a month, timing them on his stopwatch and issuing instructions through his bull-horn until evacuation procedures became second nature for everyone involved. Even the most senior executives participated.

On the day the planes hit, Rescorla hustled virtually every Dean Witter employee out of the building before it collapsed. His colleagues remember him as a voice of calm, singing snatches of songs to keep their spirits up as he urged them down the stairs.

Ever the leader, Rescorla then took his bull-horn back inside to search for stragglers. That's when the tower collapsed around him.

Rescorla was one of more than 2,700 people who died that day, when the tragedy of which he had vainly warned finally came to pass.

MORE OF THE STORY

As a second lieutenant in the 7th Cavalry, Rescorla became a battlefield legend in Vietnam. His men called him "Hard Corps." At the battle of Ia Drang (depicted in the movie *We Were Soldiers*), his platoon held off wave after wave of attacks by the Vietcong and Rescorla earned a silver star. But of course that wasn't the end of his heroism or his human-ism. During the first bombing of the World Trade Center in 1993, Rescorla found himself unable to get the attention of panicked Dean Witter employees. So he leaped up on a desk and yelled: "Do I have to drop my trousers to get your attention?" That did the trick, and he then led an evacuation of the building.

Britain's most famous naval officer, Lord Nelson

Chapter 8

How and Why
The Reasons Behind the Facts

No curious person ever gets too old to ask "Why is that so?" and
"How did that happen?" These are the stories that answer those
questions. From how the famous Boston Garden floor came to be
to why "Hail to the Chief" is played for the presidential entrance and
from who decided where the keys on a typewriter go to why elephants
and donkeys symbolize political parties, these fascinating and fun
tales run the gamut from war to sports, art to science and adventure
to tragedy. Whether it involves a famous person or simply explains
a common happening, you'll want to know the how and why of each
of these unforgettable tales.

Spoils of War

An Islamic invasion leads to one of the world's wonders.

An army of Arabs, Berbers and Spanish Moors invaded Sicily in 832. This fearsome group was known as the Saracens. Within 50 years they had taken over most of the island and ruled it in the name of Islam for two centuries.

In 1004, the Saracens sacked Pisa. The citizens there thought of themselves as traders, not fighters, but in response to the Saracen attacks they built up a navy to defend themselves. Then they turned the tables on their one-time invaders, undertaking a daring raid on Palermo, the capital of Saracen Sicily. They ravaged the city, sinking many ships. Only a single enemy vessel remained afloat, and it was used to bring back a shipload of plunder.

Back home the powers-that-be decided that a portion of the booty should be used to fund the construction of a grand cathedral, which was duly built. A cathedral wouldn't be complete without a bell tower, and in 1172 a wealthy widow named Berta di Bernardo left "60 coins" in her will for the construction of one. Work began immediately but kept getting interrupted. It took almost two centuries to finish it.

Maybe that's where the problem began. Or maybe it would have happened anyway, what with the structure's shallow foundation and shifting subsoil. For of course the cathedral bell tower that the Pisans built had a flaw. A flaw that would one day be seen as its greatest glory, and make it known around the world. From an Islamic invasion and a widow's will: the Leaning Tower of Pisa.

OTHER PLAYERS, OTHER PLACES

In the summer of 1944, the fate of the tower was in the hands of U.S. Army sergeant Leon Weckstein. The Germans were thought to be using the tower as an observation post. Weckstein was sent forward with orders to call in an artillery barrage if he saw any movement in it. "Had I seen the glitter of one shiny button, even for a second, the tower would have become a pile of gravel," he said later. Seeing nothing suspicious, however, Weckstein held off giving the order for the tower's destruction.

Children's Crusade

A tragic journey gives birth to a legendary story.

In 1212, a French shepherd boy named Stephen of Cloyes had a vision. The intense blue-eyed youth told everyone that Jesus had called on him to raise an army of children to win back the Holy Land. He began preaching to crowds of people. His appeal struck a chord among devout Christians ashamed of the atrocities of earlier Crusades. Perhaps the pure of heart could succeed where the corrupt armies that had gone before had failed.

Tens of thousands of children were enlisted in the Children's Crusade. Across France and Germany village after village was emptied of its young people. Some were orphans, but many others were sent by parents who believed they were doing God's will. The children marched off in high spirits, chanting hymns, confident of victory. But they would never see Jerusalem, and only a handful ever made it back.

Thousands of German children died during an agonizing march across the Alps. Fate had even worse things in store for the French children. More than a thousand, including Stephen, perished when their ships sank crossing the stormy Mediterranean. Several thousand survived the journey only to be sold into slavery in Egypt by Hugh "The Iron" and William "The Pig," the merchants who had transported them.

This tragedy inspired an enduring folktale, born of collective guilt and the need for someone to blame, a dark story of a town whose happy children are spirited away forever—by the Pied Piper.

Shakespeare in Print

Can you imagine a world without Macbeth, Hamlet or Romeo? It almost happened.

William Shakespeare's genius was never fully appreciated during his lifetime. People thought of him as just another of the many playwrights of the day. Since he never published his plays the only ones in print were pirated versions often missing whole scenes. Once he was dead and buried much of his work was forgotten. And it might have remained so but for two loyal friends.

After Shakespeare, The Bard of Avon passed on, actors John Heminge and Henry Condell took it upon themselves, in their words, "to keep the memory of so worthy a Friend & Fellow alive, as was our Shakespeare." They determined to publish a collection of all his dramatic works. It was a task that took them years to accomplish.

The two men had acted alongside Shakespeare in his plays, and they knew

Heminge and Condell acted in many of Shakespeare's plays at the Globe Theatre (illustrated below) and were among his closest friends.

> ## *"He was not of an age, but for all time."*
>
> —PLAYWRIGHT BEN JONSON, IN THE PREFACE OF THE *FIRST FOLIO*

his work in detail. They searched out long-lost copies, dredged up missing pages and convinced playwright Ben Jonson to help them edit the material. They scratched together funds for the project, and finally, seven years after Shakespeare's death, they were able to publish the plays in one authoritative volume, now known as the *First Folio,* in 1623.

"To be or not to be?" Much of Shakespeare wouldn't be, if not for two devoted fans.

The opening pages of the *First Folio*

JUST A TALE?

The complete collection of Shakespeare's 154 sonnets was published in 1609. But there is some controversy over whether the Shakespeare we know actually wrote most of them. The name Shakespeare is hyphenated on the cover of the book and there is a dedication to Mr. W.H. that refers to him as the "onlie begetter" of the poems. That same dedication refers to the poet as "ever-living" which are the words Shakespeare used in *Henry VI, Part 1* to describe the dead king. Some believe this means the author of the poems was already dead when the manuscript was published, but since Shakespeare lived until 1616, that would mean the sonnets were penned by another writer.

A bust of the great bard

English Kilt

Horrors! Can it be true that the Scottish kilt is really an Englishman's invention?

In the 1700s, the traditional dress of Scottish highlanders was the plaide (pronounced "play-dee"), a large blanket wrapped around the body, thrown over the shoulder and belted at the waist.

It was cheap, convenient and great for cold nights hanging out in the heath—but it could be awfully cumbersome for industrial workers. At least that's how Englishman Tom Rawlinson saw it. Rawlinson came to Scotland in 1727 to open an iron foundry. He employed a "throng of Highlanders," but found their plaides often got in their way. He summoned a tailor to help him make the traditional dress a bit more practical. The tailor responded by shearing the plaide in two, cutting the skirt into a separate garment.

So was born what we now know as the kilt. After a Scottish uprising in 1745, it was banned by the British government. That had just the impact you might expect—it made the kilt infinitely more popular with Scots hostile to British rule, even though this most traditional of Scottish garments owes its existence to an Englishman.

And if that's not bad enough—to make things even worse—bagpipes aren't Scottish either. They're from the Middle East.

Fighting Words

We can't stop talking about this outdated weapon.

The flintlock was invented in France in 1610 and came to American shores shortly thereafter. For more than 200 years the flintlock played a major role in American history. Flintlock muskets and pistols were the weapons of choice in the American Revolution, the War of 1812 and the Civil War. And though they have been obsolete for more than a century they live on in our language.

MORE OF THE STORY

It was a flintlock rifle that fired the "shot heard round the world" on April 19, 1775, that began the American Revolution. But perhaps the most famous flintlock was the "Brown Bess," used by British soldiers for more than a century and immortalized by Rudyard Kipling:

> Brown Bess was a partner whom
>   none could despise...
> With a habit of looking men straight in
>   the eyes.
> At Blenheim and Ramillies, fops would
>   confess
> They were pierced to the heart by the
>   charms of Brown Bess.

To fire a flintlock the shooter first cocked the hammer partway so that he could sprinkle powder onto the priming pan—but he had to remember to cock the hammer the rest of way before firing. Otherwise the gun would go off half-cocked.

When the trigger was pulled, the hammer brought down a piece of flint with great force, creating a shower of sparks. If the powder in the pan ignited but failed to set off the charge inside the barrel, the result was a very showy but useless flash in the pan.

When that happened, no one knew when or if the gun was going to go off. It was said to be hanging fire.

By the way, the "lock" in flintlock referred to the firing mechanism. It was one of three major parts of the gun: only if you had the lock, stock and barrel did you have everything. Remember the flintlock!

The flintlock was used by both sides during the American Revolution.

Blind Man's Bluff

In this case, it's the words he ignores that make all the difference.

"I have only one eye—I have a right to be blind sometimes."

—ADMIRAL NELSON TO HIS FLAG CAPTAIN
DURING THE BATTLE

Horatio Nelson. Admiral Nelson. Lord Nelson (right). Perhaps the most revered officer ever to tread the deck of a British naval vessel, he is best known for his famous victory at Trafalgar in 1805. It was there aboard the HMS *Victory,* that he signaled to all his ships that "England expects every man to do his duty." It was also there that he defeated Napoleon's fleet, saving England from invasion, before dying from wounds suffered in the battle.

But it was at a battle four years earlier that he added a colorful phrase to the English language.

At the Battle of Copenhagen, Nelson was second in command to an elderly admiral named Sir Hyde Parker. Nelson led a squadron of ships on a daring attack against the Danish fleet and in no time he was heavily engaged in bettle.

The Battle of Copenhagen earned Nelson a promotion and command of his own fleet.

From his flagship several miles away Admiral Parker became convinced that Nelson's squadron was being decimated and that the battle was lost. He hoisted a signal flag ordering Nelson to withdraw. The younger admiral, knowing his ships were inflicting heavy damage on the Danes, paid no attention. When one of his officers pointed it out Nelson reportedly raised his telescope to his eye and said, "I really do not see the signal." Then he proceeded with the battle.

But the officer knew, as eventually everyone in England knew, that Nelson had put the telescope to his blind eye. Thus Nelson was able to claim ignorance of the order without disobeying it outright. Within the hour he had won a great victory and given birth to a new expression. So the next time you "turn a blind eye," remember the famous British admiral who did it first—and why.

Tea Party

How did Britain's thirst for tea lead to a drug epidemic?

At the beginning of the 1700s, virtually no one in Britain drank tea. By the end of that century everyone did. The British were gulping down tea as fast as the East India Company could import it from China. It was a national love affair.

But there was a problem. The Chinese weren't particularly interested in importing European trade goods, so by the early 1800s it required the modern equivalent of $1 billion a year in hard currency to pay for the tea. Silver and gold were flowing out of England to China, creating a terrible problem in foreign debt.

The solution? The East India Company, in collusion with the British government, became the

Clipper ships such as the *Three Brothers* were the fastest and largest ships of the day.

MORE OF THE STORY

The freshest tea commanded the highest price, so the tea trade launched a fleet of "clipper" ships, which were fast cargo vessels that would race across the ocean, to see who could get the first tea of the season back to London the fastest. One of the most famous was the *Cutty Sark,* which could carry more than a million pounds of tea and sail from China to England in under 100 days.

world's biggest drug dealer. The company started producing massive amounts of opium in India and worked out a complex scheme to smuggle it into China to trade for the tea. Opium shipments increased by a factor of 250. By 1839, widespread opium addiction was a serious problem in China.

The emperor of China tried to put a stop to the drug trade that was ruining his country. His agents destroyed British stocks of opium in the trading port of Canton and kicked out the British. But would Britain stand for that? Not for all the tea in China.

Britain responded by going to war to protect its opium trade. The Opium War was an easy victory for the British, who forced China to let the trade continue for another 70 years. And that's why millions of Chinese were addicted to opium: to subsidize Britain's love for tea.

Having a Ball

A great time is had at the presidential campaign.

The presidential contest of 1840 is considered the first modern election campaign. It was also one of the wildest and most colorful campaigns in American history. This was the year that politics became public theater. There were torchlight parades, catchy slogans, campaign songs and all sorts of ballyhoo that had never been seen before.

The Whig candidate was William Henry Harrison, who back in 1811 had defeated the Shawnee Indians in the battle of Tippecanoe. With his running mate, John Tyler, he boasted one of the most memorable presidential slogans of all time: "Tippecanoe and Tyler, Too."

The Whigs seemed to have an inexhaustible supply of campaign gimmicks. One in particular caught on across the country. Supporters in various cities created giant balls, 10 feet in diameter, which could be covered in

MORE OF THE STORY

Democrats made fun of Harrison as a candidate. One paper said, "Give him a barrel of hard cider and a pension of $2,000 a year and he will sit the remainder of his days in his log cabin." Harrison's campaign team turned it to their advantage, billing him as the "Log Cabin and Hard Cider" candidate.

slogans and rolled along in parades. Energetic ball rollers pushed them great distances. One of them was rolled from Cleveland to Akron, another from Kentucky to Maryland, to drum up enthusiasm for Harrison.

"Keep the ball rolling" was the cry of the men who rolled the ball along. "Keep the ball rolling on to Washington."

Harrison rolled into the White House, and because of an odd campaign tool, we have kept the ball rolling ever since.

A Whig slogan ball on parade

Spencer's Legacy

A hanging at sea leads to the creation of the Naval Academy.

Philip Spencer was a fresh-faced 20-year-old the day he was hanged. He was a screw-up who had flunked out of two colleges before his father pulled strings to get him an appointment as a midshipman (an officer in training) in the U.S. Navy. True to form Spencer promptly got himself kicked off a ship for drinking.

Given a second chance on the brig *Somers*, he allegedly hatched a plot with some crewmates to take over the ship. Accused of mutiny by the captain, Spencer said he was just joking. "It was only a fancy," he said.

Spencer and two confederates were chained to the quarterdeck. The Somers was hundreds of miles from port, the crew was angry and resentful and it seemed to the officers that at any moment the sailors might rise up to murder them and free the three prisoners.

So Captain Alexander S. McKenzie (above) did what was within his power as commander of the ship. He ordered that Spencer and his two co-conspirators be hanged from the yardarm.

Naval Academy cadets

But Philip Spencer was not just any young man. His father was the Secretary of War, and his hanging shocked the nation. Some accused the captain of overreacting. Others wanted to know how an unqualified teenager could get an appointment as a midshipman and then be put aboard ship with no training at all.

The public cried out for reform. Secretary of War John Spencer was at the forefront of those demanding a court-martial for Captain McKenzie, but a Navy court eventually exonerated him. McKenzie's Naval career was effectively over, however, and he was never trusted with command of another warship. Philip Spencer and his co-conspirators were the last men to be hanged aboard a U.S. Naval vessel. Slightly more than two years later, in response to the Somers affair, a Naval school was founded to turn midshipmen into well-trained officers. And that's how Philip Spencer's death paved the way for the creation of the U.S. Naval Academy at Annapolis, Maryland.

Hail to the Wives!

This pair of supportive First Ladies pick a presidential theme song.

After the sudden death of President Harrison, John Tyler became the first vice president to take over the presidency. While some thought he should call himself "acting president," Tyler promptly moved into the White House and claimed the title and full powers of the office of president, setting a precedent for later VPs.

The presidency was no picnic for Tyler. People mocked him as "His Accidency." When he vetoed a bill establishing a national bank almost everyone in his cabinet resigned, his party ejected him and the first impeachment resolution against a president was introduced in the House.

Tyler's wife died early in his term. Two years later he married a vivacious young woman named Julia Gardiner (above). After their marriage, they held a series of parties at the White House. The new First Lady, trying to bolster her husband's ego and image, requested that as the president made

The music was originally written by an English composer in 1812 to accompany a stage production of Sir Walter Scott's epic poem, "The Lady of the Lake."

his entrance at parties, the Marine Corps Band should strike up a stirring song from a popular stage show. The name of that song: "Hail to the Chief."

The song happened to be a life-long favorite of the next First Lady, Sarah Polk (right). Her husband, President James Polk, did not cut a very dashing figure. In fact he had a way of entering a crowded room almost unnoticed. To help him appear more impressive she asked that the song be played every time he made an entrance. And a tradition was born.

JOHN PHILIP SOUSA
COMPOSER

OTHER PLAYERS, OTHER PLACES

John Philip Sousa, conductor of the Marine Corps Band, wrote a replacement to "Hail to the Chief" at the request of President Chester A. Arthur, who hated the song. Sousa came up with a song called "Presidential Polonaise "but it wasn't one of his great efforts and failed to make any more of a dent than Arthur's brief presidency. However, many of Sousa's other compositions found their place in American history. "Semper Fidelis" written in 1888 became the Marine Corps march, 1896's "The Stars and Stripes Forever" became the national march and "Processional," also known as the "Wedding March," has accompanied millions of brides down the aisle since it was penned in 1918.

The Art of War

A military failure changes the course of art history.

The cadet had suffered his share of problems at West Point. Truthfully the main reason he was there was because his widowed mother wanted him to become a career military officer like his late father had been.

In his first year he got enough demerits to be kicked out. But the superintendent of the academy—a soon-to-be-famous colonel named Robert E. Lee—was kind enough to forgive some of his demerits and allow him to continue.

In his second year he fell gravely ill, and Colonel Lee had to write his mother to come get him. After he recovered, though, he passed all his exams, even finishing first in his drawing class. Things were finally looking up for the young man.

Then, at the end of his third year, came the fateful exam. It was an oral exam in chemistry, and it may go down as the shortest oral exam in West Point history. The instructor asked the young man to discuss silicon.

"Silicon is a gas," he began.

"That will do," the instructor interrupted him.

James Whistler's self-portrait

With four words the cadet had managed to fail chemistry and flunk out of West Point. "Had silicon been a gas," he said later, "I would have been a major-general."

But what the military world lost, the art world gained. The cadet put his skill at drawing and painting to good use, becoming one of America's best artists: James McNeill Whistler (below).

And his mother, Anna, who wished for him a career in the military? She is remembered as his most famous subject: Whistler's Mother. And that's how a famous portrait came to be.

The famous painting of Whistler's mother, is now housed in Paris in the Musée d'Orsay.

OTHER PLAYERS, OTHER PLACES

Whistler wasn't the only creative man to be dropped from the academy. Other famous West Point flunk-outs include author and poet Edgar Allan Poe and 1960s counter-culture guru Timothy Leary. Poe had already published an unsuccessful volume of poetry when, completely broke from paying the costs of publication, he joined the Army. However, the drudgery of the enlisted man was no life for him and he contrived to enter West Point. But his poet's heart couldn't withstand tragedy. Unhappy after the death of his mother and subsequent remarriage of his stepfather, Poe neglected all his duties and was court-martialed in 1831. Leary entered West Point after a brief stint at the conservative Catholic college Holy Cross. After imbibing too much at a party and not making reveille the next morning, Leary was punished by a "silencing" in which he was forbidden to speak to any cadets or they to him. He resigned from the Academy in 1941.

A Touch of Grace

The face we all know is remade by a little girl.

The clean-shaven Lincoln

Norman Bedell was working as a stove maker in Westfield, New York, in 1860. He was an ardent Republican, and that was enough to make his 11-year-old daughter, Grace, one as well. One day her dad brought home a campaign poster with a picture of presidential candidate Abraham Lincoln. Grace counted herself a zealous champion of Lincoln's candidacy, but when she peered at her hero she noticed something she didn't like.

Lincoln was clean-shaven.

Beards were growing in popularity, but Lincoln didn't have one. Shortly before the election, Grace sat down and wrote the candidate a letter explaining why he ought to remedy the situation. "All the ladies like whiskers," she wrote, "and they would tease their husbands to vote for you and then you would be President."

Grace's famous letter encouraged Lincoln to grow a fashionable beard.

A few days later Grace was astounded to receive a response from Lincoln himself, wondering if whiskers were really a good idea. "Having never worn any, do you not think people might call it a piece of silly affectation should I begin wearing them now?"

But the little girl's letter struck a chord with Lincoln. After he was elected, he acted on her suggestion and began to grow a beard for the first time in his life. The angular face of the president-to-be was transformed to the bearded visage we know so well today—all thanks to Grace.

This statue in Westfield, New York commemorates Lincoln's meeting with Grace.

MORE OF THE STORY

The train that carried Lincoln to Washington for his inauguration stopped in Westfield, New York and Lincoln got out to speak to the assembled crowd. He told them he had "a little correspondent" who had suggested he grow the beard and asked if she was in the crowd. When Grace was pointed out Lincoln stepped down from the train platform and made his way toward her. Lincoln kissed the little girl and she touched his beard: "You see, I let those whiskers grow for you, Grace." The little girl treasured the moment her whole life, until she died in 1936 at the age of 88.

Qwerty

A key part of your computer is more than a century old.

The modern typewriter was born in the back of Kleinsteuber's Machine Shop in Milwaukee, Wisconsin. That's where Christopher Sholes took some piano wire and a telegraph key and built a crude typing device in 1868. It could type only one letter—a rather fuzzy-looking "w"—but it was still pretty amazing for its time. Sholes and his partners designed a more ambitious model with all the letters in the alphabet.

The typewriter had a problem, though. When typing quickly the bars banged into one another and got stuck. The solution to that problem resulted in the keyboard we know today.

Sholes consulted with an educator who helped him analyze the most common pairings of letters in the English language. He then split up those letters so that their type bars were farther apart and less likely to jam. That in turn dictated the layout of the keyboard—known as QWERTY, for the first six letters in the upper row. In a manner of speaking he slowed down the typists to prevent jamming and thus sped up the typing.

In 1873, the Sholes & Glidden Type Writer became the first to be mass-produced, and its keyboard layout was soon standard on all typewriters. Other keyboard layouts have been created since, such as the Blickensderfer Scientific and the Dvorak, and some are demonstrably more efficient, but the original continues to thrive. It is a telling illustration of the power of inertia and the reward of being first.

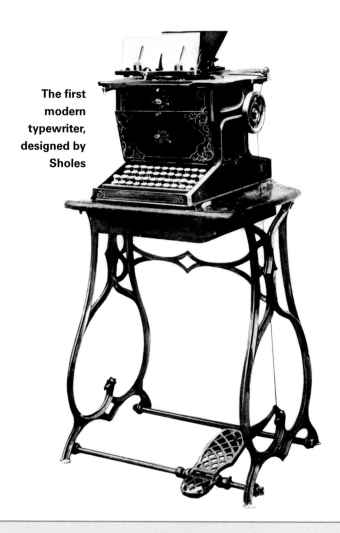

The first modern typewriter, designed by Sholes

Cartoon Characters

One man's imagination turns politics into an animal farm.

In the years between the Civil War and the start of the 20th century, Thomas Nast was the nation's most influential political cartoonist. In fact the influence of his powerful cartoons is still felt today.

Nast, a die-hard Republican, liked to use the jackass to portray Democratic policies he considered hotheaded or downright stubborn. When others picked up on the symbol the Democrats tried to make the best of it, portraying themselves as donkeys, not asses.

A few weeks before election day in 1874, Nast drew a cartoon for *Harper's Weekly* in which he used a rogue elephant to represent Republican voters he felt were being panicked by phony charges from the Democrats. The cartoon was meant as a rebuke, but the idea of a pachyderm representing the GOP soon took on a life of its own.

The issues and controversies of those days have long since faded, but the elephant and donkey have proved amazingly durable.

MORE OF THE STORY

The German-born Nast also helped shape our image of Santa Claus. Trying to capture the "jolly old elf" of Clement Moore's poem "A Visit from St. Nicholas" he created the face of Santa we've come to take for granted. He did more than just shape American popular culture, though. He may well have influenced the style of artist Vincent van Gogh. Van Gogh systematically collected Nast's work, even saving a collection of his illustrations in a bound volume for reference.

Nast drew this Santa in 1872.

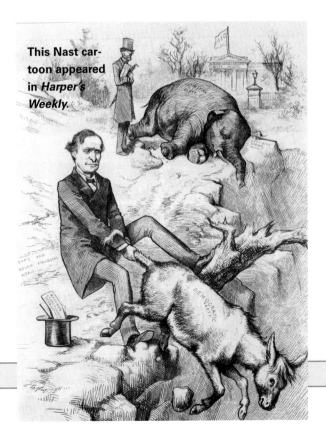

This Nast cartoon appeared in *Harper's Weekly*.

Let the Good Times Roll

A White House tradition is created by a Congressional snit.

In the 1870s, the children of Washington, D.C., would turn the Capitol grounds into their own personal playground the day after Easter. Families would set up picnics while children rolled decorated eggs around the grounds, egg rolling being a long-standing Washington custom.

In 1876, the assembled throngs left the Capitol grounds a mess. Congressmen, more comfortable with high rollers than egg rollers, promptly passed a law known as the Turf Protection Act. (Politicians, after all, love to protect their turf.) The new law sternly asserted that the Capitol grounds could no longer be used as a children's playground. As Easter 1878 rolled around, Congress took out newspaper ads making it plain that Easter Monday egg rolling would not be tolerated at the Capitol. What were the revelers to do?

A group of children approached President Rutherford B. Hayes while he was out on his daily constitutional. They begged him to let them use the White House lawn.

The president proved he wasn't as hardboiled as the eggheads on the other end of Pennsylvania Avenue. Hayes and his wife, Lucy, opened the south lawn of the White House to the egg rollers, and a new tradition was born. A few hundred children and parents came that first year. By the 1930s, as many as 50,000 were showing up for the White House egg roll. It's been a festive annual event ever since, except when weather, war or White House renovations got in the way—leaving Congress with just a little bit of egg on its face.

The festivities on the lawn, circa 1921

All Buttoned Up

A businesswoman's patent leads to a campaigning mainstay.

Amanda Lougee didn't set out to forever change presidential campaigns. But this Bostonian nevertheless helped do just that.

Lougee was something of a rarity for her time—a female entrepreneur. She took over a small rubber factory after the death of her brother, and built it up into a nationally known company that employed nearly 300 people, making almost everything from clothing to electrical tape. In her spare time she was an avid supporter of the suffragette movement, even contributing a fruitcake recipe to *The Woman's Suffrage Cookbook.*

She was also a bit of an inventor. In 1893, she filed a patent for a new way of making a button covered with material. A New Jersey printing company called Whitehead and Hoag saw a use for her idea that she never anticipated. They snapped up her patent as well as two others and in 1896 came out with something completely brand new: the modern campaign button.

The buttons were inexpensive to make and soon became all the rage. Perhaps no innovation in politics ever gained acceptance more quickly. More than a thousand different kinds of buttons were made for the 1896 presidential campaign pitting William McKinley against William Jennings Bryan. And they've been a campaign staple ever since.

Court of Appeal

Given a choice, this president prefers another job.

All his life William Howard Taft had one great ambition: to be chief justice of the United States. President Theodore Roosevelt thought Taft would be a great Supreme Court justice and wanted to appoint him to the court. But one person stood in his way: Taft's wife, Nellie.

When Nellie Taft was 17 she confided to her girlfriends that her goal in life was to marry a man who would become president. She didn't want her husband on the court. She wanted him in the White House. And she was determined she would have her way.

In 1906, TR offered Taft the next opening on the court. Taft wanted to accept. His wife told him he would be making the biggest mistake of his life.

It led to a West Wing showdown between Nellie Taft and Theodore Roosevelt. One night at a White House dinner TR teased the Tafts by saying he saw a silver string above Taft's head. He said he couldn't tell if it said "president" or "chief justice." "Make it the presidency," said Nellie. "Make it the chief justiceship," said Taft. But according to White House chief usher Ike Hoover, "It was only through the pleadings of Mrs. Taft that he was not appointed [to the court]."

Nellie Taft had her wish fulfilled. Her husband was elected president. Taft got his way, too. After being defeated in a reelection bid he was appointed chief justice by President Woodrow Wilson, becoming the only man to serve in both positions.

MORE OF THE STORY

As First Lady, Nellie Taft helped transform a muddy patch of land alongside the Potomac into a park with a grandstand. She suggested lining the road to the park with Japanese cherry-blossom trees. The Japanese government offered the trees as a gift, and she and the Viscountess Chinda, wife of the Japanese ambassador, planted the first two in 1912. Within a few years the cherry-blossom trees had become one of Washington's most distinctive tourist attractions. They are the showcase of a two-week festival that heralds spring for many in the capital.

This political cartoon shows President Theodore Roosevelt, a good friend of Taft's, using his political clout to advance Taft's career.

Eiffel or Eyesore?

A reviled structure, saved from certain destruction, becomes a beloved landmark.

It is hard to imagine Paris without its most famous landmark, the Eiffel Tower. But when it was going up, there were many who thought it would be the ruin of the great city.

The famous tower was built for the Paris Centennial Exhibition in 1889. It was scheduled to

Tourists never had any doubt about the tower. When it opened in 1889, 2 million people visited.

"This stupefying folly...this odious column of bolted metal."

—ARTISTS' PROTEST AGAINST THE EIFFEL TOWER

stand for only 20 years—but for critics that was 20 years too long. Construction was barely under way when a committee of 50 writers and artists launched a public campaign against what they called "the useless and monstrous Eiffel Tower." They bemoaned its "barbarous mass overwhelming and humiliating all our monuments." Other critics referred to the tower as "a lamp post stuck in the belly of Paris" and "a giant ungainly skeleton."

The tower proved wildly popular among visitors, but many Parisians continued to regard it with a jaundiced eye. Its opponents kept up a drumbeat of criticism, and the government was determined that when the 20 years were up, the tower was coming down. Nothing could save it.

That is until radio was invented, which proved to be the tower's salvation. The 1,000-foot structure turned out to be an excellent radio tower that could receive messages from far, far away. In 1907, the French government decided the tower could not come down—it was too valuable as an antenna. Function followed form this time around, and saved a Paris monument from certain destruction.

The Shape of the Presidency

This is the story of the famous Oval Office, from Washington to Watergate.

It's the most famous room in the White House, perhaps even the world. Decisions made in the Oval Office impact everyone on the globe. But how did the president's office come to be an oval, and when did we start referring to it that way?

It all has to do with George Washington and the formal way he preferred to greet people.

Upon becoming president Washington moved into a house in Philadelphia, then serving as the nation's capital. Washington liked to hold formal receptions where guests gathered in a circle to meet him. He replaced the square corners of two rooms in the house with semicircular walls to make them more suitable for these levees. When James Hoban designed the White House, he catered to Washington's desires by including an oval drawing room, the Blue Room.

More than a century later, in 1909, when architect Nathan Wyeth was designing a new West Wing office for the president, he wanted to give it a "dignified treatment" in keeping with its high purpose. In tribute to the Blue Room and Washington he created an oval office. But the term "Oval Office" was not widely used—not for 60 years.

During the Watergate scandal aides to President Nixon started using the phrase "Oval Office" to talk about the involvement of the president without actually using his name. The phrase exploded into public usage and has been with us ever since.

The *Resolute* desk in the Oval Office was a gift from Britain's Queen Victoria to Rutherford B. Hayes.

Republican Charles Evans Hughes campaigns in Hampton Beach, New Hampshire, in 1916. He lost the election to Woodrow Wilson.

First in the Nation

A state with a reputation for frugality gives birth to a presidential rite of passage.

It all began in 1906, when Winston Churchill decided he wanted to run for governor of New Hampshire. No, not that Winston Churchill. This Winston Churchill was a popular American writer of the same name.

When he sought the Republican nomination for governor, however, he was defeated at a rigged convention. The resulting outrage eventually led reformers to establish New Hampshire's first political primary. Initially it was just for state offices. Then in 1913, the presidential race was added.

The state's first presidential primary was scheduled for May 1916. But someone suggested that it would be cheaper to hold the primary on the same

George W. Bush rallies the crowd on the campaign trail in New Hampshire.

New Hampshire is one of the smallest states in the Union, but its primary had made and broken many candidates since 1952, while offering more than its share of media moments. In 1968, President Lyndon Johnson dropped out of the race after challenger Eugene McCarthy came from nowhere to garner a better-than-expected 38 percent of the Democratic vote. In 1972, Democratic front-runner Senator Ed Muskie choked up while responding to personal attacks by the *Manchester Union Leader*. The "Muskie Crying Incident," as it came to be called, suggested that he couldn't handle the pressure of the campaign and proved devastating to his candidacy. In 1976, a win in the New Hampshire primary helped catapult a little-known Southern governor named Jimmy Carter to front-runner status. But after a disastrous showing in the Iowa caucuses Vice President Bush rebounded to defeat Senator Bob Dole in the 1988 New Hampshire primary, going on to win the nomination and the election. Who knows what will happen next?

day all the towns in New Hampshire held their annual town meetings: the second Tuesday in March. Granite Staters pride themselves on their frugality, and the date was changed. So it came to be that New Hampshire had the first presidential primary in the country.

At first nobody cared. The voting was only for delegates, and most of them ran as uncommitted. Interest and turnout were so low that in 1949 the legislature added a "beauty contest," where people could also vote for which presidential candidate they preferred.

This innovation caught the nation's eye. In 1952 the "first in the nation" primary gave an important public boost to the candidacy of General Dwight Eisenhower and abruptly ended the high, third-term hopes of incumbent Harry S. Truman. It has been in the political spotlight ever since.

Strike Song

Please rise and hear how the national anthem came to be played before ball games.

"We'll play...for the sake of the wounded sailors and soldiers who are in the grandstands."

—HARRY HOOPER, RED SOX OUTFIELDER

On September 11, 1918, game five of the World Series was scheduled for Fenway Park in Boston. The Red Sox were going to play the Chicago Cubs, and since this was during World War I, many wounded veterans would be in the stands.

The start of the game was delayed when a dispute arose over—guess what? Money. (As you can see, little has changed in sports.) Players were upset that they weren't getting a bigger share of the World Series purse, so they decided to strike and refused to take the field. Hasty negotiations took place under the stands as fans grew more and more impatient.

After about an hour, the players reluctantly agreed to play ball for the sake of the vets. Caught up by the patriotic fervor (and no doubt trying to placate the restless crowd), the happy Red Sox owner had the band strike up "The Star-Spangled Banner." It was the first time the song is known to have been played before a ball game.

The wartime fans rose and doffed their hats out of respect for the nation and its anthem, and a new tradition was born. The Red Sox went on to win the Series, the last one they would capture in the 20th century.

According to the United States Code, all men except those in military uniform should doff their hats and place them over their hearts while the anthem plays.

Revolutionary Cold War

Backing a monarchy ultimately leads to icy relations.

American soldiers fight the decisive war against communism in Russia. It sounds like a Tom Clancy fantasy, but it actually happened.

World War I was barely over when President Woodrow Wilson decided the United States should intervene in the Russian Civil War. He sent thousands of American troops to help overthrow the new communist regime under Lenin. Britain, France and Japan sent troops as well.

The Allied Expeditionary Force fought a series of bloody engagements with the White Russians against the Bolsheviks in north Russia, losing hundreds of men. Another American division in Siberia also took casualties. The military effort also had a propaganda component. The troops sent to Russia were accompanied by Signal Corps camera crews to bring back images of American boys going to war against communism.

The halfhearted efforts proved too small to prevent a communist takeover, and the troops were pulled out by 1920. Quickly forgotten in the United States the fighting was long remembered in the Soviet Union. It cemented Soviet distrust of the West, creating suspicions that eventually helped to fuel the Cold War.

U.S. soldiers on board a Siberian troop train

Convoy

This is the road trip that changed America.

In the summer of 1919, the U.S. Army organized a coast-to-coast expedition of military vehicles to show off its equipment and demonstrate the need for better roads.

More than half the trip was over dirt roads that were little better than trails. Broken-down bridges had to be repaired along the way and soldiers often had to dig trucks out of the mud or even push them through difficult sections. In the end it took the 81 vehicles of the Transcontinental Motor Convoy a grueling 62 days to cross the entire country.

The journey was to have a major impact on the American landscape. One young Army officer accompanied the mission "partly as a lark and partly to learn." His name was Dwight Eisenhower and the long, hard trip convinced him that better roads were an important national priority. That conviction was strengthened by his experience as supreme allied commander in Europe. "The old convoy had started me thinking about good two-lane highways, but Germany had made me see the wisdom of broader ribbons across the land."

And so it was that 35 years after the convoy struggled across the nation, President Eisenhower took up the cause of a modern interstate highway system for the country. His efforts resulted in the construction of more than 40,000 miles of interstate highways, making the family car trip a reality for millions. Small signs along those highways mark them as part of the Eisenhower Interstate System—and now you know the story behind that.

A young Eisenhower (far right), poses at a stop on the Army's transcontinental motor convoy.

Man's Best Friend

The world's most grueling race is inspired by a mission of mercy.

In January 1925, a deadly diphtheria epidemic broke out among the children of Nome, Alaska. The nearest lifesaving serum was in Anchorage, some 700 miles away. The snow-covered landscape was almost impassable, and a ship would take too long. To make matters even worse the only two airplanes in the state were in storage for the long, frigid winter.

The governor decided the serum would have to be "mushed" to Nome by a series of dogsled teams. Messages flew across telegraph lines to arrange the relay. The serum was rushed by rail to the town of Nenana. There it was handed to Wild Bill Shannon, whose dog team was the first of 18 teams that would carry the serum 674 miles across the frozen tundra.

The conditions were frightening. The temperature dipped as low as 40 degrees Farenheit below zero. Gale-force winds and blinding snow hampered the drivers. The whole world was riveted by their dramatic race against time and the elements; the progress of the sleds muscled other stories off front pages everywhere. On the fifth day all contact with the sled carrying the serum was lost, and many feared the worst. But at 5:30 in the morning on February 1—a full 127 hours after the dogsled marathon began, in fact, more than five full days—

"I gave Balto his head and trusted him. He never faltered ...the credit is his."

—GUNNAR KAASSEN

Gunnar Kaassen emerged from the darkness to deliver the serum to Nome, led by his dog, Balto.

Today, the epic journey is commemorated annually in the great Anchorage-to-Nome dogsled race named after the trail on which much of it is run: the Iditarod.

A statue of Balto, in New York City's Central Park

Lights On

Night baseball has its fans because of FDR.

FDR throws out the first ball April 14, 1935.

After the United States entered World War II baseball commissioner Kenesaw Mountain Landis wrote to President Franklin Roosevelt asking if Major League Baseball should go ahead with the forthcoming baseball season.

Roosevelt replied with what has become known as the "green-light letter," telling baseball owners, "It would be best for the country to keep baseball going." He explained that he thought baseball offered a valuable recreational outlet for a nation committing itself to an all-out war effort. Almost as an aside, FDR offered a suggestion. "Incidentally, I hope that night games can be extended because it gives an opportunity to the day shift to see a game occasionally."

Those words had a profound effect on the game of baseball. Up to this time each team was limited to seven night games. Many owners strongly opposed increasing that number, but in response to the president's suggestion they doubled the limit to 14 for each team. The following season the American League removed the limit entirely. Some teams played more than 40 night games a season.

The expansion of night baseball was a home run. Night games were better attended than day games. Nevertheless after the war ended many team owners advocated returning to the prewar limits. When they deadlocked on the question the new baseball commissioner, Albert "Happy" Chandler, ruled teams could play ball under the lights as often as they liked. The war was over. FDR was dead. But night baseball was here to stay.

OTHER PLAYERS, OTHER PLACES

The Chicago Cubs had planned to install lights at Wrigley Field in 1942, but with the outbreak of war, the team decided instead to donate the lights to the federal government. In 1944 the Cubs were denied permission to install lights because of wartime shortages of critical material. And so began, quite by accident, the tradition of daytime-only baseball at Wrigley. Lights were not installed there until 1988.

Floor It

A wartime shortage turns leftovers into legend.

In the days following World War II, good lumber was in short supply and usually had a high price attached to it. So when Anthony DiNatale got an order in 1946 for a large wooden floor to be built

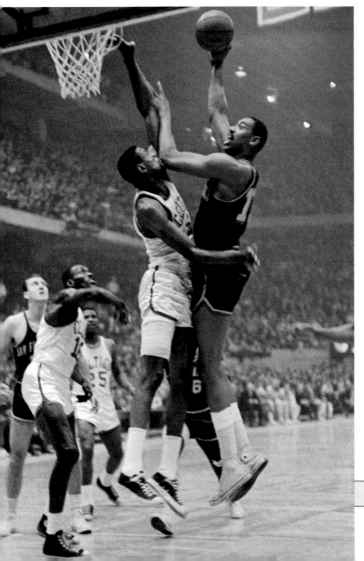

at the lowest possible cost he had to use some imagination. He located some scraps of wood left over from the construction of Army barracks. Although it was sturdy hardwood from Tennessee, all the pieces were short.

The workmen at DiNatale Flooring in Boston then fitted the scraps together in an alternating pattern and constructed a series of five-foot-square panels that could be bolted together to form the entire floor. In doing so they constructed what may be the single most well-known floor in the world— in the sports world, that is.

It became known the world over as the famous parquet floor of Boston Garden. The floor on which the Boston Celtics won an NBA-record 16 championships. A floor unlike that of any other basketball court on earth, trod by the likes of Bill Russell, Bob Cousy, Larry Bird and Kevin McHale.

DiNatale charged the Celtics $11,000 for the now-famous floor. After it was replaced by a new parquet floor in 1999, autographed pieces of the original sold for as much as $300,000 each. A few pieces of the old floor were integrated into the new one to keep the memory of the old one alive.

Fans and players have speculated the Celtics had a home-court advantage because they knew where the floor's "dead spots" were. But Celtic Bob Cousy says flatly: "The idea of dead spots is pure, unadulterated crap."

PHOTO CREDITS

Art Director: Lynn Blake, Lynn Blake Design; **Chief Photo Researcher:** Jody Potter/J Group Photo; **Additional Photo Research by**: Dian Lofton, The Right Pics; **Additional Writing by** Tara Gadomski

INDEX